DAUGHTER
of
SONG

A Cambodian Refugee Family,
Their Daughter, Crime and Injustice

DOUG HOOD

FOREWARD by WALLY LAMB

ISBN (eBook): 979-8-9868203-0-9
ISBN (Paperback): 979-8-9868203-1-6
ISBN (Hardcover): 979-8-9868203-2-3
ISBN (Large Print): 979-8-9868203-3-0

Library of Congress Control Number: 2022917954

Front Cover Photo by Chan Krom

Front and Back Cover and Logo Design by Peter Selgin

Title Production by The Bookwhisperer.ink

Published by Atacama Books, LLC

PRAISE FOR DAUGHTER OF SONG

"Compelling ... gripping ... incredible reporting ... very fine writing."

— AMY NUTT, *WASHINGTON POST* COLUMNIST, AUTHOR, PULITZER PRIZE WINNER

"I just had the pleasure of reading your manuscript. It's incredible; the story itself is powerful and moving. Congratulations on completing such a wonderful book; I'm inspired by your example."

— RACHEL E. BARKOW, VICE DEAN CHARLES SELIGSON PROFESSOR OF LAW, NYU SCHOOL OF LAW

"A true crime tale told with earnest compassion and cultural sensitivity ... with a great deal of empathy, as well as an ample amount of detail ... offering an intimacy that many true-crime stories lack."

— KIRKUS REVIEWS

"Wow. I just finished reading the entire book. The writing was so compelling and the details so expertly woven in that I found myself unable to put it down. It is a powerful and beautifully executed piece of work. I can't praise this work enough. Just want to see it get out there!

— MICHELLE OBERMAN, KATHERINE AND GEORGE ALEXANDER PROFESSOR OF LAW, SANTA CLARA UNIVERSITY SCHOOL OF LAW, AUTHOR OF *MOTHERS WHO KILL THEIR CHILDREN*

"The writing in *Daughter of Song* is beautiful and riveting. The details are so wonderful — the prose is gripping. Hood is a beautiful writer/storyteller. The short chapters create a whodunit that drives the story along. Congratulations to the author on putting this all together in a page-turner."

— RANDI EPSTEIN MD, MPH, WRITER IN RESIDENCE, YALE SCHOOL OF MEDICINE

"I have taken great pleasure in reading your very fine manuscript. It is gripping, well written and inspiring. The bottom line is the work speaks for itself and deserves to be read by many."

— THOMAS DUFFY M.D, EMERITUS PROFESSOR OF MEDICINE AND MEDICAL HUMANITIES, YALE UNIVERSITY

"Part police procedural, part biography, part plea for social justice, *Daughter of Song* unfolds an unforgettable tale of crime and redemption. Doug Hood, a gifted non-fiction writer, brings to bear an elegantly unembellished style, a keen ability to track a tough story, and long experience with today's unfair carceral system. The result is a captivating book that merits wide attention for its rich characters and trenchant critique of public policy."

— MARK ATWOOD LAWRENCE, DIRECTOR, LBJ
PRESIDENTIAL LIBRARY, AUTHOR OF *THE
VIETNAM WAR*

"I just finished *Daughter of Song*. It was meant to be enjoyable, and it was. Also educational, perhaps even enlightening. It is a very compelling story, and very well told. This book needs to be, and deserves to be published. Congratulations on your work and on the book."

— MARK R. MERCURIO, CHIEF OF NEONATAL-
PERINATAL MEDICINE, DIRECTOR FOR
BIOMEDICAL ETHICS, YALE SCHOOL OF
MEDICINE

"I have finished [*Daughter of Song*] and LOVED it. The language is terrific. The writing is fluid and sound."

— KATIE HALL, FORMER SENIOR EDITOR,
RANDOM HOUSE AND DOUBLEDAY

"This is a landmark investigative work beautifully told by Doug Hood through a captivating narrative, opening our eyes to a misunderstood crime as well as the plight of refugees. It deserves a special place for those studying criminal clemency procedure and working with teen pregnancies."

— EDWARD ZIGLER, STERLING PROFESSOR OF
PSYCHOLOGY, YALE UNIVERSITY

"Doug has a remarkable ability to transcend cultural and gender barriers, entering the world of Panna on her own terms. His unassuming and empathetic portrayal of his protagonist allows the reader to see Panna as an individual, not just a symbol of the social and judicial systems that betrayed her. Be sure to add *Daughter of Song* to the top of your reading list. You won't regret it."

— MARY C. OLMSTEAD, PROFESSOR,
PSYCHOLOGY & NEUROSCIENCE, QUEEN'S
UNIVERSITY, KINGSTON, CANADA

"*Daughter of Song* is amazing. Absolutely riveting! Seriously, I didn't want to put it down.

I thought the overall structure was strong, and the prose was clear and engaging—it really pulls the reader right along. Panna and her family are deeply drawn characters and unforgettable. I was so impressed with, not only the writing, but the tremendous amount of work done for Panna's case."

— KATHLEEN WEIDNER ZOEHFELD, AWARD-
WINNING CHILDREN'S BOOK AUTHOR

"Doug ... I read and enjoyed [*Daughter of Song*]."

— JOHN MERRIMAN, CHARLES SEYMOUR
PROFESSOR OF HISTORY, YALE UNIVERSITY

"I found *Daughter of Song* engaging, informative, and compelling—a real page-turner! The research you've done to uncover the other neonaticide cases in Connecticut was really incredible."

— AMY SMOYER, ASSOCIATE PROFESSOR IN SOCIOLOGY, SOUTHERN CONNECTICUT STATE UNIVERSITY

"Doug Hood has written a riveting book that defies categorization because it's bigger than any single genre. It has all the suspense of a police procedural, but it's also a thoughtful look at the American justice system, a history of Cambodia, an exploration of multigenerational trauma, and even a bit of first-person memoir—albeit written by a modest man determined to keep the spotlight off himself. Ultimately, it's a love story about one remarkably close and resilient Cambodian-American family and the man who changed his life to allow them to rescue their teenage daughter from a system that doesn't always mete out justice fairly."

— MICHELE HERMAN, NOVELIST, POET COLUMNIST AND EDITOR, AUTHOR OF *SAVE THE VILLAGES*

For Suki and Lee Clyde

"The world needs to know the plight of the little people who are walked upon like grass."
James Wright Foley, Journalist
1973 Illinois–2014 Syria

A NOTE FROM THE AUTHOR

This is narrative nonfiction, not a novelization. It is based on the author's own investigative research and observations, personal interactions, police reports, legal documents, library research, press and other media reports, published documents, oral testimony and interviews using notes and transcribed tapes. Only sparingly has non-essential dialogue been recreated and storyline timing minimally refashioned to make for a more readable and concise narrative while remaining faithful to the true story. The scenes involving the interactions of Panna and her family with the lawyers, the judicial, and criminal personnel were recreated to the best of their recall. Some names and addresses have been changed—specifically those charged with crimes associated with neonaticide and their families, the boyfriend, and some detectives and clinicians. For many within the Krom immediate and extended family, the names have been withheld, as they are very private people. No pertinent facts have been knowingly added or changed.

Special thanks to Panna Krom for being the only woman that I know of, out of the hundreds I encountered in reports, accused or convicted of a crime associated with neonaticide, who has had the courage to let others use her story to educate young women like herself about this unfortunate and misunderstood crime.

FOREWORD

I had known Doug Hood going back awhile, but I'd never seen him like this. He had joined our four-person group a few years back, in a class at York Correctional Institute, a women's prison. We met every two weeks and taught essay writing to the incarcerated women.

I guess it was 2012, a lazy mid-July afternoon, and the day before I'd received a cryptic email from him. Could I meet him at a nearby restaurant, which he specified, the sooner the better? He had something important he wanted to discuss with me. Driving to that lunch date, I suspected whatever sandwich I ordered was going to come with a side of indigestion.

Doug and I had met twenty years earlier at a prestigious writers' conference. As a fellow, I'd been allowed entrance to a cottage where faculty could consume lunchtime Bloody Mary's. Uncomfortable with the ossified distinctions in place at this conference, I declined the cocktails and hung out with the students. Among these, Doug was the most interesting and admirable.

My friendship with him has been an unlikely one. Although we had a common interest in writing, we were otherwise a study of opposites. Whereas he was a locally famed runner, I'm put out when I have to get off the couch to retrieve the TV remote. Doug is deep-thinking and shy;

I'm a jokester and a performer. When it comes to travel, I'm a stick-in-the-mud. By contrast, being from a military family made him a sort of world citizen. He and his adopted daughter Suki sent me cards from such places as Mongolia and Oman.

But what was this mysterious behavior of his at the restaurant all about?

It was a legal case, concerning a Cambodian family in Connecticut, he explained. Their American-born daughter got a long sentence. She's at York.

"She may be at York, but she's not a member of our class," I noted, with a deliberate ring of finality. No, he told me. I asked where he heard about her. In Hartford, he said, when her lawyer brought up her case. He added that he suspected there was a preponderant cultural bias. And he wanted to keep going, to show what he suspected, that her sentence was overly harsh. He asked what I thought about him working on this case. It was—as he freely admitted—half-baked. I must say, I was barely interested and was ready to leave.

York has plenty of cases that are full of holes, but we're not agents for fair sentencing nor are we advocates. But more importantly, his involvement in this woman's case might jeopardize the writing program. The Department of Corrections makes it clear that volunteers must stay in their lanes and not become personally involved in their students' lives or cases. And the woman, Panna, wasn't even our student!

I got up to go, looking down at the barely touched sandwich on my plate. Doug waved off my motion to pay, dropped some bills on the table and walked me out. In an effort to keep the conversation from dying, I asked, "So, you've met her family?" He nodded. "And they're okay with you poking around?"

"Plus, her attorney, who told me about the taboos."

"Taboos?"

Sensing that I wasn't jumping on board, he slowed to a stop and said, "I'll kill it."

I asked him, "What's driving you?"

"What?"

"Driving you. Why do you want this?"

"I don't know." I love the tales and facilitating the women in telling them; it's what I do. For him, I guess that's not enough. I sensed that he wasn't letting go of this, no matter what I said.

Unconvinced that I was making a wise decision, I told him, "Run with it."

The result of Doug Hood's mission is the story that follows. It asks the readers to have patience, and it asks them to contemplate nuance and extenuating circumstances as they consider what is justice and what is injustice. Beyond that, and perhaps most importantly, *Daughter of Song* is a love story.

Wally Lamb
Storrs, Connecticut

MAP OF CAMBODIA

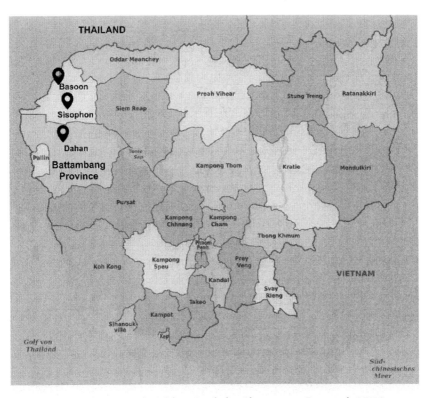

Source: This image is adapted from Cambodia Administrative Divisions by TUBS.

PART ONE
THE OUTSIDER

CHAPTER ONE

CHARLIE'S DINER

York Correctional Institution, Connecticut's only women's prison, sits on a gentle rise in wooded acreage in Niantic, an old fishing village on Long Island Sound. From the main road a few hundred yards away, the low-lying facility hardly catches the eye. Despite the original designs for a bucolic prison beside the oddly named Bride Lake, it's treeless and monolithic, constructed with ash-gray stone and encircled by double-link fences topped with rolls of razor wire. It's also spotless, with so few signs of life that a casual observer might think no one is there. In fact, it is home to more than a thousand women.

The first time I went inside, in the summer of 2011, I immediately felt an institutional chill in the hallways and classrooms—yet it percolated with life. A bounty of stories begging to be heard. I never found the prison uninviting. Instead, I had a paradoxical sense of belonging and an urgent need to find a role.

My path to York that summer began with a pair of well-known locals with peculiar ties to the place: Wally, a novelist, and Willie, who was once the most wanted man in the state. At the time, I was working as a physician assistant, doing in-patient consultations and seeing acute strokes at the Yale New Haven Medical Center, less than an hour away down I-95.

Wally and I first met in the early 90s, over lunch at a writing conference in Vermont. Within minutes, we had a solid friendship. About that time, a publisher picked up his debut novel, followed by a second book six years later. In 2010 we reconnected, and he invited me to join his long standing writing group in the York prison. York had me do an orientation class with other volunteers and I got a picture badge. I was blindly going through the paces of my life, cheerlessly approaching the end of a career and with no forethought of any redirection; I was in the "drizzly November in my soul," to borrow words from Melville.

My first day in the prison writing group began at Charlie's Diner in Niantic, where four of us shared a booth to lay out plans for that day's class. It was me and Wally, along with the other two writing facilitators, Careen and Susan, both retired colleagues of his. After introductions, lesson preparations, and a bite, we drove the two miles to York.

Shortly after his first book's release, Wally had been cajoled into giving a talk to the York women about writing their personal stories. Captivated by what he heard, he returned every two weeks for the next twenty years to listen to the women's narratives. Out of that collaboration came two anthologies of essays.

Wally introduced me to the class of around fifteen women, asking me to talk about myself and read something. I told them I grew up as a military brat with a scattered childhood: several years overseas, in and out of about two dozen schools. As for my writing, I had published some short stories, an essay here and there, and a children's book, but I had been away from it for a while, maybe ten years, while raising my little girl. Wally had assumed that I would bring something to read. I didn't think of myself as a writer and came unprepared, nothing on hand. Sorry ladies.

After class dismissal, while most split into groups of two or three for some light-hearted exchanges, I sidled to the back of the room for a one-on-one with Robin, a thirty-something rap poet with straightened jet-black hair. We chatted about her situation; she had been there for a long time and was still in for a long haul.

"Anyone helping you? I asked.

I was green; she could tell. "Here," she said. She scribbled something. "Wanna do something? Start with this."

4

A phone number. I wasn't sure if she was playing me. That was okay. I took it.

I called the number and got Robin's dad, Willie Ledbetter. He told me the issue was that his "baby" had been prosecuted as an adult, not a juvenile—although she was fourteen at the time. That's a difference in sentencing, he said, of roughly forty-eight years. Willie was grasping for a quick fix to this mess. But I had no ideas; this was all new to me. I didn't know much about courts and sentencing, and besides, her case, as he had told me, was on appeal. Still, I said I'd stick with him, and I did. After a few calls back and forth, we arranged to meet.

I found out that other women in the class had their own messy deals. One even offloaded her entire trial transcript on me and was far down the hall before I realized what I was holding: an incarcerated woman's legal file, which was considered contraband. For one or two others, I got their consent, delved into their cases, but quickly hit roadblocks: lawyers who never returned calls, families I couldn't reach or who didn't trust me, boxes of files sitting somewhere in storerooms. Locked-up women were very limited in what they could do to seek any remedy. They had to deal with a system that was unwieldy, riddled with holes, and (no surprise) not friendly. On top of that, York lacked internet and law books. None of the women I talked to made any claims of innocence—not what I expected to hear. A surprising number in our class, like Robin, were there for a lengthy sentence but had no one on the outside helping them, not even family. For someone willing to help, there was plenty to do, anything from placing a phone call to diving into their files.

CHAPTER TWO
THE PROMISE ZONE

The first time I met Willie was at his mother's apartment, located in a "broken windows" part of Hartford, newly named the Promise Zone. His stories were raw, but entertaining. He had pissed away decades, as he put it, drinking and getting by on petty theft. Dealing crack earned him time in and out of a dozen prisons. Willie's body was beat; his face was etched with mileage; and he knew time was not on his side. Yet, his mother, Robin's grandmother, was a model of composure—their anchor, I like to think. Her apartment was scrupulously neat with hundreds of knickknacks on the walls and tables. But I kept going back to one item: a photo of a beaming five-year-old Robin. Those must have been her few days of innocence and promise; I bet it could have been any one of many women at York.

Now counting off his ninth year of sobriety, Willie was sporting a bow tie and playing chess on The Common in Pittsfield, Massachusetts. He was picking up the homeless and dropping them off at detox or shelters. Despite his suspended license, every Friday he drove the two hours to visit Robin in Niantic. Together, Willie and Robin provided a snapshot of what many of us "on the outside" never see, though we four in the prison writing group did hear the stories: abuse and addiction, fractured families, street survival, the vortex of the criminal justice system with sloppy police work (I saw Robin's investigation report), then, late in life, the picking up of the pieces. Willie was the first of several who made me pause to rethink my preconceptions about the incarcerated: he had a disturbing past, yet I trusted the guy.

A few months later, Willie called. The Civil Justice Clinic at Quinnipiac University Law School had invited him to a legislative hearing about sentence reform in Hartford. Because of the notoriety of Robin's 50-year sentence—a black eye for the Connecticut justice system—the clinic people saw value in Willie's testimony. He wanted to make sure I'd come. Of course, I would. The legal team welcomed my participation, unconcerned that I knew close to nothing about prison issues.

The Hartford Legislative Office Building, the LOB, is where the state makes its laws. The bustling marble-floored lobby with two showy escalators is a beehive, where the ambitious can gladhand and trade business cards, maybe bump into a senator. We were there to speak before a panel of lawmakers, mostly state elected officials. The docket that day, November 9, 2012, featured a draft proposal for a bill called Second Look, which introduced parole opportunities for juvenile offenders with lengthy sentences. An often-referenced federal case, known as Graham *v.* Florida had introduced the now-widely-recognized concept of the immature, impulsive brain to criminal defenses, setting a precedent for states to follow. Once the bill became law, Connecticut would offer a parole hearing for Robin, who was now thirty-two, by age forty-five—plus another 260 incarcerated men and women throughout the state, who, like Robin, were under eighteen when they committed a violent crime.

Sarah Russell, a law professor in the Civil Justice Clinic, submitted our names, probably fifteen in all, securing our spots chosen by a lottery for the docket. Most in our cohort were law students. Because Willie and I were the two with no legal credentials, Attorney Russell put our names at the bottom of the day's roster. Some eighty speakers were listed ahead of us; it would be a long day. As it turned out, those eight hours of talks from that mix of activists would alter the course of my life.

A cable channel, CT-N, televised the session throughout Connecticut. The audience in the hearing room was a gathering of extremes:

retired doctors, hard-scrabble single moms, undergrads, attorneys, and the formerly incarcerated. Loved ones of the incarcerated were in abundance—moms fed up with the courts and public defenders. They had spontaneity; voices that never flinched. Things would get slow with the attorneys or legislative staffers who were flat and tedious. But interspersed were three or four who made me sit up: they were in tailored suits with du-rags or Islamic skullcaps. They told us about doing hard time but somehow had beat a bad rap and now spoke with a ring of truth on their side.

But no one was fooled. This was theater, more about political posturing, blustery talk, or grabbing a TV interview. Nothing was going to happen, nothing beyond head-nodding, some eloquent and sympathetic verbiage, and being shown the door. By late afternoon, the audience, which early on had lined the back walls, was down to a hardy few, people like me and Willie.

Then I heard the name that drew me into a new world: Panna Krom.

———

Moments before Willie and I were to talk, a tidy thirty-something lawyer in a gray suit with a coffee cup in one hand, placed her briefcase on the table, straightened her skirt, took her seat, and gently inched the mic toward her.

She eyed the panel. "Good afternoon."

She began, "My name is Jennifer Tunnard. I am an attorney in Fairfield County. My office is located in Litchfield, Connecticut. I am here to speak about Panna Krom. I represented her during the years of 2006 to 2008. On December 28, 2006, Panna committed a crime. She was seventeen. Her story is one of sadness and shame."

The attorney related Panna's story to the panel, in brief: She had been a popular student at Danbury High School, but naïve, living in fear of the sexual taboos in her culture, her parents' fanatical sheltering, the strict rules which they had carried from old-world Cambodia and Thailand. She was never allowed to see boys, not even to go out to a game or a dance. However, for four years she had had a secret boyfriend.

At sixteen she got pregnant, hid the pregnancy, lived in denial, and sank into isolation. Alone in the bathroom, she had a surge of panic, leading to the tragic outcome of a drowned baby at her hands. As Attorney Tunnard explained, the causes for her actions were complex and blame was widespread. Panna was charged with murder and was given a sentence of eighteen years. She said that there was much more to the story than the sensationalized headlines put out by the prosecutor and press.

She ended by saying, "Panna is doing well. She wants to help other girls who, like her, have unwanted pregnancies. Her family visits her every week and waits for her to come home."

A panel member asked the attorney, "Did you consider a sentence modification?"

"The prosecutor did not want to hear it," said the attorney.

Another said, "Your decision about a trial?"

She said, "She took a plea. We were afraid. We were looking at twenty-five years to life."

————

The eighteen-year sentence had to be harsh, I thought. Plus, I wasn't buying into the charge—that this high school daughter of immigrants was a premeditated or even an intentional killer. That was the charge —murder.

After Attorney Tunnard's testimony, only Willie and I plus a couple of stragglers were left. As he was taking the seat and tapping the mic, my eyes followed the attorney; she was off to one side near the exit, latching her briefcase, dropping her cup in the trash, and gathering her coat. I got up, made a start to dash over for a quick word. In a blink she was gone.

The bad-guy-turned-saint, who was in no hurry, told the panel, "Scuse me, I'm gettin' forgetful." It would look bad if they rang the three-minute bell on Willie. His plea came with unintentional long pauses and mispronunciations that lent a gritty magnetism. His point was clear. In 1997, fourteen-year-old Robin with her felony murder charge was transferred out of the juvenile court to the adult system. Juvenile court meant youthful confinement, probation and guardianship. What she ended up with was an adult sentence of fifty years with no parole. "If she were in the adult, she'd of paroled out." He implored the panel, "It's time she got home." After he slowly straightened his arthritic frame, he leaned into the mic one more time and said, "I ain't got forever." He walked away, patting me as I passed him.

My notepad sheet was cluttered with last-minute revisions and scribbly long arrows to the margins. I mostly talked about what the women had written in our writing class. Nothing about me drew attention—I suffer from that. I'm the "potted plant" famed lawyer Roy Black referred to when he felt unnoticed. When I looked up, of the ten original members on the panel, maybe four were left, and they were looking down at their phones or leaning over and, for all I could see, sharing quips.

Just as Willie and I were headed out to the parking lot, Sarah Russell, the Quinnipiac law professor and one-time Yale hockey team captain, burst out of the conference room doors into the corridor, calling out to us, "Thank you guys for sticking around all day." Catching her breath, she said, "You were great."

I wondered about the bill's chances of passage. "So-so," was her response. "The senate could be a problem; nixed it last time, two years ago."

As she was turning to leave, I asked, "Sarah, do you know the Panna Krom case?" She said, "Which case?"

"Krom, the teen with the baby. She got eighteen years."

She said, "Yes, I know of it. Why?"

"Eighteen? That sound right?"

"Tough one. No, makes no sense. But I don't have access to the particular details."

"Have you heard of any other cases like it?"

"Like that?" she said. She appeared in a rush to get back, but gave it a second. "No, none."

The mystery of Attorney Tunnard in the LOB would never go away. Why had she taken the day off, trekked up to Hartford in nasty weather, waited out the session and talked for three-plus minutes about a client she hadn't seen for six years? I replayed her words: "Sad and shameful." Shameful? And Panna Krom was Southeast Asian, her family from a part of the world dear to me. My dad did four military tours in Asia, I did most of my schooling there, and my adopted daughter and my wife were both from the Far East.

I felt sympathy, perhaps outrage, for this family and their plight. Was I alone? Or maybe the better question: *why* was I alone? I needed to know more.

As I pulled onto I-91 South heading back home, the questions lingered. Where was Panna? What about her family? What's their story? How were they dealing with this? Why did she do this? Can I talk to her? My mind was spinning. She must be at York. She has to be at York.

CHAPTER THREE

THE HALLWAY

The women's prison was an odd place, as it should be. There were strict rules, and though I had gone through a prison orientation for the volunteer writing class, I was never confident of them. So I moved with over-vigilance; I was careful where I stepped, whom I talked to or gawked at, what I said or touched. I waited for entrances to snap open, afraid I would look stupid pulling on a locked door. There were white buttons I wasn't sure if I should push. Areas on the floor were painted with yellow stripes; I was never sure if I should stand inside or outside. Officious-acting corrections officers—COs—ignored me as I waited for a signal to move. Other shadowy COs sat behind one-way glass. It had shades of the Stasi, the secret police I remembered from when I was in communist East Berlin. To avoid any missteps, I copied the person in front of me. In our class, an incarcerated woman sitting next to me wanted my paperclip and my plastic ruler, assuring me over and over that it was okay (I timidly slipped her the ruler)—but was it? Answer: No. After about a year of this cautious movement, I first laid eyes on Panna Krom. She was in her sixth year at York.

A couple of weeks after Attorney Tunnard's testimony, I asked the woman next to me in the writing class if she knew of a Thai—

"Panna!" she immediately blurted, before I could finish my question.

I told her yeah.

"Do you want to meet her?" she asked.

I said yes, I did. She darted out of the room and within minutes was back in her seat with an impish grin. "When you leave, she'll be down the hall. She knows."

Wow, I thought. This happened to be Shannon, one of Panna's best friends, something I would find out some time down the road.

Normally at the end of class, the four writing facilitators, along with a Department of Corrections (DOC) teacher/escort, would meander into the hallway and casually find their way through the locked doors, while making small talk. The women would head off to their tiers, their blocks. This time, however, I slipped out the door first, unnoticed.

I spotted Panna thirty feet down the hall. Pretty unmistakable: small stature, hair in a whale spout, Asian appearance, wearing the standard-issue grandma jeans and ample burgundy t-shirt. She held a ship-deck-sized mop, using her foot to slide a plastic pail of water. The floor around her glistened and smelled of an industrial disinfectant. She appeared earnest about her work, and as I approached, she slowed, offering a warm smile. I expected someone in the group to call me out. But no one did.

Panna stood straight, squeezing the mop into the pail. I said, "Excuse me. You're Panna?"

"Excuse me?" she said with a laugh. "I am."

"I'm Doug. From a class, over here. I heard your attorney testify about you." I came off as rushed.

With both hands on the mop handle, she tilted her head with a look of surprise and said, "Me? You sure?"

"Of course I'm sure. You didn't know? I hope I'm not telling you something I shouldn't." How could she *not* know? I thought. I kept looking back at the group.

"No, no idea," she said, quickly adding, "But it's okay." Pointing down the hall, she asked, "You in Wally's class?"

What I was doing, being unescorted and mixing with an incarcerated woman not in my class—was a little treacherous. She could get a ticket; I could get the boot. Glancing back again at my group, I saw that they had stopped, had formed a tight circle and were laughing, oblivious to my absence. I told her, "Yeah. Volunteer."

"Where did you hear this testimony?" she asked.

"A public hearing in Hartford. Late in the day, a woman lawyer brought up your case."

"Was it Tunnard?"

"Yes, exactly. She was good."

"Gosh, I haven't heard from her in six years. Didn't know she was still my lawyer. Is something going on?"

I said, "Not that I know of."

"But why would my lawyer be saying something about me? And why now?"

"I thought you'd know?"

"Me? I'm the last to know."

"Another question, before I forget. Are you Cambodian or Thai? Tunnard mentioned both."

She laughed. "Yeah, both. It's confusing."

Then I heard Wally call out, "Doug, what are you *doing*?"

I turned and held up my index finger to indicate that I was on my way.

"I better get back. I'll bring in the transcript."

She said, "Great!"

I was half turned. "I can do that?"

She nodded.

As I made my way back to the group, I was worried that the DOC escort would question me: Why are you talking to an inmate not in our class?

The woman was using the wrong detergent, I'd tell her. But she never asked.

CHAPTER FOUR

SONG AND CHAN

Two weeks after my chance encounter with Panna in November 2012, I returned to York, as I said I would, with a copy of Tunnard's transcript sandwiched between my class notes. She was in the hallway mopping, same as before. With words kept to a minimum and a quick handover, she took the packet, then asked if I had a pen. I did and she told me, "Take this number." She said, "It's my mom's. Don't call yet. I have to speak to her." Not looking up, she slapped her mop on the floor and said, "Otherwise, she'll never talk to you."

Before trying to contact Panna Krom's parents, I sent an email to her attorney, Jennifer Tunnard. I informed her I had been in the LOB in Hartford that afternoon when she testified about her client Panna Krom, and that I'd briefly met Panna at York. I told her I wasn't in the legal profession but was interested in her case, and I left my cell phone number. To my surprise, she called back and said she would be happy to meet with me. She mentioned a video reenactment of the case shown on the Discovery Channel, in a streaming series with the unfortunate title *Killer Kids*. She had agreed to go along with it, she told me, in a desperate attempt to get the word out about Panna.

I watched the episode she mentioned, concluding that it was an amateurish attempt at true crime. It played up the drama while being careless with facts. I surmised that the human elements of Panna's immigrant family were too ponderous to be captured in a one-hour program —and that bothered me. However, it was legitimized by Attorney Tunnard's narration, and in the closing minutes, surprisingly, a calm voiceover by Panna. An assertion in the final minutes was disturbing: it said Panna came from a "troubled" family but gave no further explanation.

Attorney Tunnard's office, newly relocated to Main Street in Danbury, took up the ground floor of a restored Victorian with a wraparound front porch. She lugged a huge cardboard box full of files into the wood-paneled conference room, dropped it on the table in front of me, exhaled, and said, "I'll never let go of this." Tunnard was eye-catching, classy, bright, and sharp-tongued. Though she had Castilian blood, she was originally from the Dominican Republic, then attended college and law school in New York. Part of her practice came from Danbury's Hispanics, who make up about thirty percent of the city's population. Back in 2007, after Panna's initial lawyer, Vicki Hutchinson, was dropped, the Kroms, now desperate, reached out to her and she was retained.

As she pulled item after item out of the box, I was taken aback at how casually she trusted me. I had said nothing about who I was or what I did, just called, expressed interest, and left my name. I barely kept up with the daunting array of documents she rapidly passed over to me: police affidavits, court records, DNA results, and even—after she asked me if it was okay—autopsy photos of the deceased baby. "Dead baby photos are grisly," she said. "Prosecutors love them." She readily agreed to get Panna to sign a release, allowing me access to her records, including the psychological evaluation, autopsy report, and any personal notes.

Once I had Attorney Tunnard's okay and Panna's release, the next step would be getting the cooperation of her family. Tunnard briefly told me about their travails and their utter devotion to Panna, making it obvious she had spent many hours with them. "Panna is like my own kid," she said. As I was leaving, she asked, "You want to work on her case?"

I said, "Yeah, I do."

"In what way?"

"No idea, really," I told her. "I'll see how it goes with her parents. Start there."

"We were forced to take a plea," she explained, seeming to invite my participation. "There's a lot of lingering questions that we could never look at, or use. Her whole psych state, the high school, this type of crime, plus her statement. I even wonder about the autopsy. Little quick and too tidy."

"Sounds like a lot," I said.

"It *is* a lot. You sure you want to do this?"

"Yeah, I'm sure."

"Just curious. Why? I mean I don't want to discourage you."

"It hits home for me." I didn't know what else to say.

She shrugged at that. "Okay."

We agreed to stay in touch. It was clear that the next move, if there was one, would be mine. Suddenly, I wondered, am I in over my head?

———

A few weeks later, in December, I was still holding onto the phone number Panna had given me for her parents, Song and Chan Krom. Attorney Tunnard had told me that, because of the intrusive press coverage, they were distrustful of the media, or really anyone. There was a good chance they wouldn't see me. And the story would stop there.

It turns out that on one of the parents' Saturday visits to the prison, Panna described our brief encounter in the hallway, referring to me as her "guardian angel." If I had heard that, I would have dismissed it as youthful wistfulness. But for her family, it carried deep-seated spiritual meaning. Later, I heard a related tale involving a family fortune teller who gave them advance notice of my arrival. Such omens paved the way for me to become the first outsider welcomed into their home. Little did I know, they were waiting for me to call, even *before* Panna described our meeting.

I dialed the number. "Hello?" said the accented female voice.

I introduced myself. Chan, like me, was a person of few words, but she invited me to come anytime. A few days later, I made the hour-long drive toward western Connecticut. Their township was a woodsy scattering of houses that would have been easy to miss if not for the lone sign on a curvy road: Entering Bethel, Est. 1855.

At the end of winding Whittlesey Drive stood their complex of buildings, all shaped like Monopoly hotels, with a sign at the entrance: Oak Woods Estates. Colored a rustic pastel green, it was set on hilly grounds with sparse well-tended landscaping and a backdrop of maple and scraggly oak. The mostly compact cars in the parking lot, some with baby seats, told a lot of the residents were young and not staying long.

As I rounded the stairway on the second floor, the scent of what I thought was nutmeg grew stronger. The door to apartment number 18 was cracked and I heard the TV. I tapped lightly. The TV went dead and the door opened. Chan, with a faint smile, greeted me. As I stepped inside and clumsily removed my sneakers, it was obvious that we were both trying to not appear awkward. I was wearing jeans, my favorite long-sleeve Polo shirt, and the North Face fleece jacket so popular with teens—hardly officious or intimidating.

Chan's face, both bravely radiant and weary, gave good cover for her hard years. Barefoot, she wore a Hollister hoodie, and being under five feet, had gray sweats with the waistband rolled down. Panna's father, Song, emerged from the kitchen, wiping his hands on a dishtowel. He had a boxer's face with a Marlon Brando nose, a starter mustache, and biceps. He appeared ageless (though I found out later he was near fifty), a couple of inches shorter than me, compact and tanned, in a tight faded t-shirt that said Boss. When we clasped hands, my grip was little match for his. From that moment on, Song, constantly injecting a childlike enthusiasm, never failed to up the mood, forcing me to take measure of my worries that seemed trivial. But validation for each of my steps in this long project of getting it right for their daughter came from Chan. Diminutive Chan was a thinker and a stern gatekeeper. For each new idea—and I had many—I'd learn to read her facial expression and hope for her gentle nod of approval. But with Song everything was great.

The small apartment was tiny and warm. Song caught me gazing over at their array of pictures and religious artifacts and offered to show me around.

Every room was within steps of the living area where we were. A mini-gym sat on one side, with Song's barbell set, free weights, and a bench. The couch was the centerpiece of the room—for TV viewing, next-of-kin sleepovers, or visitors like me. Right around the wall was a miniature kitchen with rice in a steamer. Down a six-foot hall, past two twenty-pound bags of rice, was the bathroom, and a bit farther the only bedroom.

Each wall had one or two pictures. A few were new, but many black-and-white family portraits, probably dating from the 1970s or 80s. The one of Song's dad, next to that of his wife, was grainy and enlarged from his passport—you could see part of the stamp.

A pure radiance came from a far corner. That was their equivalent of the Wailing Wall, a spot Song, by now more relaxed, proudly went over in minute detail. Placed on what looked like a throwaway dorm bookshelf was, I surmised, every meaningful item in their life.

Burning candles and sticks of incense splaying from little bowls sat on top, backed by two statues of Buddha. At first, I thought a wall poster showed a woman in a meditative pose on a lotus flower. But it was Buddha. His hands were in front, right strategically over left. This was the moment when he attained enlightenment after sitting under the bodhi, a fig tree in Nepal. He had stood under that tree for one week without blinking, his gratitude on display.

The two six-inch Buddha statues were made from precious Abri marble from India, a mottled burnt orange with deep brown swirls, gleaming from their ritual of daily dusting. One was seated in the lotus posture with the thumbs and fingers forming a circle, meant to promote meditation and deep contemplation. The other was walking with his right hand partly raised to the chest and the left palm out. This was *abhaya,* a sign for protection and deep inner security. Chan told me it was the Buddha position for Monday, the day she was born. As I continued my tour, I almost felt touched by the reassuring hand of Buddha.

To the right, along the top shelf away from the statues, stood an arresting picture. Panna had to be maybe four, wearing an orange outfit with beach shorts, her hair with a cute burst on top. In mid-stride, turning back, the camera captured her wonderment, but on the whole it was in a frustrating blur. Not a great photo, but a memorable one, a keeper. Chan said they had few photos of Panna as a little girl. Plus, since her incarceration, taking pictures was allowed only on open family days, every June. The next photo was one of those, showing a radiant Panna flanked by five family visitors on an outing to what they called the "school" at York. The incarcerated women had put on a show with music, singing, and dancing. Panna did a reading, since she can't sing or dance. In these June DOC photos, Panna managed to look fresh despite prison-grade makeup and her tiresome uniform.

One shelf down was a plain brown marble box, about the size of a softball, tucked away toward the side among a few toys. The box rested on a pink chevron-patterned Afghan crocheted by Panna in her cell. Song and Chan told me it was the urn for baby Angel. Gifts, mostly stuffed cartoon-like characters, including a yellow rubber duck and green bug-eyed frog, surrounded her. On the 28th of every month they held quiet celebrations, with prayer, music, and a special family dinner. They continued to speak to Angel as if she were a little girl, now six. They told me, "We take her everywhere in the car, on the front seat. One time to York to be near her mother." In the Buddhist religion, Chan explained, after you die, your spirit is still alive.

An intriguing folder sat on the next shelf down. They told me it contained Panna's cards sent from York, for occasions like Mother's day and Valentine's Day.

After being granted an intimate tour of their private life, I felt I had earned their trust. We sat down, with Song and Chan taking spots on the floor below me. I explained my role, careful not to overplay it. "I'm a regular guy, half retired. I'm not a lawyer. Not anything."

"Will you help us?" asked Chan.

"I can't get her out," I said, sure that that's what they meant. "First, I don't even know her story." I asked if it was okay to take notes or record on my phone. They said it was. "I saw Attorney Tunnard several weeks ago talk about Panna," I told them. "And I even met with her."

"What did she say?" asked Song.

"Not a whole lot. It was only twenty minutes. Though she raised a lot of questions. She gave me the go-ahead and showed me Panna's files. My first question is why. Why did she do this? The prosecutor doesn't care, but we do. I'm curious: Are there other cases like Panna's?"

"We don't know that," said Song. "We don't know much legal. We go to the court every time. We hope each time, something happen, and they let Panna come home."

"So you showed up every day?"

"Every day, I tell you," said Song.

"You guys doing okay?" I looked around the apartment. "Things seem okay here."

Song shook his head and said, "No."

Chan jumped in. "You see, we get very sick. I mean, not sick like you think. But we—"

Song cut her off. "A lot of stress. We can't sleep. Nothing. Work. Nothing. I get up and bang my head against the wall. But we don't want Panna to know."

"Do you see a doctor?"

"We don't go," said Song. "I blame myself."

"Don't do that," I told him.

"I was hard on her, angry, and scare her. I do this to her."

"There are a lot of factors, plenty of blame. This is bigger than you, bigger than her. What's your contact with her now? Phone calls, visits?"

Chan said, "She call every night—if no lockdown. We see her every Saturday."

"And financial?" I asked.

"You mean money?" said Song. I nodded. "Oh. We have nothing. Family, everyone chip in. Nothing left. We still pay."

I said, "How about Panna? She better?"

"Panna? It's hard. She's better, try hard," said Song. "She do prison programs, college work, and tutoring older women. Volunteer for everything."

Chan said, "She want to come home. Every day it's 'Mom, get me out of here!'"

Just as I was leaving—it was after ten, going on three hours—I turned and asked them if I could see that folder with Panna's cards. They pulled out the stuffed manila folder. I slipped off a heavy rubber band and a stack of cards slid out. There were cards sent to Panna and to her parents, plus her drawings and diary, grades and scores from elementary and middle school, attendance records, honors, and diplomas, as well as legal letters and court papers. A funeral bill for Angel. In one printout of an email to the prosecutor, Panna's first attorney Vicki Hutchinson pointed out that there was no video of Panna's interview. I found a letter from a social worker at York who said Panna was the best incarcerated woman he had ever worked with. One card I liked was addressed to the "world's best mom." Then there was "Noi Noi Panna!" in heavy ink, a greeting from cousin Nancy. Chan explained, "It mean Sweet Young Panna." The only thing they told me they discarded were the newspaper headlines with photos, from her arrest in 2007 and sentencing in 2008. Song had stopped at every newspaper vending machine in town, put a quarter in, grabbed all the papers, brought them home, and in a tearful frenzy, took scissors to the articles and photos of Panna. "I don't care," he said. "Arrest me." As for the one photo on the TV news, he told me, "They stole it from Panna's yearbook."

I apologized for taking so long with the folder, but they encouraged me to keep going.

Panna's letters, some never opened, were clipped together in a neat pack. "We don't read," said Song.

Chan added, "We do. But not like that." She pointed to an official letter.

The letter had been sitting at the bottom, still in its sealed envelope. They let me open it. It was dated December 5, 2006 and signed by the assistant principal at Danbury High School. He was notifying the parents that their daughter had missed twenty-one days during the first semester of her senior year, even citing a Connecticut law informing them that her attendance was their responsibility. They didn't remember the envelope, they said—reminding me again that they would never read something like that. Normal measures to notify them had apparently failed. I asked them if the school had called them. They said, no. Thinking about that date, it became painfully obvious: it was early December 2006 and they were unaware of any problem. A month later, in early January, Panna sat in prison, charged with murder.

———

Hope for the Krom's was no small item. As I would find out, it stemmed largely from an intertwining of a fortune teller's vision and a resolute faith in karma. Hope was nourishment and I was now part of that feed. I saw the school letter as a flag telling me there must be more to their story. It gave me pause. I got up to leave, picked up my jacket, and said to Song and Chan, "I better go."

Song looked perplexed and said, "That's it?"

I said, "I see problems."

"What do you mean? This is bad?" he said. He stood.

"Not exactly. Just that I'm bothered." I looked at Chan, her face was stony. It was like she was telling me to play my hand. So I did. "I don't believe she should be in prison."

They both put their hands in a prayer position and bowed. Song repeated, "Thank you."

That wasn't so much a thanks but a plea. Tearing myself away was now looking nearly impossible. "Lots of loose ends," I told them. I thought for a minute and asked, "Did anyone look at all of this?"

Chan said, "Jennifer. She spent a lot of time with us."

"No, not her. Her focus was on whether to go to trial. Anyone else?"

Song added, "Only you."

"Me?" I laughed. "Look, there are questions."

I had made a bold declaration and it put me in foreign territory. But I had the right ingredients: the incarcerated girl, her devout family, the files, a lawyer on board, and a messy story that I was certain I could make sense out of. Their *wai*, that prayer-like gesture, would be a constant reminder. I wanted this case.

"I may get nowhere," I told them. "Or I might dig up bad stuff, like on Panna. More than likely nothing changes. You know that. She gets out in 2024 or whenever it is. I'm not changing that."

Song said, "We know."

"You guys may end up wishing you never met me."

"We don't worry," said Chan.

"Okay. I'll come back. In two weeks, Tuesday. I'll be here, same time. I won't even call ahead. Just show up. I've put in a request for the police report. We'll begin at the beginning—the crime and what the police said. If it gets ugly, it gets ugly. You guys okay?" I was all in.

Song shook my hand.

Chan said, "I will make you special dinner."

PART TWO
THE CRIME

CHAPTER FIVE

PANIC ROOM

When I returned to Song and Chan Krom's apartment on that designated Tuesday evening, I brought the Danbury Police crime report, which described the investigation and arrest. I let them thumb through it and asked if they were present when their daughter was interviewed. Chan told me that the police moved her to the next room. I had been reading up on police interview practices (police carefully avoid the term "interrogation") and told the Kroms, "They can't make you leave the room. No way. That was wrong." They nodded. "In fact, a lawyer should have been there. Would be a different story."

I patted the report and said, "We may not like it but we have to accept this as is." They understood and we began.

What follows—the next nine chapters—describes the crime, the scene, interviews, autopsy and arrest, all derived from the document I got from the Danbury Police. I've added what Song and Chan were able to recall during those seven days—from the night of the crime until her arrest. There's no way to independently corroborate either account, the parents' or that of the police. This is a systemic problem with police investigations—a natural bias, a "noble cause corruption"—as they work in concert with the prosecutor. I largely avoided questioning the obvious person who could refute the statements in the document—Panna herself—because as I would learn from forensic psychiatrists, Panna had been subject to trauma and likely persuasive questioning by the authorities. Her memory would be unreliable.

———

It was early morning, three days after Christmas in 2006, and Song was up. Slipping on a pair of jeans, he went about his routine: in and out of the bathroom, starting the coffee maker while downing a couple of meds, then rinsing the rice and pouring it into the steamer for later. In the living room he pulled the curtain to see what it was doing outside, turned the TV on mute, and while a *Survivor* rerun played, he counted off fifty dumbbell curls in each arm, did sit-ups and stretched his hamstrings. With a quick dash outside, he scraped the ice off the two cars. No peep from the girls. Following a morning prayer and meditation before a Buddha statue in the corner of the living room, he eased Panna's door open and whispered, "Hey, Sweetie... Noi Noi, sh-sh."

Panna was in her senior year at Danbury High. Though considered artsy and cool, she mostly hung out with her peers, the Asians, a largely unnoticed group. And instead of being her best year, the winter had been bleak. Holding down two jobs to get her mind off things and get her through this holiday season wasn't working; matters were getting worse. Personal problems during the semester—problems she couldn't discuss with her parents or really anyone—had left her scared and increasingly isolated. Her longtime boyfriend, a six-foot-something quarterback at another school, who she had kept a big secret from her parents, had dumped her, and she heard that he was parading down the halls with another girl. That she could deal with.

But Panna herself had attracted unwanted attention at Danbury High, all the way up to the assistant principal. She had missed so many days that her grades were crashing, killing a decent GPA. Her counselor warned her that she may not graduate, something that should have upset her, but it didn't show. There was a buzz going around the school, harsh rumors about her—only they were true. She was avoiding eye contact, and, when she had to, coming up with stories, like saying she was headed to Boston College, when she hadn't even taken the SATs. In the halls, she kept her head down, lost in the din of the chatter. In the cafeteria she sat alone. In the classrooms, she was last in, first out.

At night, Panna took orders, cleared tables, and stacked chairs at KFC until closing. She would drive herself home after her parents were asleep, then after a fitful night, be up before them. They'd ask her, "You okay?"

She'd say, "Yeah, why?"

At KayBee Toys in the Danbury Fair Mall, her day job was shelving the returned boxes. For weeks, store employees had been increasingly cautious with her, whispering to each other about how "hormonal" she looked. Even though it was stuffy in the store, Panna wore a droopy sweater, at times one over another.

That day, a Thursday in late December 2006, she stretched to catch a box coming off an overhead shelf when a horse kicked her in the belly; at least that's what it felt like. An older co-worker who saw that she was in trouble—pale, almost doubled over—told her to go home, and even offered to drive her.

Panna, fighting back waves of belly cramps, made it to her own car and cranked up the heat. First stop was her cousin's, where she knocked once on the door, but no one came. In the car, she tried to down a few old crackers, then remembered she had to get her mom. She drove to Hologic, the medical device factory where her mother worked, in nearby Ridgefield, and sat out front with the car idling. A receptionist spotted her. Chan hustled out into the dim light. Coatless and shivering, she leaned through the half-open window, asking Panna, "Why are you here? It's way early. Eight-thirty, remember? You okay?"

Her mom spoke Thai. Panna responded in English: "Yeah, I'm fine. I'll come back. Mom, get back inside, you'll catch pneumonia. Bye." As she rolled up the window to speed off, her mom told her, "Seat belt!"

Hunched over the wheel in pain, Panna made it to their brick apartment building on quiet Fifth Avenue. As she struggled up the single flight of stairs, her legs became soaked. She hit the bathroom and headed straight to bed. Her coat and sweater were thrown onto the couch and the wet jeans and socks lay crumpled on the bathroom floor; she was half-dressed.

In her bedroom, with no light except for bluish metallic rays coming off an alley lamp, Panna remained restless, nauseated, writhing, and so alone. She heard her dad, Song, arrive home around 6:00 p.m. He called to her but she begged him off, groaning, "So tired, Dad." He let her be; she deserved the rest, he thought. He prepared dinner. Later, she heard the phone ring. That must be her mom. Song left to pick her up.

Panna was still awake when she heard them return. She did her best to remain frozen and not breathe. She didn't want them to check on her. But Chan did, briefly stopping outside her door. Cracking it, she peeked into the darkened room, saw and heard nothing, and eased the door closed.

Sliding herself out of bed in the near-darkness, Panna shuffled back and forth across the hall to the bathroom, barely making a sound and holding her belly like a cantaloupe. She ran a hot shower and repeatedly flushed the toilet.

Hearing the stop and start of the water from in the bathroom, Song tapped on the door: "Panna. Panna?" Panna stood still.

Her mom came to the door next, knocked harder and cried, "Panna, what are you doing?" She tried the handle but the door was locked.

"Mom, I'm having a bad period. Grab a towel."

Chan pulled one from the closet. Panna cracked the door while Chan handed her a white towel. While Panna struggled to cover herself, Chan leaned on the door. Spotting the glistening blood all over the floor, tub and toilet, Chan recoiled. "Why is there all this blood?"

Panna whispered, "I told you, Mom, my period." The towel partially covered her as she stayed behind the door.

"You need to talk to me?" Chan asked.

"No," said Panna. She flipped her wet hair out of her face. "It's a mess, I know. You can go."

Chan leaned in, wiped up a quarter-sized blob on the floor with a tissue and tossed it to the wastebasket. She rinsed her hand and closed the door.

The shower and exhaust fan were going. Panna flushed the toilet, then again, and again. The bathroom was a panic room.

Panna emerged, half-wrapped in the towel, turning her back to her mom, her hair stringy and soaked, chin dripping, her arms around a bundle of wet clothes, a twisted sweatshirt, and streaked towels. Song heard Panna's bedroom door close hard, got up, then spotted drops of blood in the hall. On the bathroom floor, in the tub, and down the toilet were rivulets of mixed water and blood. He turned off the water for the shower and sink.

When he opened Panna's door, she was sitting up with her back to the wall, her wet hair falling over her face. She cried, "I'm cut!"

This wasn't his daughter. Feeling lightheaded, Song scooped her up and frantically called out to Chan, "Something's wrong!"

While they sped the two minutes to the hospital, Chan cradled Panna, throwing Song's coat over her. The streets were empty, it was pitch black, and they said nothing. She could see the strain on her husband's face, the glare in his eyes; this was not good.

CHAPTER SIX

EMERGENCY ROOM

S ong emerged out of the late night blackness, followed closely by Chan, through the automatic doors into the Danbury Hospital Emergency Department. His daughter was draped in his arms. Her hands were loosely around his neck, her head smothered by his coat and her legs limp and dangling. A triage technician at the desk jumped up and helped her into a wheelchair. Spotting the reddish streaks on her legs and discoloration of her socks, he motioned for the parents to stay back. Wheeling her into a bathroom, he handed her a cup and told her he needed some pee. When Panna finished, he scribbled her name and birthdate on it, and guided her into the gynecological exam room. Taking her vitals, which were okay, he cleaned the blood off her legs and left a gown. A nurse came in, offered her two warmed blankets, took down some preliminary history, then helped her onto the exam table, placing her feet in the stirrups and draping a sheet over her legs.

At the check-in desk, a nervous Chan registered Panna. For chief complaint she told the clerk female bleeding. Song and Chan took seats in the middle of an empty waiting room. Song's coat, which had covered Panna, was now draped over Chan's shoulders while his hand, slipped underneath it, tried to ease her, working her neck and back. Repeatedly, he bolted up and paced the floor, muttering, as if mad at himself.

The emergency department attending, Dr. Broderick, entered the exam room, introduced himself to Panna and took down details about her bleeding. By now it was after ten. Someone came in to attach an ID band to her wrist. A phlebotomist drew blood. A tech needed another urine sample. Panna described her symptoms: abdominal pains, diarrhea and vaginal bleeding. He asked her how long she had been hemorrhaging. Two months. Though one month ago she was certain she had a normal period.

After a light tap on the door, it cracked open and the technician handed Dr. Broderick a slip and said, "HCG, doc." The doctor looked at the lab result and asked Panna, "Did you know you were pregnant?" No, she said. "No?"

While the nurse guided Panna, Dr. Broderick performed a speculum exam—her first one, she nervously admitted. He discovered cervical engorgement and an enlarged uterus, both consistent with a recent delivery, though she quickly denied it. He asked her, Is there a baby? An immediate no.

He asked her about the jagged tear in her vaginal area. She told him she accidentally cut herself with a razor, but as she was explaining, she became flustered: her story changed and soon made little sense. He asked if her parents knew she was pregnant. They didn't, she said. He let her know that he would need to tell them, and Panna, in a flat voice, told him, yeah, go ahead.

He snipped off some placental tissue, dropped it in a cup for the lab, and left to put in an urgent call to the obstetrician resident, Dr. Sontiero, who was in house and came right down.

When Dr. Sontiero examined Panna, he agreed with Dr. Broderick's findings, specifically that she was now hours post-delivery. He palpated her abdomen for the uterus edge, finding it consistent with an estimate of twenty-four weeks pregnant. She then admitted to him that something came out —not a baby, she insisted—and said that it went down the toilet.

In the hallway outside the exam room, the two doctors exchanged their thoughts. Dr. Broderick said, "The patient's lying."

"Lying?" said Dr. Sontiero, with his Portuguese accent. "I'd say delirious. And I'm not so sure about a miscarriage."

"Why's that?" asked Dr. Broderick.

"Twenty-four weeks is a bit on the late side. And it's not going down the toilet. I think there's a baby somewhere. She's clearly in denial. Not sure if she knows what's what." He advised Dr. Broderick to call the police. "Missing baby," he said. "That's for the cops, not us. Give her pads, analgesics; have her follow up in our clinic."

The call came into the Danbury Police Department at 12:06 a.m. and Sergeant Mark Casey took it. Dr. Broderick was to the point: "Sergeant, we've got a seventeen-year-old female—she's just delivered. But no baby."

"No baby. What do you mean?" the detective asked.

"You need to talk to her."

In the waiting room, Dr. Broderick spotted Song and Chan, the only two there, and broke the news: that their daughter had delivered a baby. With stony silence, they looked quizzically at each other trying to process the information. The doctor asked them if they know where the baby was. They shook their heads, saying they knew nothing about a baby, not a thing. Song told the doctor, "We want to take our daughter home. Can we?"

"We'll see. Cops are on their way. They need to talk to her."

Cops? About what? Song wondered.

Sergeant Casey arrived at the hospital, leaving his car out at the entrance, running with the red-and-blue strobe-light bar flickering. Mark Casey was not a big guy, but solidly built, like a big league catcher. He had ten years under his belt and this was what he thrived on, being first at a scene, sorting through the chaos. Song's and Chan's eyes followed him as he hurried past them to the Emergency Department door and got buzzed in. He was there to see Panna; they knew.

Sergeant Casey spoke briefly with Dr. Broderick and got the okay to talk to Panna Krom. He asked her a few direct questions—she was vague —then got the apartment key from Song and rushed out. With lights flashing, he sped the short mile to the apartment to do a welfare check for the newborn.

The place was tiny, which made it quick work. In the bathroom Casey found a clump of towels, some wet clothes, a clogged tub, nothing in the toilet, and some scattered blood and goop. He looked in all the trash cans, under the bed, and in the closet, thinking he would surely find something. But he came up empty.

At 1:02 a.m., he woke up his supervisor, Detective Sergeant Rachel Wallace of the Youth Bureau Institute, informing her of what he had. They agreed to meet at the hospital.

Although they had the same rank, Wallace was senior to Casey and had a reputation for being a pugnacious, detail-oriented person and all business. He liked to joke and she didn't, but they had worked many cases together and they clicked. Casey briefed Wallace on what he knew so far. He told her the obstetrician said that Panna is post-delivery and put the fetus at about twenty-four weeks. Casey went on to explain that Panna and her parents, who spoke broken English, all denied the existence of any baby and that he found nothing indicating that a baby was brought to the hospital—nothing in their car and nothing in the apartment. So all they had was what the obstetrician said and a bloody mess in the bathroom.

Sergeant Wallace made a quick call to tell officers to secure the apartment as a crime scene.

Sergeant Casey didn't know whom to believe and was at a total loss as to where the baby was. Miss Krom hadn't been straight with the docs, he told Wallace, and they needed to push her, do their own questions. Wallace decided that they would take Panna, plus her parents, to the station. She said, they'd then go through the apartment, top to bottom.

———

The two detectives found Panna and her parents in the Family Room. Panna was in a wheelchair, clearly spent and writhing in discomfort. A nurse entered to inform Panna's parents that she was being discharged—there was no reason to keep her. She handed Chan two pages of instructions and a supply of pads.

Sergeant Wallace asked Panna and her parents to come to the police station to answer some questions. She recognized Panna's long night—it was near 2 a.m.—and apologized, telling them this was voluntary and they were free to not come. The police were also interested in searching their apartment and collecting any blood or human tissue they might find. For that, they would need a Consent to Search document, a search warrant. The Kroms had a longstanding fear of and utter obedience for anyone in a uniform, going back to their days in Cambodia. They stated that they understood and were willing: they signed her document on each line where she pointed.

In their own vehicle, the Krom family followed the squad car to the police station. Panna needed a parent on either side to make it over the icy macadam in the parking lot. Once inside, her mother helped her maneuver into the bathroom to deal with the private mess. The station had no pads; she had left hers in the car. After cleaning up, Panna was pushed in a wheelchair to an Interview Room. Her parents were led down the hall to Sergeant Wallace's office.

During the interview, Panna sobbed and squirmed, afraid they would see the blood stains she had no way to stop, now seeping through her sweatpants. The questioning opened with the detectives asking how she was and noting Panna's reply, "I'm okay."

First, Sergeant Wallace handed Panna a pre-typed statement, asking her to read it back. She read, "I have come with my parents to Danbury Police Department to speak with Detective Wallace. I am seventeen years old and a senior at Danbury High School. I speak English." While she did this, Sergeant Casey stationed himself to one side typing her statements.

Sergeant Wallace asked Panna to explain the events of the last evening, using leading questions to help her.

Panna cooperated (it never registered that she was under no obligation to talk), telling the detective how she had pains at work, drove to a cousin's house, then to her mom's workplace, then home. Her parents came home later. She had waves of pain and spent time in the bathroom dealing with the bleeding.

She told them, "The bleeding was steady. I saw blood clots and globs of stuff. Which got heavier and heavier. And then something long and oblong came out. It hurt my groin. I didn't know what it was. I was freaking out. It looked like a blood clot. Not like a baby. Just a big clot. I had to push a little to get it out. When it came out, it splashed into the toilet. I tried to flush it. It got stuck and I flushed it again and it went down. I was still bleeding. I ran hot water and got in the tub, which was full of blood and clots. I tried, but did a poor job, had to clean up with some towels."

Sergeant Wallace said, "When did you know you might be pregnant?"

"Back in August I started thinking I may be pregnant. I began to feel sick and nauseous and stopped having my period. I remember this because school was just starting."

"Did you take a pregnancy test?"

"No."

"Why not?"

"I was too scared. I started to see changes in my body. I got a little fat and my period just wouldn't come. I mentioned it to my boyfriend, Jason, and he said he would support me if I was pregnant."

"What do you think happened in the bathroom?"

"I don't know. I started to feel sick. I don't know what came out of me, but it could have been a baby."

"Was it a baby?"

"I mean, it didn't look like a baby. It was like a bloody covered oblong clot or something."

That was the conclusion of Panna's statement.

———

Afterwards, Detective Wallace met Panna's parents in her office. "Before tonight," she asked, "Did you know Panna was pregnant?"

After an initial silence, they stated that they did not know. Song had noticed her gaining weight in her stomach and thought she might have been eating too much of the wrong food. They had suggested to her that she watch her diet.

Sergeant Wallace said, "The doctors told Sergeant Casey, the other detective, that it was clear that she had been pregnant and delivered. You understand? This was not food. This was not just gaining weight."

They nodded and told her they understood. They both said they were afraid for her. But no, they never saw a baby.

Sergeant Wallace told them, "Look, she may have miscarried the baby. That means it died at birth. But we have to take a further look.

We're going to the apartment this morning. You can't go back there. Do you have another place to stay? I know it's late."

Chan said, "My sister," and gave her the phone number.

Song asked, "Panna is my baby girl. Will she be okay?"

The sergeant said, "We'll take care of her."

CHAPTER SEVEN

THE SCENE

.

Hours later, that same morning, while Sergeant Casey stood in front of the apartment building, Sergeant Wallace pulled in. They were expecting a plumber and the sewer guys, able to get them on short notice. Since the apartment was taped off as a crime scene, Panna and her family had spent the night at her aunt's house. Sergeant Casey called there to see if they were okay, but mostly to make sure they hadn't left town. He explained again about the need to go through the apartment including the plumbing—all pretty routine, he reassured them.

In the hospital the night before, Casey had been told that the fetus was about twenty-four weeks gestation. After looking it up, Casey came up with a size of about eight inches and maybe a pound and a half—a very large potato. He tried to conceptualize whether something that size would get hung up in the plumbing system.

When the plumber arrived, Wallace led him to the second-floor apartment while Casey checked the environs.

In the apartment, the toilet had leaked onto the floor. Donning gloves, the detective discovered a clump of wet clothes and jelly-like goop in the wastebasket and blood stains on the towels, the tissues, and around the tub. But otherwise the bathroom was clean, at least on the surface. Inside the toilet bowl and tank were clean. Walking through the front half of the apartment—a closet, the kitchen, and parents' bedroom—Wallace saw nothing suspicious, and she returned to focus on where the delivery would have taken place.

Drops of blood led to Panna's bedroom. Her room was small, somewhat cluttered with a night table, two dressers, and posters of basketball players on the wall. The bed was unmade—just as Panna left it when she was rushed to the hospital—and the sheets had blood stains. The detective pulled out every drawer, looked under the bed, felt the pillows, even opened the windows. Inside the closet, she saw disarray. Some clothes were neat and some scattered loosely, while many were in a disordered heap on the floor. She checked the shelf above her, opened a couple of boxes, slid the hanging clothes aside, felt inside all the shoes, and flipped through a stack of jeans. With her baton, she poked the loose pile of clothes on the floor several times, lifting and dropping a number of pieces.

After the plumber removed and reattached the clogged drain in the tub, he called out to Sergeant Wallace to get her okay before unbolting the toilet from the floor. She wanted to watch and positioned herself behind him. He lifted it and demonstrated just how tight the S-bend trap was. Using his snake camera, he could see down the entire soil stack. Wallace, tracking it on the video monitor, was convinced that there was no obstruction. She tagged along as he walked down two flights to the basement. There, he reset the camera and video to check the discharge line to the street. It was clean.

Workers from a drain-service company and public utilities were outside the apartment, inspecting the lines leaving the building, including all the traps, pipes, and valves, and the connection with the main line. They lifted the manhole cover and used video to make sure there was no obstruction going out to the first intersection. The utilities supervisor told Wallace that they would install a screen at the end to make sure nothing got past. If anything managed to get that far, he said, it'd be nearly impossible to find, but said he'd go ahead and notify the crew at the city plant to check the mesh there. He added, "Really, at that point, it's pretty high volume and rapid churning water."

As the plumber was loading his van, Wallace wandered over. He told her, "Sarge, you're clear." She wanted his thoughts. "Ma'am, if something gets by the toilet trap, it's gone. But if you want to know the truth, no baby is getting past that S-bend. We're talking one-and-a-quarter inch."

Wallace had not spoken with the hospital doctors, so she called Danbury Hospital and was put through to Dr. Sontiero, the obstetrics resident. He reaffirmed what Sergeant Casey had been told: his findings on Panna Krom were consistent with a twenty-four-week pregnancy, maybe twenty. He explained that miscarriages do not normally occur after sixteen to twenty weeks. He said, "Can I say something?"

"Sure."

"This case bothers me. I have no idea what you're going to find, but I don't think this girl knew what she was doing in the bathroom. In fact, she may have tried to rescue the newborn out of the water. Kind of hard to do, especially in her state."

"Gotcha. Thanks for your help. We're not coming up with much."

Following their thorough inspection of the Krom home—including the trash, the dumpster, and grounds, by Sergeant Casey—the detectives were satisfied and agreed that there was no newborn in the apartment.

As they stood together on the porch, Casey took out his notes. "Just thinking out loud," he said. "Try to make some sense of this." In the hospital, Panna Krom had claimed her last period was in November, a normal period. That would put her at seven to eight weeks—pretty unlikely. In her interview at the station, her story changed. She thought she might have gotten pregnant in August. That's fourteen to seventeen weeks. The obstetrician put her at twenty to twenty-four weeks. But he said miscarriages don't occur that late. Then she tells us baby, then no baby. That it went down the toilet. Now the plumber, saying it had to be tiny. Look, the one indisputable fact is this: we found no baby.

Wallace said, "What about this cousin's place? Said she went there before coming home. Remember?"

"I checked it out before I came here. They were home. Never saw her, even though she told us she knocked."

"Good." To the detectives, with all the uncertainty in the numbers, a miscarriage seemed the most likely scenario. "The fetus was little—it got away," said Sergeant Wallace, with a shrug.

"Had to," Casey agreed. They were satisfied. There was no criminal element to this case.

"A couple things don't add up," said Wallace in parting, "but they never do. Let's close the case." Their final report concluded: "No baby was found."

CHAPTER EIGHT
THE BEDROOM

Sunday morning, New Year's Eve, Song was up before the others. Hoping things were getting back to normal, he did a few reps with his dumbbells then went into the kitchen to make some pancake mix. Still no word from Panna—this was going on day three for her in Song and Chan's bedroom, with only brief somber appearances for a bite and shower.

Chan got up. She did her prayer ritual in the corner of the living room, then with a brush, a pail of warm water and detergent, got down on her hands and knees in the hallway to scrub the blood stains out of the carpet. She got the plastic basket to gather the week's laundry, starting in the bathroom, then moving to her own bedroom where the girls were—now in a better mood she was happy to see—and finally to Panna's room, which had remained shut since the police search two days earlier.

Chan opened the closet door just to the right and pulled the string for the light. It was a mess, with Panna's dirty clothes piled up (not at all like her), many tossed about by the police during their rummaging. The carpet underneath her had drops of dried blood which she would need to get to. Starting at the top of the pile, she picked up various pieces, shaking and inspecting them, and tossing them one by one into her basket, darks on one side, lights on the other. More dirty clothes were bunched on top of a bluish plastic container. She lifted the first few, but streaks of recent-appearing blood made her recoil. She uncurled a mildewy-smelling sweatshirt and a towel, both of which were wet and heavy.

She froze. A baby's head. Chan dropped her basket and inched the towel down. She screamed out to Song, running into the living room and dropping to her knees. "A baby!" she cried, trembling, her eyes squeezed shut, grabbing the back of her neck and pressing her forehead into the floor.

Panna heard the screams and wept. Exhausted and spent, she let her head flop down on the pillow, curled up and didn't say a word.

Song gingerly moved Chan aside and slowly entered the bedroom. He saw the laundry by the closet, basket tipped over. Looking inside, he could see part of the baby's head. He eased the towel down for a better view. The baby was light brown with shiny skin, eyes closed, mouth open, with no obvious injuries; the limbs were held outward. Carefully unwrapping the sweatshirt, he saw that it was a girl. He lifted her—she was waxy—and lightly rubbed his fingers over her eyes. He inspected the body, kissed her head, then gently placed her back down in the closet and covered her.

Chan remained on the living room floor, shaking. Song lowered down to her level and whispered, "Our baby." After a pause he said, "I'll call the detective."

Sergeant Casey's business card lay on the kitchen counter. Song tried the number but got no answer. Sergeant Wallace's card was underneath it. He tried that number, but again, no answer. He heard a voice mail prompt but left no message. He called the main number for the police department that he found at the bottom of the card, but the operator said she couldn't give out the detectives' private numbers. She asked what the problem was; Song choked up and disconnected. Then he called Chan's sister struggling to get the words out: "We found the baby." He hung up.

Within minutes, the sister showed up with her husband and Chan's other sister. They all sat in the living room for two hours, not knowing what to say.

The men broke off into a group in the kitchen. Speaking Cambodian, they were coming up with options as to what to do: call an ambulance, call the police, call a monk from the temple. Together they decided to do the right thing, a bit fearful, and said that they would call the police. "The police said they'd help us," said Song.

"Okay, let's call them."

Song found Wallace's card on the refrigerator, called Panna out of the bedroom, and handed her the card. "Call the cops." She looked over at the others, who nodded. She got voice mail. She told them, "I'm calling 9-1-1."

The dispatcher answered. Maintaining a calm voice, said, "Hello. We found a dead baby."

"You sure it's dead?"

"Yes."

"Whose baby is it?"

"Mine."

"What's the address there?"

"Six, Fifth Avenue."

"Danbury?"

"Yes."

"And, you're sure? It's dead."

"Yes, ma'am."

"What's your name?"

"Panna Krom." She spelled it and gave her the cellphone number.

"Don't touch anything. A squad car is on the way. Stay on the line."

No one knew what to say. Chan went back into the bedroom with Panna. One of the men said, "It's done. We can't reverse it."

Within twenty minutes, a squad car was out front. Before getting out, Officer Gary Coe pulled up the address and got the detectives' report from two days ago. "Suspicious activity" had occurred; "a missing baby. No baby was found." Case was closed.

Officer Coe tapped once on the apartment door and walked in. "Someone called."

Panna said, "I did, sir."

"A baby was found?"

Song stood up and told him, "Sir, we find a baby in the bedroom."

"Dead?"

"Yes sir." He led the cop to Panna's bedroom.

Officer Coe entered the room and Song pointed to the closet. The officer put on his latex gloves and pulled a few pieces of clothing from a pile on the floor. He uncovered the deceased newborn and lightly touched it.

Field Supervisor Sergeant Sturdevant arrived. Officer Coe told him to notify a YBI detective and the crime scene personnel. Sturdevant did, then looked at Chan and asked what happened and she explained it.

"You knew nothing of this before today?"

"No, sir."

"Who's the mother?"

"My daughter, Panna."

"Where is she?"

"There." She pointed at the bedroom.

The sergeant asked, "Your daughter, Panna, has she been out of the apartment since Friday?"

Song spoke up. "No sir, she never leave."

———

At 1:30 p.m., Sergeant Casey got the call. He immediately got hold of Sergeant Wallace, telling her, "Rachel, remember that little place on Fifth Avenue? They found the baby." She asked where. "The closet, dead."

"Meet me there ASAP."

Entering the apartment, Sergeant Wallace saw Song and Chan sitting on the couch, both teary-eyed. Chan, relieved to see the detective, jumped up to hug her.

Sergeant Wallace's remained stoned-faced and responded with coolness. She turned to Song, pointed to a Consent to Search form on her clipboard and told him she needed their signatures. "We do anything you want," said Song. She handed them her pen and pointed to the sheet. They each signed.

Wallace entered the bedroom. She inspected the layout of the closet and saw the baby girl lying on her right side. The head was full of black hair, her umbilical cord still attached. She appeared to have been dead for, "some time," as she would note in her report. As for dimensions, Sergeant Wallace assessed her to be full term, estimating six-and-a-half to seven pounds. Another officer took pictures.

While the family waited in the living room, Sergeant Wallace gathered the four officers outside, out of earshot, to discuss the case. "i think Panna lied." Sergeant Wallace was blunt. "She must be covering up something. The question is, was the baby alive or a stillbirth? And did she do something to intentionally kill the baby? This is no miscarriage." The detective instructed one of the officers to search the apartment, especially the closet, for any evidence. He agreed and informed Wallace that he had called the medical examiner. She said, "Get all your material first and strike the scene before they touch the body."

Wallace returned inside and informed Panna and her parents, "We have more questions. We need another interview. You'll have to come to the police station, all of you." They agreed. She told them they could drive their own car. Chan told Panna, "Let's get you fresh, baby." Panna took a shower. She walked out of the apartment arm-in-arm with her mother.

Officer Coe stayed back with Song. Alfred Carmago, the assistant medical examiner, arrived. He inspected the baby's body and features to determine time of death. In his notes, he pointed out a mark on the right side of the neck and a scratch at the front base of the neck.

The medical examiner's team transported the baby to Farmington for an autopsy while Coe took Song to the police station, where he'd meet the rest of his family.

PART THREE
INVESTIGATION

CHAPTER NINE
INTERVIEW ROOM

T hat Sunday afternoon, hours after Chan found the baby, she and Panna, as instructed, followed a pair of squad cars for the ten-minute ride to the Danbury Police Department. Police led them upstairs. A small sign said Interview Room. It was bare, flat blue with no clock, window, pictures or camera, only a metal table and three chairs. Days before, Panna had sat in the same room answering questions.

As she closed the door, the detective, Sergeant Rachel Wallace, reminded the mother and daughter that this was a voluntary interview and they were not compelled to speak. The police were only fact-finding, she said. They could stop at any time and they could leave at any time. She pointed to the door. "You're not under custody." They nodded that they understood.

Chan later explained to me, "We don't know any rules. We just say yes whatever they tell us."

Wallace asked, "Panna, is there anything you want to say?"

Panna whispered, "I can talk."

Chan was led down the hall to the Youth Bureau office, leaving her daughter on her own.

Wallace pulled out a chair and directed Panna to have a seat.

Sergeant Mark Casey, the detective who first encountered Panna at the hospital the night she gave birth, entered the room with a portable computer to type notes.

As before, Panna was handed a prepared statement and asked to read it back. The last part read: "I am talking to Detective Wallace today because I was not truthful with her and the others on Friday, December 29, 2006."

Wallace motioned to her to put the paper down. "Good. How about we start with the boyfriend?"

The following statements (Panna's, her family's and the Wyatt family's, in this chapter and the following one) were extracted from the interview transcripts in the police report and edited for clarity.

"I've been dating another student, named Jason. We broke up in October and we haven't really been together since. In June last year, I found out I was pregnant from a test kit I got at Walmart. I was shocked and scared. A couple days later, I told Jason. He wasn't too happy about it. I'd say he was angry, but he said he'd be supportive. We talked about getting an abortion, but they're expensive and we couldn't afford it. We had no money. Besides, I'm against it because of my religion. We talked about open adoption. I was for it but Jason said he couldn't do it.

"We continued dating, but our relationship changed. He turned away from me. I don't think the pregnancy was the main reason. We argued about other things. Jason and I didn't talk about the pregnancy a lot, maybe a few times. There was no plan about what I would do with the baby.

"I did feel the baby move in my belly; I don't remember when. I thought my due date was mid-January, but I didn't know for sure. I never went to see a doctor and never got any medical help throughout the whole pregnancy. When Jason and I broke up, he never said a thing about the baby or what he'd do. We just never talked about it after that. I felt so lonely."

"When did you last talk to him?"

"On Wednesday."

"The 27th."

"Yeah. We still didn't talk about the pregnancy. I had no plans on what to do for the delivery, never spoke with anyone about going to the hospital."

"And Thursday night, tell me what happened," said Wallace.

Panna described her symptoms, which began at work. She continued. "Both of my parents were in the house when it got bad. I thought at one point I should tell them what was happening but didn't want to get them angry."

Panna asked for water. "About 10:30, I felt like I couldn't lie in my bed anymore, it was so uncomfortable. I went into the bathroom and just sat on the toilet. Blood was coming out of my vagina and getting heavier. I had a strong sensation to push and I started to do that. Real hard for like fifteen minutes. Because the apartment is so small, I had to be quiet. I thought I was going to die. Then as I was pushing, I saw the head of the baby coming out of me. I pushed and held the baby around the shoulders and helped it out. Again and again, and the baby came out quickly. Slipped out of my hands and fell into the toilet, headfirst."

"The baby was moving?" asked the detective.

"Yeah." Panna looked up. "Her arms and legs were going, you know." Panna moved her arms. "Her face and head were submerged in the toilet water. I got up. The toilet was filled. I didn't know what to do with the baby. I reached for, but she was slippery. She was in there for five to eight minutes. Not moving. I left her there. I was bleeding a lot. I was frantic and got in the bathtub. I had to clean up some of the blood. When I turned on the bath water, my father knocked on the door. He asked why I was running the bath water. I didn't answer him. I was worried about him getting in and seeing the baby. The door was locked. I sat there with the water running. I thought about killing myself but I couldn't bring myself to do it. I did cut myself down there a little with the razor because I had so much on my mind. I stayed in the tub for about five minutes. When I got out, I turned on the shower and put on my bra and underwear. My mother knocked on the door."

Panna squirmed, took a breath, and continued. "My mother asked why I was taking so long and what I was doing. I told her nothing was wrong. She told me to come out of the bathroom now. I didn't know what to do with the baby. I took her out of the toilet and wrapped her in my large grey sweatshirt. I knew she was dead. I didn't know what to do.

She was limp. I wrapped a towel around the sweatshirt. I didn't want them to see the blood. When I opened the door, my mother was there. She looked at me strangely, like a confused look. She didn't know what was going on. She asked me about the blood. I told her I had a heavy period and I cut myself. I think she believed me but my father said I should go to the hospital. I walked right past my mother with the baby wrapped up in my arms. When I got in my room, I put the baby down in my closet next to a laundry basket, then got dressed and we all went to the hospital. I never told anyone. I was afraid of what my father would think. I realize now my parents would have been supportive. I don't know what made me think differently. My parents have never hit me or abused me. I didn't want to disappoint them. I wasn't thinking."

"How about this morning when they found the baby?"

Panna said, "When I came home from talking with the police on Friday, I was worried about someone finding the baby. I couldn't go back to my room, so I slept in my parents' room the last two nights. My parents slept with me. They didn't want me to be alone. My cousin came over at one point. I knew the baby was still in my closet and they would eventually find her. When my mom found the baby, I heard her cry and call for my dad. She and Daddy were crying. I knew that would happen and that would be the end of all of this."

She looked up. "I don't know why I did this." She went on, "I didn't do this because of Jason or because he told me to do this. Nobody told me to do this with the baby. I did this solely because I didn't want my parents to be angry with me. Now, I know there were options, like adoption and abortion. I researched some of those, but never went through with any of it. I don't know why. I know I am wrong."

Sergeant Wallace stood up and read the transcript back to her. Panna followed along on the computer screen. Sergeant Casey printed out the typed pages. Panna swore the statement was the truth, and as instructed, signed the printed copy. They asked Panna permission for a cheek swab DNA sample, which she allowed them to do.

———

Sergeant Mark Casey left to obtain a written statement from Chan Prum. According to the police report, he established that she went by the both last names, Krom and Prum (her family name). She described the events. "On Thursday night I found Panna in the bathroom with the door locked for about thirty-five or forty minutes. I knocked on the bathroom door for about five or ten minutes before she opened it. When she did, I saw blood on the floor, on her legs, and in the bathtub. My husband and I drove her to the Danbury Hospital."

Chan continued with her statement. "After the doctor examined her, he told me and my husband Panna was sick and bleeding because Panna was pregnant and she lost the baby. Detectives Casey and Wallace told us Panna miscarried her pregnancy on Thursday night and flushed it down the toilet. Panna didn't say a thing. My husband, Panna, and I gave police permission to search the house. The police went there. We stayed at my sister's. I have not talked to Panna about being pregnant or what she did.

"This morning, I was getting the dirty clothes from the basket. I saw some clothes on a blue plastic container that had blood on them. When I moved them to see what it was, I saw the baby's head. I didn't check to see if the baby was alive. I ran out to my husband and told him what I saw. He then went into the room to see for himself. The police came to my apartment today after we had my daughter call them."

Sergeant Casey said, "Okay, this concludes your statement."

In his report, he added some comments: "Chan Prum told me she doesn't know why her daughter did this. Ms. Prum stated she and her husband try to be good parents and do everything they can for her. Ms. Prum stated Panna never came to her to ask her for help. She and her husband would have helped if they knew and said they would have taken care of the baby. She's never gotten the image of the baby out of her mind. She was trying to think of what she did wrong in raising her daughter to be able to do this. Ms. Prum stated she must be a bad mother to have a daughter like this. She was crying and very emotional." Casey and Wallace met in one of the rooms, read each other's reports and signed them, dated January 1, 2007.

———

When Song arrived at the police station, he was lead to the interview room and discovered Panna weak, still bleeding, crying, and sleep-deprived. He carried her downstairs to the lobby where they waited for Chan and the okay to go. Once Chan returned from her interview, Sergeant Casey took the parents aside. He informed them that, in his opinion, Panna had intentionally killed her baby and that they were probably going to arrest her. He said they were waiting on a couple of reports. For now, she was free to go, but she should not leave the apartment. Seeing that Panna was distraught, he told them he was worried for her and advised them to take her to the Danbury Hospital to be evaluated.

Panna was seen briefly by a psychiatric consultation in the emergency department. They put her on Zoloft, referred her to a counselor in Family and Children services, and gave her an appointment for January 4.

CHAPTER TEN
THE WYATTS

A t 11:00 a.m. New Year's Day, Sergeant Wallace arrived at the Wyatt residence in Danbury. Boyfriend Jason Wyatt, as named by Panna, was the presumptive father of the deceased baby. Their house, a 1950s colonial with landscaped hedges and two new cars in the driveway, was on Highland Street, not far from the high school, though he went to a private high school in the area. The detective needed his statement.

A dark-complexioned man in a dress shirt answered the door. He gave his name as Daniel Wyatt; he was Jason's father. Wallace, apologizing for the unannounced visit on a holiday, briefly explained that she had some urgent questions regarding Panna Krom. Mr. Wyatt reacted with a concerned look. She assured him that no one in the Wyatt household was in trouble and asked if he, his wife, Macie, and son, Jason, would mind coming to the police station. He was agreeable.

At the station, Wallace went over general details about what happened to Panna's baby, informing them that there were some uncertainties about Panna's situation and emphasizing that neither she nor anyone else had been charged with a crime. She added that they had no evidence that Jason was the father, just a boyfriend.

Macie and Daniel Wyatt, seated in a separate room from Jason, upon learning about Panna's baby, expressed shock. Macie explained that Panna often picked Jason up from school and spent hours at their home. She said she understood Panna had received a scholarship to attend Boston College and they were excited for her. Although Panna often came to their home, according to Macie, Jason never once visited her home. They thought that was strange. And in May, when the two of them went to the prom together, Jason did not go to her home to meet the family, nor were any photos taken. Macie Wyatt told the detective that recently when Panna came and left her house, she never saw her. Panna would slip in, quickly yell out, "Hello" on her way upstairs to Jason's room and a simple rushed "Good-bye!" on her way out.

The Wyatts said they could not understand why Panna hid her pregnancy and went on to do whatever she did. They would have helped. They never challenged the assumption that Jason was the father. Daniel and Macie even claimed they would have raised the baby, allowing their son to finish school and do whatever he needed to do. Macie cried in front of the detective; Daniel comforted her and was visibly shaken. To Wallace, they appeared to be supportive, loving people who were truly shocked by the incident.

After the interview with the parents, Wallace met Jason in a separate room. Per her instructions, he recited, "I came here to talk to Detective Wallace about what happened with my ex-girlfriend Panna Krom," then was asked about his relationship with Panna.

"I first met Panna when we were both in the eighth grade at Broadview Middle School. We started dating by the end of that year but stopped being together in anything serious about my junior year. Right now, I'm eighteen and she's seventeen."

"Did you break up with her?"

Jason said, "We did break up. We weren't getting along very well, arguing about things. We fought about me and other girls. Even though we broke up, we were still talking and seeing each other off and on."

"Were you still having sexual relations with her?"

"Yeah."

"When was the last time?"

"The last time? About one week ago."

"When did you know she was pregnant?"

"Panna told me she was pregnant in the beginning of last summer, in 2006, maybe June."

"What was your reaction?"

"Me? I was surprised and scared. We talked about abortion but we didn't have the money. I don't remember her telling me how much it would cost but she said she didn't have the money. She told me that she met someone at her school, I think a teacher or someone older, someone who told Panna they could help her with adoption. She had help from this person and was thinking of putting the baby up for adoption."

"When was this?"

"Around November. She had me believing she was going to put the baby up for adoption. She told me she was going to the hospital, getting checked. She never told me how she was paying for the doctor."

"Did you ask her?"

"No. I assumed that when Panna had the baby, she'd give it up to a family for adoption. She told me she was due in February. Sometimes when she was with me, she'd talk about pregnancy stuff. I remember her saying she felt sick and I remember her telling me she felt the baby moving. I could see these changes in her, her face, body, her belly getting bigger."

Wallace asked, "When did you last hear from her?"

"Last time she sent an email to me was Friday, the 29th, or maybe it was Saturday. Even then, Panna and I were arguing."

Sergeant Wallace said, "That was the day after the incident. What did she tell you?"

"She told me she had a miscarriage. She said the baby went into the toilet. She didn't tell me any other details, other than she needed to go to the hospital and get stitches."

"What did you say?"

"I told her that I didn't think we should see each other anymore because of everything that's happened. She got real upset and, I think, confused. She thought that I didn't care. I told her I did. But I didn't know what to do. She told me how the cops were investigating and how she had to go to the police station and was questioned. I asked her if she was going to jail and she said she didn't know. She thought the cops were thinking she killed the baby. But what she told me was that she didn't kill the baby. Some of what she said didn't make sense."

Wallace printed out a sheet, handed it to him and said, "Okay, Jason. I need you to read this statement and sign it."

Jason held it, drumming the table, and hesitated.

"This is the truth, right Jason?" He was staring at the printout. "You have a problem? You can add something if you want."

"No, it looks true. I'll sign," he said.

"I think this concludes your statement. But we will need to look at your computer and emails. We may need to remove them."

"Yeah. Okay."

CHAPTER ELEVEN
AUTOPSY

Two detectives stood at the entrance of the University of Connecticut Medical Examiner facility. A woman at the desk buzzed them in. They told her they had called ahead; they were Danbury detectives, there to view the Krom baby autopsy, and gave her the case number 16240. Dr. Frank Mangela, the associate medical examiner, came right up, checked their badges, and asked if they had been to an autopsy before; they had. Even though it was late in the day on New Year's Eve, he seemed in no rush as he led them to the suite in the basement. He told them, "Got a call this morning from the DA. Put a rush on it, he said."

Frank Mangela was a large man, bow-tied, and chatty. He was thirty-seven, had trained at Georgetown, and told the detectives he ended up in pathology instead of psychiatry because he liked solving problems, the messier the better. Stopping at the insulated door entrance, he said, "I spoke with your colleague, Sergeant Wallace. Here's what I know so far. A teen showed up at the ER, vaginal bleeding. That was three nights ago. She had signs of delivery, but with no baby. Hospital called the police. In the apartment, no body was found. Assumed, at that point, a miscarriage. Remind me, is she Thai?"

"Thai, Cambodian, not sure. Refugee family, I believe," said a detective.

"Any odd beliefs, superstitions?"

"No idea."

"Might be worth checking out. Drugs involved?"

"Tox screen was clean."

"Where was I? Three days later, this morning in fact, we now have a body. So, she did deliver—full term in fact, female— and said in her interview earlier today that she saw the baby move, maybe a twitch, but told the detective the baby became limp. Never heard her cry or scream. Said she left her in the toilet water. Wrapped it, put her in the closet. Mom finds her. We get the call. So, here we are. What'd I leave out?"

The detectives both agreed, that was about right.

Entering the autopsy suite, Dr. Mangela, apologizing for the chill and strong disinfectant smell, handed out gloves, gowns, and face shields. He flicked on the operating light and slid the plastic sheet down to expose the tiny body, quickly setting aside two blood-stained items, a sweatshirt and towel. "This is the way I got her," he said. In a recorder he described the general appearance: the baby was female with normal morphology, the muscle tone was rigid; she had tawny skin, looked to be mixed-race, lips were blackened with eschar, and her arms were held in a semi-flexed sort of Moro-reflex posture.

"Couple things jump out, telling me the baby was alive at birth," said the medical examiner. "See the bruise here?" He pointed to the forehead. "And here," this time pointing to the neck. "Abrasions. That means there was blood flow, the heart was pumping."

The doctor separated the umbilical cord and placenta from the body and weighed the baby. "Three point two kilos. Little over seven pounds." He checked the skin, eyes, and neck and measured the head circumference, saying, "Nothing out of the ordinary." Using a scalpel, he dissected the nasal region and with a magnifying glass inspected the septum, then dictated, "Dependent fluid in the sinuses."

"That mean anything?" asked a detective.

"Drowned. Maybe."

Dr. Mangela motioned for the detectives to step back while he pulled down a rotary saw that was suspended from overhead. He applied it to the middle of the chest, making a standard Y-shaped incision, then opened the rib cage and exposed the lung cavities. "See how the lungs are expanded and abutting? I don't know if you can appreciate that, they're so tiny," he said. "Means she took a breath." With his fingers, he excised and cradled the pair of lungs, easing them into a container of water, telling the detectives, "This is a hydrostatic test. The lungs float, see? Means they took in air. Kind of elementary, I know." He inspected the major organs and the brain.

Lifting his face shield, he told them, "All right, detectives, that's pretty much it. I just need to grab samples for toxicology and histology. Should wrap this up and get you a preliminary report, I'd say three or four days."

Two days later, State's Attorney Stephen Sedensky called Dr. Mangela to ask about the cause of death. The doctor explained that they were waiting on the toxicology report and that he would need to go over the case with another medical examiner. "Purely routine," he said.

The following day Sergeant Casey called and asked the same question. Before hanging up, the medical examiner reassured the detective. "Listen sergeant, unless something unexpected turns up, this is a drowning."

CHAPTER TWELVE

ARREST

On January 4, 2007, one week after Panna's tragic delivery, Sergeant Wallace, quietly sitting at her desk in the Danbury Police Department, got an incoming call. It was the medical examiner's office with Dr. Mangela on the line. "Sergeant, good morning," he said. "Baby Krom. I just completed the autopsy report."

"What'd you come up with?"

"Water in the lungs—I'm putting down the cause as drowning."

"Okay. How about the mode of death?" asked Sergeant Wallace.

"Well, from the way it was described in the police report, pretty deliberate actions of the suspect, Ms. Krom, I have to go with homicide."

"Homicide. Okay, thank you, doctor."

"I'll have them fax it over."

From her top drawer, Sergeant Wallace took out an arrest warrant affidavit. At the top, she typed in the name Panna Angel Krom. Referring to her own co-signed police report, she filled in twelve factual points to support the arrest, one of them being the deliberate actions of Panna Krom, using her own words from the interview. The item she saved for last was the "specified reason," in the larger box directly under the name. She called the prosecutor, Stephen Sedensky, went over the case with him, and asked what he wanted for the charge. He told her. So, in all caps, she entered MURDER, SECOND DEGREE. She drove to Danbury Superior Court, where she promptly found a judge. He reviewed it, signed off, and thanked her.

That morning, Panna had an appointment at the hospital mental health clinic—this had been part of her discharge instructions. She was there for a little over an hour, while Song sat in the waiting area. It was encouraging; Song could see it in her face the minute she walked out. They got in the car. He looked in the rearview mirror. Ever since the day the baby had been found, Song later told me, the police had been tailing them—and making no effort to conceal it.

He and Panna were on their way to pick up Chan. First, they pulled into the Beijing Chinese Restaurant for some takeout. After that, while driving eastward on White Street, the tailing squad car surged to just inches behind them, then flashed its lights. The siren blasted, quick, for two seconds. Song immediately turned into the entrance of the Three Brothers Diner parking lot. A second cruiser rushed in from the opposite direction to block their front end, like in a TV drama, positioned in case Song and Panna decided to make a run for it.

Officers from each squad car walked toward Song's car. The first, one they hadn't seen before, stopped at the driver's side. Song rolled down the window and asked, "I do anything wrong, officer?" It was a busy intersection. The day was gray with low clouds, chilly, no breeze. His patrol car, with its blue and red lights rotating, was blocking half of the right lane of White Street, so traffic going both ways was backed up and crawling around the scene. Bystanders stopped what they were doing. People looked out the windows of the dinner; some came out and stood on the front steps.

"Mr. Krom." He paused. "Do I have that right?"

"Yes, sir."

"Your daughter is not supposed to leave her house. You knew that."

Song reached into his pocket and pulled out a paper. "She have appointment for counselor. At the hospital. Here."

The policeman didn't look. Instead, he leaned down to eye Panna. "Good morning, Miss Krom."

"Good morning," she replied, her voice barely audible.

"Where are you off to?"

"Nowhere."

Sergeant Wallace, standing on the passenger side of the car, tapped on Panna's window. Panna recognized her and teared up, then looked over to her dad. Sergeant Wallace tapped again, this time a little more forcefully. "Miss Krom, you want to open the door? I need you to step out of the car." Panna put her face into her hands and cried.

"Miss Krom. I have a warrant." She showed a paper. Panna cracked the door and the sergeant opened it. "Panna Krom, please come out."

She stepped out and Sergeant Wallace, as in a formal dictation, told her, "You're under arrest for murder. You'll need to come with us." Panna was shaking. Assisting her to turn around, Wallace said, "Put your hands behind you." Handcuffs were snapped onto her wrists. Panna gathered herself, looked at her dad and, in Thai, said, "Daddy, I'm going to be gone for a long time."

Sergeant Wallace led her to the cruiser and they drove off.

Song was able to stay two cars behind the squad car, on their way to the Danbury Police Station. His eyes locked onto Panna in the back seat. A pink wool cap was easily visible, bobbing and twisting, as she made an effort to see if her dad was behind. He waved, but she never saw him. Parking in the far end of the lot, Song missed seeing Panna being led through a side entrance, then into the holding cell.

He phoned Chan, who was waiting for them to pick her up. With desperation in his voice, he told his wife, "They got Panna." Choking, unable to pronounce another word, he hung up. Gathering himself, in a few minutes he called again, telling her he was at the police station and rattling off names for Chan to call: sisters, brothers, anyone. Song hung up and, his eyes watering up, walked into the lobby.

Sergeant Casey, though standing right in front of him, looked past Song, as if he were invisible. Song was frozen, at a loss as to what to do. Sitting behind bulletproof glass was a policeman who never looked up. Two cops chatted in the middle of the lobby, two people sat on the benches, but they ignored him. Then, without saying a word, Casey held up what looked like loose-leaf paper that had one scribbled word and a number: "Bond $750,000." The state's attorney had suggested the figure after talking to the detectives. Flight risk was what they claimed.

Judges generally follow prosecutors' bond recommendations, especially for a murder charge. The judge had signed off.

"What's that?" asked Song, eyeing the number.

"A bond," said Sergeant Casey. "For murder."

Song looked puzzled. "Murder?"

The sergeant said, "That's how much you need."

Song gazed again at the big number and shook his head. "Where is my daughter?"

Sergeant Casey said, "In back."

"In back?"

"Being processed, then she's off to York. You can see her there."

"York? What's that?"

"Prison. She'll be there. Unless you come up with this." He handed the paper to Song. "Here, take it."

"I can't see her now?"

Sergeant Casey said, "Nope." He nodded at the cop behind the window and was buzzed through the security door. He told Song, "Get a lawyer."

Prison? Song turned to look at the other people. They were now watching him.

At the same time, two marshals were leading Panna, sobbing, her hands cuffed behind her, into a small room. She was logged in, fingerprinted, and had mug shots.

Panna had been wearing two bracelets and a necklace that day— actually for the last week: talismanic images of Buddha and the revered Thai monk Koon. Each had been touched and blessed, for protection and to ward off evil. She never saw them again.

CHAPTER THIRTEEN
HUTCHINSON

After the arrest, Song dashed back to their apartment on Fifth Avenue, just blocks away. Two reporters camped out in an Eyewitness News van jumped out and caught up with him. They pressed a small recorder in his face and angled for photos while yelling out, "Mr. Krom! What about Panna's baby?!" Song turned his back, waved them off and shielded his face while he slipped into the entrance of the building.

Chan was inside with about ten relatives.

"Where's Panna?" they asked.

Song gasped, "Jail."

His niece jumped up and said, "Jail? For what? They tell you?"

"Murder." His voice quivered. "They gave me this." He showed the crumpled paper that said $750,000.

The niece said, "Oh god. That's the bond? Okay, that's it." Desperately flipping through the Yellow Pages, she informed everyone, "We have to have a lawyer." An ad for Vicki Hutchinson caught her eye: "An Experienced Attorney Protecting All Your Rights." She called the number.

A secretary put her through to Attorney Hutchinson. She blurted, "We need an attorney."

"What's going on?"

"My cousin's been arrested."

"What's the charge?"

"Murder."

"Murder? How old is he? What did he do?"

"She. She's seventeen and she..."

"Come to my office right now." Vicki Hutchinson gave her the address and the niece headed straight to the office on Old Maple Road in Danbury, bringing her uncle and aunt, Song and Chan.

As they entered through the glass double-doors, a secretary directed them to head right in. Vicki Hutchinson introduced herself, motioning for them to take off their coats and make themselves comfortable. The secretary brought in a tray of Evian. Hutchinson was an unflappable woman, obviously bright, maybe in her mid-fifties, with a pixie hairdo and a durable smile, dressed conservatively in a seafoam-green wrap dress. The Krom family, with their heavy accents and ordinary clothes, were readily identifiable to her as Southeast Asians, obviously of modest means. The thirty-year-old niece, in her crisp English, did the talking. Within minutes, the lawyer got what she needed and phoned the Danbury police station. "You have Panna Krom in custody. This is Attorney Hutchinson. Who's her arresting officer?

A few minutes passed. "Casey."

"Sergeant, this is Attorney Hutchinson. You or no one else is to ask my client, Panna Krom, any further questions. Do you understand?"

"Yes, ma'am."

"I am on my way to the station to talk to her."

"She's not going anywhere."

Hutchinson asked the family, "Did you give a statement to the police? Did you talk?"

Song said, "They take us in a room, ask us questions and we tell them."

Hutchinson shook her head, then told the family, "Look, this is not cheap. Up front, I'll need $5,000. It's a lot. Do you have that kind of money?"

Song said, "Yes, ma'am, we get it."

"Okay, let's go see her."

Attorney Hutchinson arrived at the lockup, where she saw Panna alone. The police opened the cell door, letting her in. She found Panna to be an attractive young girl, petite, her face masked with fright, her eyes inflamed and puffy from crying. She needed a hug; Hutchinson gave her one and handed her a tissue. While pulling papers out of her briefcase, Hutchinson explained who she was and what they would do, then had her initial some documents. She went straight to a few pointed questions.

"Did you talk to the police?"

"Yes."

"What did you say?"

"Pretty much whatever they asked." Panna, gathering her composure, described what she told them about that night one week ago. She could tell by Hutchinson's reaction that they had a problem. Hutchinson asked her, were your parents in the interview room with you? Panna said no. Stopping short of an all-out scolding of her naïve client, the attorney told her, "Don't talk to anyone. No one." The visit was quick, twenty minutes. But seconds after she stepped out, Hutchinson walked back to the cell and asked Panna about the two days after the crime; she was clearly in trouble, yet she did nothing.

Panna shrugged and told her, "I just wanted it over." Panna suddenly felt like this—her confession to the police—was her second major problem.

Hutchinson said, "Listen, I'll get the crime and autopsy reports, see what kind of case they have. We'll go from there."

She told the family, waiting in the lobby, "I'll represent her." They smiled in relief and nodded. She added, "I'll call you before any hearings. They'll be at the courthouse, just up on White Street. You understand so far?" They nodded. "Don't talk to the news, to the police, no one." Hutchinson handed them her card and said, "Call me anytime. I will see Ms. Krom tomorrow. Listen, this will take a long time, figure months, maybe years."

She stopped at the desk and asked Sergeant Casey for the police report. He retrieved a copy. "Here's a draft," he said, handing over the fifty or so pages. She asked him if they taped the interview. He smiled and told her, "Talk to the DA."

Attorney Hutchinson returned to her office. As her secretary was packing her bag to leave for the night, she asked, "Vicki, how's this new client?"

"Panna? She's just a kid. As far as her family ... pretty simple," said Hutchinson. "But the case is a nightmare."

"How so?"

"Murder. They've already got her statement and charged her. And a bond for seven-fifty thousand."

"Wow."

"Yeah, wow." She held up the police packet and said, "Can't wait to see what's in this. See you in the morning."

Hutchinson poured hot tea, sat down, flicked on her desk lamp. Outside there was barely any light. She took a sip and began reading—bracing herself for what she would be up against.

After retaining Attorney Hutchinson, the family gathered at the apartment. The brothers, sisters, their spouses, and cousins all sat in a tight circle around the kitchen table and pooled their money, each chipping in checks, some loose bills, or scraps of paper with handwritten pledges. It made for a thin stack. They added up the numbers, just short of $2,000. Song put a paper clip on it and said he would drop it off at the lawyer's office.

The following day's headline in the *News-Times*, the Danbury paper, was "Teen Murder Suspect in Court." A grainy picture showed a glum Chan Krom, hand raised over her head and eyes downcast, hurrying down the steps of the Danbury Superior Courthouse. Accompanying the photo, the *News-Times* ran the story:

Hutchinson described Panna as an A's and B's student with no record of disciplinary action. Panna was charged with murder and risk of injury to a minor, both felonies. She said Ms. Krom was probably 24 weeks along when the baby was born. Police initially characterized the incident as a possible miscarriage and stillbirth. Autopsy results were expected in the next six to ten weeks [they became preliminarily available in days].

Hutchinson requested the court lower the bail to $100,000 with electronic monitoring. She told the court Krom planned to have the baby and things went wrong. She said, "She is not at risk of harming anybody in the community." She turned to point to Chan and Song, walked over to them and said, "Your honor, they are both factory workers and do not have three quarters of a million dollars. Also, your honor, can we please provide an interpreter for them as they cannot understand these proceedings?"

Song and Chan kept hearing the name Sedensky. They weren't exactly sure who he was, what his role was, or whose side he was on. In one hearing they spotted him, sitting across the courtroom, wearing a blue suit. Okay, pretty nice guy, they thought.

At the bond hearing, while the judge listened to Attorney Hutchinson's plea to lower the $750,000, State's Attorney Stephen Sedensky rose to his feet, cutting her off and pointing his finger at Panna. She was a flight risk, he said. She has a passport; she has family in Cambodia; she speaks the language. Song looked at Chan—none of that was true. The judge struck his gavel and confirmed the amount as it stood. Now they knew Sedensky.

The report in the *News-Times* continued:

Several high school boys and girls sat together in the back weeping quietly. Afterwards they huddled in the hallway, shocked this could happen to a Danbury High student, especially somebody sweet like Panna.

The reporter caught Hutchinson and asked, "Attorney, can you comment please? What's Miss Krom's state of mind?"

"Right now, she's just in shock." Vicki Hutchinson moved on.

———

According to notes, Hutchinson left messages for the prosecutor with a series of questions: Who was present at Panna's interview? Her parents? Was there a video? A recording? Do you have the detectives' handwritten notes? Were Danbury police officers present at the autopsy? Is Sergeant Casey capable of typing at conversational speed? She demanded: I need these answers and items handed over.

Nothing was handed over. Panna's bleeding continued—one full week now. After the hearing, two marshals transported Panna back to the emergency room. An on-call resident performed a routine pelvic exam, told her everything was fine, and discharged her back to custody. She spent her first few nights in the police department jail and the next morning a squad car took her back to the courthouse.

———

Panna's entanglement within the Connecticut legal system began with Sergeant Casey that night in the emergency room, late December 2006. Just days after that, Attorney Vicki Hutchinson came on board. But during that sliver of time, virtually all the key evidence had been obtained by the state's attorney, Stephen Sedensky. And he made noise, talking to the press, saying he had the signed confession and autopsy results. After poring over the reports, seeing the headlines, then imagining herself across the aisle from him in a trial, Hutchinson, being called late to the game, would surely muse about how unfair the competition was.

Vicki Hutchinson was a scrapper. She had done four years in the Navy and eight years in the Naval Reserve, used the GI Bill to put herself through the University of California-San Diego, paid her way through University of Bridgeport Law School, and started her solo practice—while raising three children. Criminal casework was what she did, anything from DUIs to double murders. She was no-frills, no-nonsense, tough when she needed to be, and won a lot. On her desk was a model of the USS Maine, a battleship.

At the time of Panna's arrest, Song was working for a watch company in New York City. His boss and company's owner, Steve Ogden, had a law degree from prestigious College of William & Mary. But he had never used it—in fact, had never sat for the bar exam. When the Kroms were desperate for help, Ogden stepped up—much to their relief—appointing himself as their legal advisor. His style, as depicted by Chan, was, "When Steve want something, he want it *now!*" thrusting her fist on the table. His dive into Panna's case was a setup for a collision. Hutchinson was a careful tactician and had little tolerance for Ogden, the showman. He badgered her, she ignored him.

At one point, Ogden insisted that Hutchinson go to the autopsy suite, something she called ridiculous. She said lawyers don't just show up days late at a medical examiner's office. But Ogden wouldn't hear it, telling her, "The cops were there." He told her they had to agitate, maybe get a second opinion. Down the line, they did get one, from a pricey celebrity medical examiner in New York. He reviewed the slides and found no water in the lungs—in other words, not a drowning. And when asked if a girl performing a self-delivery might leave scratches on the baby's neck, he answered, "Absolutely."

Ogden had a point, Hutchinson conceded—maybe a big one—and there would be others. Prosecutors will challenge such evidence, Hutchinson said, but rounding up experts costs money, and we have none. After more weeks of the back-and-forth vitriol, the Kroms were hearing from Ogden much more than from Hutchinson and they began to believe him. They gave in and with a sense that they were making a mistake, the two parted ways. Someday, she would be back. But not for a long time. Meanwhile, the pre-trial hearings went on. Panna's name still came up on the docket, only now she had no counsel. A continuance was called and a new court appearance date was set.

Feeling Panna needed another private lawyer (not a public defender), the family were given a name and made a distress call. She told them she did only real estate, but referred them to a criminal law attorney: Jennifer Tunnard. The cousin and Steve Ogden met with her in the tony township of Litchfield and they immediately liked her. They liked her take on the case, but also liked that her cover-girl looks and fancy diplomas didn't stop her from using rough language. They were not at all certain where they stood on funds; they still owed Attorney Hutchinson thousands even though Ogden had contributed thousands. Nevertheless, each wrote a check to retain her.

Every hearing took place in Court No. 2 on the second floor of the Danbury Courthouse. Attorney Tunnard told Panna it would look

74

good if her family was there. Every court date, her cousins, aunts, uncles, co-workers, and friends crowded into the back two rows, even though not much happened—usually another delay and both sides agreeing on a date for the next session. Other than a few detached relatives everyone in the family did their duty in the gallery. Plus, Steve Ogden was there, clutching Chan's hand and instructing her: "Head up, Chan. Keep your head up," which she willed herself to do. When she left the courthouse after the bond hearing and a photographer hounded her, she did exactly what she was told and maintained an unflinching steely gaze. Ogden himself made every hearing, all the way through the sentencing, and eventually chipped in what the family figured was nearly $10,000. On top of that, if Tunnard and Panna decided to go to trial, he told them he was all set to mortgage his house.

But after the sentencing day, which was some two years after Panna's arrest, fiery Steve Ogden, the self-proclaimed Krom team captain-for-life, was never heard from again. It was a mystery to them why Steve was all in one day and gone the next. Where did he go?

Years later, Ogden was located on Facebook. He resembled the *Parts Unknown* chef, Anthony Bourdain, sporting a skin tight t-shirt over a well-ribbed chest wall, along with gray spiky hair, and, of course, the smart-aleck smile. A friend request was made, but he never responded. The Kroms remained at a loss—what ever happened to Steve? They wouldn't find an answer.

Meanwhile, Song was missing so many days of work at Steve Ogden's watch company since Panna's detention that he eventually stopped showing up altogether. The flood of police, reporters, lawyers, hearings—but especially the sight of Panna in cuffs—it was just too much. Feeling defeated, wracked with guilt, he hit a low point one day in downtown Manhattan; he seriously considered riding an elevator to the top of any random skyscraper and jumping. Song then thought he received inspiration through a prayer. Thereafter, he told himself, I am not afraid anymore.

———

A few days after Panna was taken into custody, two police officers, carrying Dunkin Donuts coffee, showed up at Chan's workplace in Brookfield and asked to see her at the front desk. The clerk called a supervisor, who came out, talked to them, then brought Chan out to the front desk. The supervisor had a custodian unlock a utility room.

The two cops followed Chan into the room and closed the door. Exactly one week before, when the investigators had arrived at the Kroms' apartment on that dreadful morning when they realized they were grandparents of a dead baby, Song and Chan felt a pall, a wave of dread. They realized that the Danbury police, once their friends and protectors, had switched sides. They sensed a betrayal.

Chan whipped around, a scowl on her face, her hands firmly on her hips.

The two immense officers closed in, towering over four-foot-ten Chan. They had bulletproof vests, nightsticks, and handguns the size of her forearm.

"Miss Krom," said one. She didn't budge. "You're Miss Krom, right?"

"Prum."

"You the mother of Panna Krom?"

She nodded.

"Okay, Miss Prum. We got some questions."

She glared at them.

"Did Panna deliberately hide her pregnancy from you?"

"Why don't you leave us alone?"

"I don't think you understand the seriousness of what's going on. You need to answer these questions."

"I say everything," she told them. "I have no more."

"Listen lady, you don't want to cooperate with us, that's perfectly fine. Not a problem. We can arrest you too."

Chan thrust her wrists up and screamed, "Then arrest me!"

The police looked at each other. One of them smirked and said, "Fuck this shit. Let's go." They threw their cups in the trash and were gone.

When Chan came out, one worker in the hall who overheard the exchange, quipped, "Our finest, making us safe."

Chan, sobbing and trembling, slowly made her way back to her workstation. Her table was full of items she had been in the middle of assembling. A couple of the women stopped what they were doing to put their arms around her. Her boss came over to console her, telling her to take the day off.

CHAPTER FOURTEEN
ANGEL NAHNG-FAH KROM

T he name Baby Girl Krom on the autopsy report was changed to one chosen by her family: Angel Nahng-Fah Krom.

After that brief, frantic moment in the apartment when Song lifted his granddaughter's lifeless body, he never saw her again. Baby Girl Krom was zipped up in a body bag and taken to the medical examiner's office in Farmington for her autopsy. The Green Leaf Funeral Home was to pick her up for her cremation, but before that, as required in all homicide cases, they needed to clear the paperwork, something that took months. After her cremation, the Krom family was planning to have a funeral ceremony in their apartment.

The Kroms inquired with the Wyatts, since they were possibly the family of the father, as to what kind of service they preferred—and would they be willing to contribute to the funeral home expenses ($3,800, later reduced to $3,100)? The Wyatts, who had obtained legal counsel after Panna's arrest, never responded.

Hearing this, Chan said, "We don't think about Jason again," adding, "We can't say a word to Panna about the boyfriend."

Song told the family, "We'll let it go. Angel is our baby. We'll take care of her."

The day before the cremation, Panna's cousin had placed a call to

York to see if Panna could attend. After all, it was her child. When Panna called later that day, Chan let her know that they had heard from the warden—she would not be able to attend. This was despite a prison policy that allows inmates to attend funerals (in shackles) for immediate family.

Chan told Panna, "It is very important: we want her to have clothes on when she gets to her new home. What clothes do you want her to wear?" Panna was specific, going from head to toe, emphasizing to her mom that she wanted everything to be pink.

In the infant section at Target, Song and Chan pushed their cart around, running down Panna's list, crossing off each item. They chose the tiniest leather shoes the store had. They found a binky rimmed with pink, a solid pink bib, a knitted cap and a tiny pink-capped bottle which they would fill halfway with milk. Finally, the dress: frilly, saturated with pink hearts, tied in back with a scarlet ribbon. Tom, the funeral director, had told them that only one item was not allowed: flowers. He didn't say why. Later that day, Song proudly handed the items over to Tom, all folded and in perfect order. Tom took them, shook Song's hand, hugged Chan, and assured them that each item would be with little Angel.

Months later, Angel's body, which had never again been viewed by the family, was quietly cremated. After a cool-down, her remains were put into the urn picked out by the Kroms, a small light-brown marble box. They were told they could pick it up in two days.

When they did, Song drove home carefully while Chan held little Angel on her lap, singing to her.

Once they were home, Angel had her own shelf in the middle of the living room, lovingly prepared with gifts, directly under the Buddha picture and beside a statue—a spot that guaranteed daily attention.

———

At dawn on the day of Angel's funeral ceremony, the core of Panna's family arrived at the apartment. Both of Chan's sisters showed up with their kids. Angel's great-grandfather was in Thailand, but her great-grandmother, Chem, was there in a wheelchair, being assisted. Panna's trusted cousins were there. Meanwhile, in the kitchen, Chan and her sister put the final touches on six elaborate Thai dishes.

Just before 11:00 a.m., Nareen, a Theravada monk arrived, closely followed by three novices. All had shaved heads and rattan seed prayer beads, and even though it was a chilly March day, wore sandals and thin saffron robes. Bowing and clasping hands, they were warmly invited in. By tradition, the monk comes to where the ashes, and one of the spirits, are. Chan hurriedly brought them the first course, acutely aware of their daily deadline for eating by exactly noon, and taking care, as a woman should, not to touch them. Using chopsticks, Nareen benignly smiled and described his journey to America: a trail of desperation out of war-torn Laos, four years in a Bangkok monastery, more years in a Thai refugee camp, finally arriving to live with a sponsoring family in Connecticut.

Chan brought out the other dishes: chicken curry, Thai salad with fried chicken, scoops of in-season jasmine sweet rice, pork stew, and Pacific halibut. Thai and Laotian were spoken, with a smattering of English among the kids, until the prayers began. After the monks had finished eating, everyone followed Nareen's lead, moving the few feet across the living room to the sacred corner immediately beneath Angel's ashes. Candles and incense burned. Mimicking the monks, the family sat cross-legged with palms up and eyes closed, then clasped hands. Nareen, his hands held in the prayer position, chanted, while everyone followed. None, except a few of the elderly, correctly uttered the ancient phrases. It is said that this dialect, known only to a small number of people on earth, is understood by the devil or the spirit above. The monk, representing the heavenly power and the way of the light, pointed to the path up above for the deceased baby. Until that moment, her spirit would not know the way. By relating to Buddha, Nareen ensured that the path for Angel was one of light—that Angel was guided to heaven.

———

Often in traditional Buddhist communities a close relative leaves a mark on a dead body, just a dark smudge, maybe under the arm or on the side, using coal or ink. It was something to look for when that person returned as a new baby. Whenever a newborn arrived in their village, friends and neighbors would gather and carefully inspect it. Once a mark was located, it was not unusual for someone to declare they knew who it was. It could be an uncle lost months prior, someone who had led a good life. That earmarked the new baby for the same good life.

On that December morning when Song lifted his granddaughter's body out of the closet, he secretly turned her over, checking for a mark, not revealing what he found.

"When someone pass away, you know," explained Chan. After three days, there's a sensation. By seven days, they return and you feel them nearby. Sometimes they appear as certain people. Chan's sister described the frequent spiritual sensations of her father. To this day, Song and Chan report that they can feel Angel. With clarity, Chan told herself, "I know she is here."

Ninety days after death, the Cambodian custom is to celebrate the life of the deceased with a big ceremony in the temple. This was never done for Angel. Chan said to her family, "We do it when Panna can be here." At that time, Panna will also decide where to spread the ashes.

PART FOUR
IN THE HOUSE

CHAPTER FIFTEEN

THE FARM

Connecticut jails date back to 1650, starting with makeshift structures intended to retain offenders for some later corporeal penalty, like a lashing. Reformers envisioned prisons as a more humane form of punishment; thus, the penitentiary movement began. In 1773, the state's first prisoner, John Hinson, entered Newgate Prison in East Granby (he later escaped). Newgate quickly earned a national reputation for its brutality, seen as a throwback to the old European dungeons—it was, in fact, an old copper mine that held the incarcerated some fifty feet underground. In an effort to refurbish that image, Connecticut opened the more modern Wethersfield State Prison in 1827, designed to be a showpiece. Perhaps more significant, by exploiting prison labor, it turned a profit, showing that prisons could make money (or were perceived to).

The American penal system was initially influenced by the Puritanical interpretation of sin and punishment. As a result, prison policy has always been the product of a moral tug-of-war between retribution (revenge) and rehabilitation (more moral and beneficial).

York Correctional Institute opened in 1918. Originally called the Connecticut State Farm and Reformatory for Women, it was one of the first women's prisons in the country, founded on the idea of isolating women in pastoral areas, away from the corruption of city life. Beginning in the 1970s, retribution had the muscle. Women could be imprisoned for "lascivious carriage, manifest danger of falling into habits of vice, intoxication, vagrancy, street walking, being lewd, or even if she possessed obscene pictures," according to local historian Paul Harrison, a former Connecticut correction officer. With this idea of punishment came what is commonly referred to as "warehousing" in maximum-security structures best suited for numbering, stripping, and caging women, with revolving-door confinements. The 80s and 90s, during the Reagan and Clinton presidencies, saw women and men alike being swept up by the "war on drugs" and other "tough on crime" policies—though in retrospect were seen by many as failures. Contributing to the trend of mass incarceration were strict criminal statutes, new mandatory sentencing rules, reduced parole opportunities, and the full immunization of police and prosecutors from corruption charges. Prison populations exploded. York swelled to 1,368 women in 2009, about the time Panna was sentenced. Gone was their cottage system with women rowing boats, planting gardens, having barbecues, and tending dairy animals—gone also was the low rate of recidivism. They referred to York as "the State Farm."

Only in the last few years, with bipartisan pressure, has the United States been able to reverse this national embarrassment. Connecticut has been a moderately progressive state, seeking to reduce its prison population, albeit, (according to the undersecretary for criminal policy), it's occurring mostly through reduced crime.

———

For years, Panna never saw the outside of York Correctional Institute and had no idea that the site had been selected for its sunshine and fresh easterly sea breeze, promoting it in its day as a retreat. The *Baltimore Sun* even dubbed it "a prison with a view," something the women inside would have found amusing.

Panna's first stop at York was Admissions and Discharges, A & D, a large, glassed-in holding area, where she squeezed onto a small bench with other women. She heard the whispers, "Is that her?" and realized that they knew her story. Sitting on that cold steel was her introduction to a major part of her new life: waiting in line. When Processing called her name, she was unshackled and uncuffed, then led to a side holding area with two more metal benches. The bathroom disgusted her. The phones had frayed wires.

In the next room, they snapped at her not to smile for her mugshot, capturing her blemished, ashen face and matted hair. She filled out the paperwork, listing her emergency contacts and checked the box "no" for previous arrests. They took a DNA sample from her inner cheek, gave her a PPD to test for tuberculosis, an ID badge with her picture, a PIN for phone calls, and her inmate number, her new identity: #347106.

What followed, for Panna, felt no different from an assault in a back alley. It was the first of what eventually totaled some 2,000 strip searches. Bending and spreading your cheeks for a "body cavity" check was a procedure that all women at York were forced to incorporate into their daily routine. They referred to it by many names, never demure. One favorite: "Show me pink." While Panna was standing bare, shivering and hugging herself—it was January—two women with cameras inspected her entire body for tattoos, snapping closeups of her private areas. She was dosed with Quell disinfectant, spray-washed, issued a uniform, and handed a linen kit. In it were motel-room-sized items: a tube of toothpaste, bar of soap, shampoo, one ratty towel, two stained sheets, a couple of laundered pre-worn granny panties, and a threadbare blanket. After being pointed to an area called Inpatient Overflow, Panna waited for her medical clearance (a once glance-over by a nurse practitioner) before moving on to Protective Custody.

Protective Custody, called PC, was just that. It provided shelter for a subset of incarcerated women who might be targeted, such as sexual predators, high-profile cases, celebrities and gang members. Teens, like Panna, were assigned there for a similar reason, being easy prey for the "mamas." It was one notch up from solitary confinement—Panna was locked in a single cell the size of a parking spot. Two cold meals and a couple of random books were all she got, no TV or radio. For an hour and a half in the afternoon and two hours in the evening, she was released onto the tier, which consisted of six cells with a common area. The staff on the tier were generally unreachable, camped out far down the hall in front of a TV. The only view of the sky or any natural light was through a six-inch pipe. Once a month Panna was taken to the library.

One special arrangement was made for Panna. A month after her admission, Danbury High School sent her textbooks and she resumed her class assignments under the remote direction of a school counselor. In June 2007, Panna earned her Danbury High School diploma, graduating on time—the first non-GED diploma awarded at York. For the ceremony, her parents and six other relatives attended; no one from her school was there.

———

Despite her segregation from the General Population (GP), Panna still got taunts, at times coming through the vents. For the first few months she sat in her cell crying, phoning home every evening only to spend the entire fifteen minutes in a sobbing duet with her mom. Those calls could be placed only to landlines, and since Song and Chan couldn't afford one, after work they went to Chan's sister's house and waited for Panna's call, until 9:00 p.m. if need be.

They did this for four years.

———

During her nearly two years in PC, Panna sat alone, absorbed by self-loathing and battling guilt and depression.

In the early summer of that first year, Panna told her counselor that her main concern was her boyfriend; she wanted to have "closure." No one dared to tell her that Jason was long out of the picture. Immediately after their police interview—despite their hand-wringing over Panna and the baby, and their professed desire to "do anything we can to help" —the Wyatt family had washed their hands of Panna and of anything having to do with the tragedy. Jason's mother, a lawyer, had made sure they had their own counsel and directed that all communications go from attorney to attorney. They did have one valid point: no attempt was made to verify who the father was. There was no reason to.

All of this, like many other things, was kept from Panna.

———

Despite the Sixth Amendment guarantee of a speedy trial, meaning roughly twelve months in Connecticut, Panna spent almost two years doing court runs while her attorney tried to gather evidence and decide whether to go to trial. The van rides for court dates became a growing source of anxiety. The intercom woke Panna at 3:30 a.m. (too early for breakfast) and took her to A & D. She was strip-searched and allowed to wear only her prison uniform with nothing heavier than the standard sweatshirt, even in winter. No shoelaces or hair ties. Wrapped in belly chains and cuffed at the wrists and ankles with what the women called the black box (a rigid metal box between the cuffs with covered key holes) she was led to the transport unit. She got in the unmarked generic-looking, much-loathed "ice cream truck." Weighed down by her cuffs, she could lift her arms or feet merely inches. She learned to double up on socks to lessen the ankle cuts. Women from PC were considered privileged, so she got to ride alone, with two CO's—unlike the other incarcerated women put into the York bus with multiple cages and stops all over the state. Still, the trips were daunting for her. There was no talking, just the blare of a rap station on the radio. With no supporting strap, the ride on the hard bench bucked her at every turn while barely any light came in through the smudged back window. It was hot, bumpy, noisy, and endless. Even the sight of a holding cell in the back of the Danbury Superior Courthouse was a relief.

She was held in Judicial Custody in the courthouse basement, better known as lockup. The ten-by-ten cell could get so crowded that there was no space to sit. Speaking through a wire mesh was the only way to talk privately to her attorney. Her one meal was slices of hardened French toast, one small box of Corn Flakes, and one piece of shriveled fruit. By mid-morning, some seven hours into their day, most of the women in lock-up were too beat-up to talk. Panna told me, "There were fights, always over something like a hand gesture or not flushing the toilet." To use the one toilet while shackled, a woman had to ask other women to pull her pants down, then pray they would give a hand to get them up. By their second or third trip to the courthouse, most learned to pack their underwear with pads.

Fortunately for Panna, until the year she turned eighteen, her lockup was a single. Still, the one dirty toilet sat like a throne in full view of a male marshal pacing by. If she wanted to use it, she had to time it precisely and move quickly. Starting the day before every court date, she stopped eating or drinking. That left her clammy and dying for anything fluid. When her name was called, she was led through a hall going up to the courtroom, with staring people she had never seen before but who gave the impression that they knew her.

At each hearing, her attorney, Jennifer Tunnard, having arrived early, made a point to lean over into the gallery to update the Krom family and lay out what to expect. They were puffy-eyed, on edge, and at a loss. She kept it simple. As Panna waited to enter, her family would be focusing on the small window on the left side of the courtroom. Standing on her tiptoes she could just catch sight of them, while all they saw was a shadow. Pressing her head against it, she moved back and forth.

With the marshal's announcement, all stood as the judge entered. Then a door opened and two marshals led Panna in, tripled chained, shuffling, her York outfit sweat-stained. Her hair, which she couldn't reach, felt petrified, which stressed her out. Her face was ghostly, her lips parched, her body frazzled and smelly. She followed Tunnard's instructions and didn't wave to her family. A quick glance and a twitch of a smile were okay.

Song grew angrier with each hearing. He later told me, "When I see the detective [Sergeant Casey], I tell you. He see me. He look down. He don't look at me."

State's Attorney Stephen Sedensky had a manner that grated on Song. In the courtroom he would roll up his sleeves, pull off his glasses for effect, and gesticulate, neck veins bulging, injecting the word "murder" at the slightest opportunity. Song, his jaws tightening, stared at this theater and wondered, "Does he have a daughter?"

Sedensky, coming from a family of prosecutors and a former linebacker at Plymouth State University, had been in office since 1984. His district had earned a reputation around the state for being tough, meaning imposing long sentences—"long ball hitters," as one defense attorney put it. However, a former prosecutor and a forensic psychiatrist I spoke with both said Sedensky was fair.

In her hearings, Panna slowly caught on to her lawyer's tactic: stalling for more time. Motions for continuance was a strategy to increase the odds against the prosecution. They might lose track of witnesses or evidence and it gave Attorney Tunnard time to contact experts for second opinions, though under a limited budget. However, Panna paid a dear price, sitting in her cell at York, at a total loss about her fate. At first she held out for hope that something good might happen, naïvely thinking the judge might release her. However, at many hearings there was no judge. She was paraded before the empty bench, hearing little more than "The defense needs more time."

Late in the process, Tunnard informed Panna, "The prosecutor's not budging." Panna confided to her prison counselor, "Court dates never go well. My attorney can't come up with new mitigating evidence, as she calls it." Another time she told her counselor, "I miss being a teenager." And on one visit Panna came into the mental-health clinic puffy-eyed, telling the therapist, "They raised my offer," likely meaning the prosecutor's time-to-serve number was going up. Tunnard had told her, we're firm on fifteen.

The bewildered Kroms interpreted this suffering as karma, retribution for their past selfish actions. They made frequent visits to the Khmer temple in Bristol, praying for a miracle. But their optimism, like Panna's, was fading.

On one visit during Panna's second month of incarceration, Tunnard took the autopsy photos of the baby out of her briefcase. She said, "You have to look at these. Sorry. I think Sedensky's pulling out them at the next hearing. He'll try to scare you."

Panna quickly glanced down, then put her hands over her face. Tears rolled down her cheeks. Tunnard dabbed them with Kleenex. Panna muttered, "I'm okay."

"No you're not," said Tunnard and hugged her. While sliding the photos off the table, Tunnard told Panna that Sedensky calls himself a child advocate. Panna missed the irony, shook her head, looked up at Tunnard, and asked what the police report said.

"It describes you pushing the baby underwater and flushing. Doesn't mince words. Is that what you said?"

"Honestly, I don't remember. If that's what they wrote, then I said it."

Tunnard said, "Not necessarily. We've tried to get a video, but it doesn't exist, at least according to them. Problem is, whether you said it or not, you *did* sign the statement. That's big. The signature."

"Jennifer, I have to live with that."

"Did you read it?"

"Yeah, I did. At that point, I didn't care. I just wanted out. I know that sounds bad."

"The other problem is the autopsy—the scratches on the baby and water in the lungs—matched the police descriptions of your actions. Frankly, I think it's all dubious. Obstetricians tell me scratches can come from a self-delivery like this. Anyway, it's there and it's persuasive."

"So, I shouldn't have talked. My parents always told me to respect..."

"Never talk to cops." Tunnard got up. "Let's see what we can do. I'll argue for whatever I can get. But it'll be your decision whether we go to trial or take a plea deal, though they haven't offered one yet."

Panna told her what the women at York had been saying. One warned, "Don't go to trial! They'll bring out every piece of dirt in your life." A cellmate told her, "It will drag on and they'll find you guilty of something anyway." And another one advised her: "Don't go anywhere where there's 'life' on the end of it."

Tunnard cautioned, "Be careful what you hear. Each one's different. Again, this is your decision."

Panna said, "I don't want to put my parents through any more."

"Panna, this is about you, not them."

"I know. I just want it over. A trial freaks me out. If I don't, what's going to happen?"

"We ask for a plea. A reduced charge, probably first-degree manslaughter."

"How many years is that?"

"Five to twenty. Figure twenty."

Panna said, "What happened to fifteen?"

Tunnard said, "He's holding all the cards. He's got the press. You've seen the headlines. Plus the ridiculous bond he gave you—that makes you scary to a jury."

Tunnard asked Panna what she would settle for and she said, "Fifteen. I'll take fifteen."

The prosecutor met with Tunnard and stuck with the murder charge. With a guilty verdict, she could be looking at twenty-to-life. Tunnard told him, give us a plea—fifteen. Sedensky countered. She had to retreat, saying they were okay with seventeen. But when she walked out, it was with eighteen.

She told Panna, "He wouldn't budge."

Panna's parents were distraught at eighteen years. Song later told me that while in a back room, he cried to Tunnard to fight for less. "I hear twenty, eighteen, I don't know, and say, 'C'mon.' I'm on my knees before Jennifer. 'Lower it!'"

Panna said she couldn't fathom eighteen years. But her parents could—Panna would be in her mid-thirties—they told her not to take it. Tunnard explained to them that the fight's over.

After that, Panna was back in the basement holding cell, then onto the van for the long ride back. She sat numbed, realizing that this was real, that Tunnard was not going to pull any miracles out of her briefcase. She was going to be locked away for a long time. Panna was lonely, spent, and defeated.

By waiting alone behind the courthouse building, Song discovered he could catch a view of the York van each time it left. It was maroon. He could never see Panna. She was weighed down on a side bench. Song charged up the small rise to the exit out of the parking lot. He watched the van disappear down White Street.

CHAPTER SIXTEEN

SATURDAY NIGHTS

F or Song and Chan, Saturdays were for Panna. Every weekend, they made the 150-mile round trip to Niantic to see her, missing it only for the occasional funeral or Buddhist holiday. "One lady at work, she tell me I should not see Panna so much," Chan said. "But I tell her, 'You don't understand.'"

On those weekend mornings when overtime hours were available, Song (or Chan) picked up a half shift. The money kept their heads above water and reassured them that the company was not in trouble. Layoffs had upended their lives before, and they had figured it out by now: if their company was outbid on a big contract it meant "belt-tightening," and assembly workers were the first to go. After putting in four hours, Song would race home and shower. Then they took off in their SUV for Niantic. Halfway there, they met my wife and me, either at our house or for lunch at Pad Thai, a mutually favorite restaurant in New Haven.

Following Panna's imprisonment at York in 2007, the Kroms had no idea how to get there. Song's boss, Steve Ogden, drove the route and sketched the directions on a map using giant arrows. He instructed them on what time to get there, what they needed, what to wear, and what not to take. For their initial visit, they had packed a dinner specially prepared for Panna. When the CO at the gate checked their IDs, he spotted the baskets of food on the back seat and informed them, "Sorry folks, you can't take that in."

Song and Chan were at York by the Saturday 6:00 p.m. check-in, sometimes bringing one of Panna's aunts or cousins. On occasion, York was on an unannounced lockdown, and they would turn around at the gate. Panna's visitor list was limited to seven names and being on it was like making an NBA team roster—to get on you had to bump someone off. Since York didn't allow incoming calls to the incarcerated women, Panna was not sure who—or if anyone—would be coming. Hearing her cell intercom announce "Krom. Visitor" gave her a rare spark of joy.

Song and Chan, generally the first ones to check in, would sit in the waiting area quietly while others slowly entered in groups of twos and threes; no one seemed to be in a hurry. Arriving in vans or pick-up trucks, many wore jeans, sported tattoos and were on the heavy side. Their kids crawled around on the floor; they took cigarette breaks. A few were still in their work clothes; definitely no Brooks Brothers, unless an occasional lawyer got waved through. On the whole, they were honest hard-working regulars, not well-resourced to deal with the inglorious criminal justice system. As the summers rolled into winters and back into summers, Song and Chan saw the same faces, aware that they, like them, were barely holding things together. To the ones they met eyes with, they would give a nod or wave, maybe a cordial word or two, but no one brought up crimes or sentences. As Chan told me, "Nobody feel sorry for you at York."

With seating for only about eight, the room quickly filled as first comers grabbed the three benches. Song always gave up his spot and joined the other guys leaning against the cinder block walls. Everyone waited for a CO to open the door and call their name; there was not much to do—no magazines or TV, no cellphones allowed. Sounds from inside the bathroom were hard to ignore. Song followed the minute hand on the clock and counted down the interminable forty-five minutes, the typical wait time, hoping for less.

A picture of the prison's namesake, Janet York, was in a glass case above one bench. She appeared to be hard-ass, but in reality, she was a reformer—"on our side," as one woman put it. On the opposite wall, ads for jail bonds and business cards for lawyers were tacked onto a bulletin board. Occasionally there would be a beefy-armed bondsman filling out paperwork at a makeshift table. They hated York, as they often were made to wait for hours. One told me, "They jerk you around. One call from York and your whole day is fucked."

Below the cork board was a machine that looked like an ATM, for depositing money directly into an incarcerated person's account. The name was inviting: Touch Pay. At first glance it was a godsend, a painless way to make sure an incarcerated loved one had "currency." Before Touch Pay, Song told me, they had to mail a cashier's check to Enfield, Connecticut, and wait weeks for the processing. "Now," Song explained, "I go up to it, punch Panna's number, swipe my debit card, and boom, it put money in her account. She get the receipt." But, as cynics point out, few things at York ever work that smoothly. Nowhere on Touch Pay did it tell the charge, even if you called the toll-free number or searched the website (which I did). Song said it was $7. Whether you deposited $10, let's say, or even the max, $50, the charge was $7. Either way, a nifty DOC profit. As a bystander put it: "On the outside that's called loan sharking." If the women had no source of money from home—and most didn't, according to Panna—life on the inside was pretty miserable. Every Saturday, Song tapped in the codes on Touch Pay and deposited $50, money that Panna often split with her cellmate.

Haphazardly taped onto a check-in window crowded with sheets of paper were two lists, warning visitors about prohibited items. They changed almost monthly; still, missing from them were the obvious: cameras, weapons, wire cutters, hacksaws. One list was a hodgepodge, things like credit cards, cash, necklaces and cell phones. The other was more anatomical, starting at the head with hooded sweatshirts, hats, or any headwear, then going down: scarves, sunglasses, tank and tube tops, spaghetti straps or anything resembling a CO uniform. They didn't allow gloves, large buckles, mini-skirts, hot pants, shorts, flip-flops, swimwear or lingerie. If an infant had a bottle, a CO had to witness the kiddo sip it. For ID, you showed your driver's license, though passports were also acceptable. But library cards—I found that funny—were not. As I observed over time, check-in was inconsistent. Our regular

Thursday foursome of writers were once halted and reprimanded for Susan's hoodie and on another occasion for Wally's baseball cap—items they had been wearing to York every two weeks for over fifteen years.

Upon seeing the Krom couple, some COs behind the Plexiglas smiled and said, "Panna, right?" Chan told me, "Many CO, they tell us, she don't belong here. All the time they tell us, she don't belong here. Some CO, they were nice, but some were mean. They don't care." A couple COs had quietly told them that they looked out for Panna—despite knowing what she was in for. Even though they were forbidden to look up the crimes. Panna laughed at that and said, "They know."

When Song and Chan heard a CO bark out "Krom," they waved their hands and stood before the metal detector. With their keys, wallets, caps, and belts already stashed in a locker, they waited for a barely attentive CO to observe them pass through. The detector, awkwardly occupying the middle third of the room, was finicky. It beeped for anything as insignificant as a metal grommet. And it was better to slip through it sideways. Especially memorable was the buxom young woman who repeatedly set off the alarm even after shedding her jewelry, sweater and shoes. Then, like it was strip poker, she slipped her bra off under her jumper—a little protest that opened plenty of eyes in the room. She danced through the stubborn contraption like Isadora Duncan, arms waving. When she was done another woman from a bench yelled out, "Honey, you need a prison bra!"

While most COs were lax, simply putting in their twenty years to get a pension, others acted officious, puffed their chests, sported their regalia, and put their hands on their spray can holsters—reminders of why the York women referred to them as "toy cops." Because we volunteers were allowed to bring in a tote bag with papers and books, I imagined that it would not take a whole lot of trickery to get contraband past the guards. One member of our writing group (I won't name names) once made it past all the layers of security with an iPad sitting in the bottom of his/her satchel.

After passing through the metal detector and the COs' office, Song and Chan proceed to a peach-toned ten-by-ten cinderblock sally port with two doors—seemingly bomb-proof slabs of steel on wheels. Operated by a shadowy figure behind one-way glass, one door would close while the other mysteriously unlocked and slid open, allowing them to enter another small anteroom in front of the visitors' area—like an amateurish *Space Odyssey* set. During that half-minute last stop, the Kroms peered through the bulletproof glass to locate Panna, as she was already seated on the burgundy-colored "inmate" side of an elongated picnic table. Song and Chan took stock of her mood. Was she beaming and waving? Or was her head in a hangdog position? This detail set the tone for their visit, the rest of the evening, and possibly the entire week.

Erasing the memory of Panna's first year behind bars had been hard. It began with a two-inch glass partition separating them and a telephone hookup. Pressing their hands and weeping together, Panna repeated, "Dad, take me home. Get me out of here. Please get me out of here. I hate it!" They told me that the crying and pleading hardly let up, from 2007 to 2012, then eased when I introduced myself.

Now at the table with no barriers between them, they were allowed to hold hands and give a quick hug at the end. Randomly scattered around the room were other incarcerated women, some weeping, some laughing, clasping hands with their lovers or family. Panna might wave to an old roomie. Far at one end, a CO was positioned on an elevated platform, where she could keep an eye on the entire room and a timer on each woman, while another CO did floor duty. Through the chatter they could never be sure of what was being said, so everyone talked freely. Since all of the incarcerated women's phone calls were taped and all mail going both ways was opened and read, this private one-on-one conversation was the only secure way to relay a crucial message to Panna. "For touchy stuff," Panna said, "we spoke Thai," adding with a vengeful chuckle, "It's pretty unlikely the roving CO understood us."

Chan told me, "Panna, she try to smile. I tell her, tell us *everything*, baby. And she tell us back, don't hide *nothing* from me, Mom." But Panna did hold back the ugly stuff, which was a lot. As did Song and Chan. "When she in a good mood," Chan said, "I know, because she makes joke with her dad and tease him."

Early in her sentence, during one wintertime visit from her family, Panna got a quick lesson. It was about her winter coat. There were green ones, which were warmer and considered "cool," and there were beige ones, which were missing insulation and drafty, a telltale sign to the other girls that you had no "pull." Being told by a CO that she couldn't take her coat to the visiting area, Panna left hers—a "cool" green one—in the hallway on a chair. When she returned, it was gone. In its place was a beige one.

At the end of each visit came a dreaded part: the strip search. It was the reason some women wanted no visitors. After a visitation, Panna was led to another room. She said, "It had partitions. Everything came off. Tampon? Out—no tissue provided. If it was my lucky day the CO, she'd cut me slack, usually the older ones, and the two of us faked it. She'd go, 'Hey P, how's your old lady?' I'd say, 'Cool, ma'am.'"

———

Beginning the day of her arrest, Panna's Danbury friends and schoolmates, who had sat in classes with her and high-fived her in the hallways, faded away. Fifteen or so showed up at her hearings—some for support, some out of curiosity, some to catch the action. And during her first year, a few mailed her Hallmark cards. But none ever visited. During her last days of freedom, close friends sent a flurry of emails, promising things like, "Hang in. You can beat this. I'll be there for you." Eventually, they all let her down. Panna dismissed this by saying, "They got jobs, got married, had kids, and moved on, while I was frozen in time. For some, their parents put the quash on it—I get it." It was one more item on a lengthy list of mini-assaults that long-term incarcerated women had to endure. Not long after her arrival one of the elders on her tier gave her a dose of reality: "Get ready. The visits'll trickle down to nothing. Then the letters. By three years you'll be lucky if your mom even talks to you." It can get worse. More than one in our writing class had a daughter she never hears from.

Beyond her parents, Panna's cousins never gave up on her. Many Fridays, one of them made the trek to York. They said, "We just try to laugh." On occasion, a relative would bring their baby so Panna could play with him in the kids area. Panna wanted to keep up with what girls were wearing, what musicians were hot, any fads. It was a painful reminder for Panna, who told one of them, "What I'd give for a friggin' day at the mall, picking out my own clothes—and not thinking about what criminal wore this crap before me."

———

The goodbyes for Song and Chan were tough: the hug, bravely holding back tears, then, knowing Panna had the strip-search and her cold cell.

Chan told me, "We cry in the car on the way back."

Song nodded and admitted, "Sometimes we pull over and just cry."

By 10:30 p.m., they would arrive back home in Bethel.

That was their Saturday. Sundays they generally slept in, prayed, cooked, and if the sun was out, went to the Danbury Reservoir.

CHAPTER SEVENTEEN
PSYCH

Nearing her two-year milestone at York, Panna felt ready for GP, the general population, tiers where she would deal with the other women and all the chaos. Due to her young age, all of her time had been spent in Protective Custody. She would leave the PC with mixed feelings. "When I got there, waiting for my sentencing," she said, "my self-esteem was low. By the time I got word that the prosecutor was looking for twenty years, it hit rock bottom. I was haunted by my dead baby, unable to get her out of my mind. I actually felt twenty wasn't enough. I deserved more time."

She went on: "However, PC *was* protection. Twenty-three hours a day locked in a cell, no one could bother me. But also, I couldn't do anything—no jobs, no programs, just an occasional book. I needed to quit hating myself, take college courses, and get on with my life. Despite the warnings I got about GP, I put in my request to leave. I was still a teenager, pretty clueless."

Her old boyfriend Jason was still an issue. She had assumed that by now he had moved on with his life and was out of hers, but a few nagging reminders told her that he hadn't. The first one came in May 2007.

Having left Niantic at 4:00 a.m., she was in the back of the York van on a court run for a pre-trial hearing, driving through familiar territory: the main thoroughfare in Danbury, near the Superior Court, a block from her old apartment. Through the iron-mesh back window she noticed a car following too closely. At the wheel was Jason. With him was another girl.

Then, a year or so into her incarceration, sitting on her bed one afternoon was a surprise: her one and only letter from Jason. In it he said, "I forgive you." She laughed and asked herself, "Forgive me? Wow. Okay." She wrote him back, with a final goodbye.

But it wasn't final. Around the time she was transitioning out of PC and patching up her tattered self-esteem, she received word that Jason got another girlfriend pregnant. Only this time, he decided that they would keep the baby.

———

Just days after her arrest and her two-day stay in the Danbury Hospital's Psychological Observation Unit, the mental health clinic at York started seeing her. She carried the diagnoses PTSD and OCD (obsessive-compulsive disorder), although no formal evaluation had been conducted. The handwritten notes, typically a few hurriedly scribbled lines, described her as tearful, but never suicidal. She was treated with the antidepressant Zoloft and given Benadryl for sleep. She said, "The clinic was mostly: 'Do you have any thoughts of hurting yourself? No? Okay, goodbye.'"

Adding to her precarious state at the beginning of her incarceration was the vaginal bleeding that wouldn't stop (the unit was chronically short of pads). Panna made at least two trips, ankle-chained in a DOC van, to the University of Connecticut Medical Center. Hospital staff informed her mother that she couldn't go in to see her. This was an odd restriction: because since Panna was only seventeen and still a minor, Chan had to be called each time they changed medications. Records showed Panna being seen on two dates, January 3 and 9, 2007, for the persistent bleeding. The Ob-Gyn service finally discovered the cause: retained placenta (something that can cause bleeding, infection and scarring). After doing a D&C (dilatation and curettage) under general anesthesia, a gynecologist told Panna that it resulted from a "botched delivery," and in a patronizing tone, indicated that it was her fault, adding that it could have been life-threatening.

In the middle of Panna's twenty-month stay in PC, because of her age and the unusual nature of her crime, the judge ordered a formal psychiatric evaluation. The state assigned Dr. Catherine Lewis, a professor of forensic psychiatry at the University of Connecticut Medical School. Dr. Lewis was brilliant (graduated *summa cum laude* from Yale), seasoned (which in forensic psychiatry meant hardened from years of dealing with major crime cases and florid, untreated psychotics), and well-published in the psychology literature. Her findings would become part of Panna's record and could factor into any trial decision, her eventual charge and sentencing, or any plea bargain. Dr. Lewis put in thirty-plus hours poring over Panna's school and hospital records, police reports, and DOC files, while getting statements from seventeen people—including, of course, Panna and her family.

———

Panna's childhood was, in her own clipped descriptions to Dr. Lewis, "nothing special"; occasionally she was a "vagabond," something that embarrassed her at the time. "Mom and Dad were frequently being laid off and looking for work. They had it hard because of their language. They were afraid of an interview or if they had to fill out a form. At the end of every month, we'd pool our money, scraping together enough to cover the rent. I worked and pitched in. And they fought. Always over money."

Dr. Lewis asked her about home life.

Panna said, "Our little place was like a monastery. Our meals always consisted of some item, maybe something my dad caught, plus rice. We did a lot of praying. The only books we had were like a couple of Thai comics." She had only a few close American friends and came up with excuses to make sure none came to her apartment. She was worried— "I'm ashamed now," she said—of what they'd think of her peasant-appearing parents who barely spoke English, and of their one-bedroom flat which at any time might be sleeping five or six. The living area had stuff that might look odd to an outsider—a pair of Buddha statues with burning incense and posters of 90-year-old monks.

In high school, though well-liked by students and considered a rising star by teachers and staff, she signed up for no activities or clubs, and never went to dances or game. Instead, after school she headed straight to work or to one of her cousins' houses to help prepare the Thai dinner. Around Danbury High it was a widely known secret that Cambodian girls were untouchable. According to the boys, they had this "forbidden thing going on." That "forbidden" tag—a strong cultural sexual taboo—had far-reaching consequences for Panna in particular.

For school breaks, her friends and their families went off to places like ski trips in Vermont or the Florida beaches in the spring. Panna remained at home or at her cousin's and had to work. In fact, her family never left Danbury; she had never been on a plane. She had seen the capital, Hartford, one time, and Massachusetts never, although both were about an hour away.

The summer before Panna's senior year, her family took a five-day camping trip to Bear Mountain in New York. That forty-four-mile trip was the biggest of her life. Panna loved the outdoors and had often gone to the Danbury Reservoir, where she hiked and fished with her dad. "With nothing but trees and nature, we felt safe," she said. Dad was like a superhero. We'd have our fishing lines in the water, Dad'd have his beer, and no one could touch us. By us, I really mean him. At the lake, there were no men in suits or uniforms to mess with him. He was his real self."

———

Eight years into her incarceration, the Khmer Health Advocates (KHA), a group of clinicians from Hartford dedicated to treating psychological trauma, particularly for Cambodian refugees, met with Panna. During their examination, the trio of women therapists were able to provide a trusting setting (a private side room in the visiting area) for Panna, allowing her to feel safe and open up.

The KHA psychologists, with Megan Berthold of UConn, learned that Panna was sexually abused as a child, starting at age six. At large family gatherings, a man in her non-nuclear family, escaping notice, stalked her and forced himself on her. This was repeated for years. At thirteen, she wriggled and cried her way out of the grasp of another predator, a distant cousin known to be a heavy drinker. (In a later discussion, she told me that both lived out of state and that nobody has heard from them.) The trauma of those events left her childhood burdened with secrets and tainted by a constant fear. As she made her way through her adolescence, she felt unable to tell her parents, due to what she perceived as the family code of silence about personal trauma. She confided to the KHA therapists, "I never told my cousin, and I told her *everything*. That's how scared I was."

Throughout her teen years, Panna harbored a general mistrust of strangers, with a surge of panic at the thought of someone approaching from behind, and she startled whenever she was blindly touched. At York, once she was in GP, those same reflexes resurfaced. She said, "I couldn't stand anyone being behind me, even standing in line, which at York was all we did." Over the years, on the tiers, she listened to other York women telling colorful and tearful tales of their sexual traumas—a revelation for her. It seemed everyone had a story. "In my house," she said, "any talk like that was not going to happen."

———

Men and women who lived through the Khmer Rouge—the brutal, genocide communist regime that ruled Cambodia from 1975 to 1979— needed lies in order to survive. Even people with strict morals had no compunction about lying, a habit passed on to their children. Chan Krom's inhibition about speaking of her trauma at the hands of the Khmer Rouge, and her subsequent fears, laid the latticework for Panna to use denial as well. During her interview with the KHA therapists, Panna displayed the defense mechanisms commonly seen in Cambodian children. As the therapists noted, these children were taught by their parents to focus only on immediate dangers and not to verbalize their fears.

As a little girl, Panna had an utter dread that her mom or dad would find out about those assaults. To talk about it was tantamount to making the trauma happen again. Following her logic, that meant by staying silent, it would never recur. To deal with the anxiety, she had long-standing obsessive thoughts. This obsessive thinking can be linked to magical thinking, a belief that "I must do this to make sure everything is alright." Magical thinking has been described in other neonaticide cases. For Panna, it led her to believe that if she didn't think about her pregnancy, everything would be okay. This, added to her suppressed trauma, fostered serious problems in her behavior leading up to and during her delivery. On the flip side, this separation of her problems and the dissociation she experienced during her pregnancy were powerful coping mechanisms.

In reviewing Dr. Lewis's analysis of Panna, the judge felt that there was enough psychological evidence to warrant mitigation. Panna's "extreme emotional distress" (the term the court used) was a major factor in lowering her charge from murder to manslaughter.

The combined work done by Dr. Lewis and later by the KHA clinicians explained Panna's complicated behavior pattern. Unfortunately for Panna, the prosecutor and the court had hastily arrived at a charge based almost exclusively on the detectives' findings during those first two days after the crime, which, in such a short time, and with no counsel, was never questioned: killing with intent.

This full psychological explanation for Panna arrived after a long wait for those of us, like myself, desperate for an answer to the vital question: Why? By this time, though, she had been locked away for ten years—and it seemed like no one else really cared.

———

When Dr. Lewis asked Panna about her parents' past, she told the psychiatrist that she knew almost nothing. "What happened in Cambodia before they got to the US, for me, is pretty much a blank. My dad, my mom, her sisters, none of them talked about it," she said. "What little I did find out came from one of my aunts. And they would say, 'Don't tell them I told you.' Kids were told to take the hardships, be strong, obedient, and silent. Basically, don't ask."

Growing up, Panna envied the freedom of her American girlfriends. Song's rigid views on male-female matters weighed on her. In rural Cambodia, as Song and Chan explained to me, little boys and girls did not mix, even in innocent games—no flirting or hand-holding, and never any kissing.

Song told me that he would not be able to cope with his daughter ever "maturing" or being "stained" (by a boy), as he put it. He laid blame squarely on himself for her imprisonment, admitting, "I didn't listen to her. I was angry. Needed someone to yell at. She was it."

During Panna's early high school years, getting a simple okay to go to something like a school play was an all-out battle. Song forbade her (but not her brother) to hang out with other kids, meaning boys, which forced her to go underground. Going back to the eighth grade, she had been secretly seeing Jason. She, like many of the Cambodian girls, packed a change of clothes, things a little more "braggy," to wear around school. "My white girlfriends knew. It was like an inside joke to them," said Panna. It didn't help matters that, just like her parents and her brother before her, by age fifteen, she had to work, usually dirty mop-up jobs, because she had to chip in for rent. At times, she would be cleaning tables in her paper cap while some Danbury High kids she knew were laughing and leaving a mess.

Her first job was at KFC, working second shift. Song would drop her off and sometimes he remained at the far end of the parking lot, sitting in the dark car with the radio off, just to watch her. He swelled with pride, seeing her vigorously sweeping the floor and stacking chairs while the others were out back smoking weed. "Do the shit work and get the shit pay," he said to himself. He worried that his pressure might "break her" but admired her for being tough, hoping she wouldn't have to do this kind of work for long.

"When it came to homework and grades, he was dead serious," Panna recalled. "Report card day was huge. The card was a confusing mess of numbers and letters, but he sure as hell knew that red honor roll stamp. Heaven help my butt if it wasn't there. In his eyes I was his Miss Perfect. The plan was simple: get A's, at twenty-five get married, then kids. He had it all figured out."

During the months I interviewed the Kroms, more than once Song freely came out with statements like: "I punched holes in the walls. I tell you, Doug. I beat my head on the door in the middle of the night. I throw the phone. I do road rage. I was so really down. I don't know why. What else?" He looked at Chan.

She added, "Drink."

He nodded. "Yeah, I drink." He told me that after the arrest, he drank more. "It relaxes my nerves," he said. Whenever we got together, he liked his beer, preferably two, but no more. On one or two occasions when he got out of the car, I smelled it on his breath. It concerned me. Once I took him aside and said something. He apologized. I know he felt he had let me down.

I had long suspected that Song and Chan were holding back more than they were revealing. I brought up the disorder known best by its initials, PTSD. "We hear of this," said a seemingly interested Chan. I asked if they had ever seen a doctor about it. They both said no. In studies, PTSD was reported at alarming levels in Cambodian refugees, and in about half of their American-born children. Over the course of our many talks, it disturbed me to hear them describe their behavior and symptoms, hallmarks of the PTSD criteria: distrust, nightmares, anxiety, flashbacks, depression, insomnia, trigger events, short temper—they had it all. I placed a few calls and referred them to the Khmer Health Advocates in Hartford, which seemed to me a heaven-sent clinic. Not only did they speak Thai, but they wouldn't bill the Kroms. Eventually Song and Chan were put on sedatives and both reported that they slept better.

———

Panna divulged to Dr. Lewis that she first became sexually active at age fourteen, with Jason. At first, she regretted this decision, but then thought it was cool to be like the other girls, though she never bragged the way they did. It wasn't long before Jason saw her on an off-and-on basis, depending, she sensed, on what was going on with other girls.

During the early stages of her pregnancy, as she grew desperate and needy, Jason's main worry was *his* life and how it could be affected. He backed off, going for weeks at a time without calling. In fact, just the word pregnancy set him off. One time, she slipped, saying *"our* baby." He cut her off, saying, "Hey, it's *your* problem," and hung up. Sinking deeper into a state of isolation and denial, she began to doubt the early pregnancy test and never retested herself. She didn't track how many weeks along she was, putting herself in a time-lost void, willing it to go away.

During one of the stretches when my only contact with Panna was via messages to Chan, she wrote a lengthy note from her cell, which was handed off to me in class. In it she stated, "He [Jason] initially told me that he would be supportive in any given situation. A few days later when it was confirmed that I was pregnant, literally at that moment, he told me that he could no longer be in a relationship with me." It got worse: he wanted nothing to do with her and even threatened her, worried about his reputation as a star athlete. From August 2006 on, she never mentioned the word pregnancy to him. The note went on, "We were in the same circle of friends and he told me I wasn't allowed to say one word to any of them. My friends told me they saw him with other girls. I asked him if we should tell our families, but he said no." He insisted she have an abortion, but she refused, telling him it was against her Buddhist religion. She researched adoption, but to that idea he flatly told her, "No f'ing way."

In the note she continued, "So once the ground rules were laid out, Jason and I went on with our lives as if everything was normal. Other than that, I was a ticking bomb." Jason's position and her submissive response and desperation, gave him a free pass; he could call her as he pleased. They continued to have sex, always at his convenience, right up to the week of her delivery. She finished the note by saying: "I had isolated myself from my friends and loved ones so much, I ran out of people to run to. Even run from. I figured that all of this was my fault, so I dealt with it on my own." She believed that if her father had any idea, he would "disown me and kick me out of the house."

———

"Dr. Lewis," Panna said. "Mom knew." That revelation came during a quiet moment in one of their many sessions.

On October 3, 2006, nearly three months before her delivery, Panna was a passenger in a car accident, a sideswipe, with her friend Brooke, who was behind the wheel. The ambulance crew, noting that Panna was pregnant, insisted on taking her to the hospital, but she refused. The paramedic maintained that, since she was under eighteen, only her parents could make that decision. Chan was called to the scene and informed that because Panna was pregnant, she needed to go to the hospital. But Chan also told them no—AMA—against medical advice, a formal notification that they had her sign for. Chan has maintained that she has no memory of ever knowing or being told about Panna's pregnancy. When I read the police report to her, with her name in it indicating that she was informed and that she signed it, she told me emphatically, "I know they say this, but I *do not* remember. I tell you."

Chan and Panna never brought up the topic again. Such was the power of repression, I thought. I couldn't help but recall stories of the "blind ladies," the Cambodian survivors who had functional blindness (commonly and erroneously termed "hysteria") believed to be related to the unspeakable horrors they had witnessed or possibly personally suffered, at the hands of the Khmer Rouge.

———

Dr. Lewis, like the police investigators who preceded her, conducted multiple interviews with teachers and staff at Danbury High School.

Going into her fifth and sixth months, Panna's high school classmates matter-of-factly asked her if she was pregnant. As long as she thought she was getting away with it, she lied. Panna said, "Everyone was looking at me and whispering. I knew; I wasn't deaf." They persisted, to the point of taunting her. When are you due? What are you doing with the baby? Is it a boy or girl? Do you have a name? She told them her family knew and that she had an adoptive family, and not to worry. "I felt very guilty because I knew I should be taking care of my baby by seeing a doctor. But I couldn't make myself do it. I couldn't make myself do anything." More and more, she stayed home, paralyzed, numb, alone and crying, at times in a fetal position under the covers.

Barbara Seabury, an instructor in the consumer science department, had Panna in her social psychology class during her senior year. Having had prior experience with pregnant teens, even running a parenting class for them, she immediately spotted Panna's baby bump, estimating her to be thirteen weeks. She was the first staff member to talk to Panna, confronting her privately in a hallway in early September. When Panna denied being pregnant, Seabury let it go. One week later, in another encounter, Panna conceded to her that she was pregnant, giving the impression that she was getting prenatal care and that her mother knew but not her father. Her boyfriend also knew, she said, but not his parents. One month later, Panna told Seabury that both her parents knew and were not happy. Panna, never forthcoming, had indicated she wasn't ready for a child since she had plans for college. One time, Panna told her she was taking a day off so her mother could take her to a doctor's appointment, but she couldn't come up with the name of the doctor or the clinic. By late October, Seabury's entire class was aware of Panna's pregnancy, particularly since she made no apparent attempt to conceal it. When I asked her why, Panna said she was not intending to signal for help but was "totally numb" and never gave it much thought. She told me that she was too ashamed to ask for help.

In early November, Ms. Seabury took an extended medical leave. When she returned in January, Panna was gone, and she heard the news.

As the school social worker and other teachers raised concerns in e-mails to one of the high school guidance counselors, who had been unable to reach Panna, matters were directed to the assistant principal, Daniel Donovan.

Donovan told the police that he first became aware of the Panna Krom problem in November, when it was reported that Panna had missed seven days within a ten-day period. He tried to reach her by phone, but both numbers he had were out of service. On December 5, the high school sent an official certified letter to her parents informing them that Panna had missed twenty-one days of classes during her senior year and was in danger of losing credit and failing the entire semester. The letter stipulated that by state law it was the parents' responsibility to ensure that a student under eighteen attended school. There was no response because Panna's parents never read it; their English was not good enough. Since it was from the school and looked important, they put it unopened into a file folder. That's where I discovered it on my first visit with them in 2012. Seeing that it was a warning sent three weeks before her tragic self-delivery, I stared in disbelief.

Assistant Principal Donovan finally reached Panna when he got her working cellphone number from one of her classmates. He left voicemail and when Panna returned the call, Donovan arranged to meet her and the guidance counselor on December 13. First, they went over her school performance. For three years, he told her, she had been a consistent honor student with no absences, in the top tier of her class. Now, in her senior year, she had all F's. Sitting across from him, she was unmoved. Although she had talked about being headed to college, they pointed out, she hadn't taken the SATs. Panna appeared to be six or seven months pregnant, which she acknowledged rather matter-of-factly. As for those missed days, she told them, they were due to morning sickness.

They devised a plan for Panna to graduate on time: to start, Panna would contact her individual teachers and determine her status in each course. As she left, Panna seemed embarrassed and lost. Donovan never heard from her again.

———

In retrospect, it was evident to the KHA team that during Panna's troubled perinatal period, she had lacked the means to respond to the school administrators and others reaching out to her, trying to rescue her—something the prosecution blamed on her. But the descriptions of her speech during that time showed that she went from being organized and articulate to fragmented and tangential.

Dr. Richard Miller, a psychiatrist with the KHA, addressed one of the most damning items from the police interview with Panna. According to the interview report, Panna said she held the baby's head underwater and flushed. Throughout Dr. Miller's examination of Panna, she was unable to recall providing that specific statement. According to his assessment, her faulty memories revealed a young woman who was in a "dissociative state, who felt totally detached, and not in control of the events that were occurring."

In his final assessment, the psychiatrist stated, "We are inclined to believe the events as Panna described them [to us]. She had no psychological preparation for giving birth and no knowledge of the birthing process. Rather than [concentrating on] care for the baby, she was intensely focused on hiding the blood and the birth from her parents. Her ignorance of childbirth made it highly likely that she was unprepared for how a newborn baby might look."

In her summary, Dr. Catherine Lewis, addressing this same critical period, stated, "Panna offered many inconsistencies, for instance, about the baby due date, her college plans, not knowing where her father worked, and when she last talked to her boyfriend. She had a child-like failure to see the gravity of her distortions. This alteration of reality made her susceptible to leading questions in an interrogation."

That conclusion by Dr. Lewis, that Panna was "susceptible to leading questions," brought to light something in the police report that for a long time bothered me. Just hours before her mother found the dead baby in Panna's closet, Panna was hemorrhaging, sleep-deprived, traumatized, and processing with an altered concept of reality. Yet, as a seventeen-year-old suspect, she sat in an interview room. Across from her were two veteran investigators, a clear mismatch. They had a mission and to extract a confession that would lead to conviction. There was no video that day (Connecticut has since passed a law mandating recordings of police felony investigations). Panna had waived her right to a lawyer. And her parents were in another room down the hallway. That vulnerability played into the hands of the detectives.

We can never know precisely what dialogue was exchanged in that interview room, nor what means were used to obtain it—the police report says one thing and Panna remembers another.

In the end, the detectives obtained a murder confession and Panna signed it.

CHAPTER EIGHTEEN
THE JUDGE

On August 28, 2008, twenty months after her arrest, Panna stood before Judge Frank Ianotti in Danbury Superior Court, with Jennifer Tunnard at her side. Ianotti was known as a people's judge, a soft-spoken gentleman with a friendly, rubbery face, someone who had previously worked on "both sides of the *v.*" After lengthy discussions with her attorney and family, Panna was ready to enter her plea. She had learned a lot about the criminal process and the courts—much of it by way of "war" stories from the women at York. Her case, as she found out, was riddled with problems. Going into this hearing, the one word that she felt best described her whole situation was "chaos." Nothing good was coming out of this.

Earlier in the day, Judge Ianotti and the two opposing attorneys had convened in a hurried three-way conversation. Assistant State's Attorney Colleen Zingaro had accepted the defense plea, lowering the charge to manslaughter in the first degree. Judge Ianotti then explained to the defense, "It was the state's attorney's call because they controlled a murder charge," and noted the now agreed-upon sentence. Looking at Attorney Zingaro, he said, "Eighteen years flat-to-serve, right?"

Attorney Zingaro told him, "That's correct, Your Honor."

When handed the pre-sentence investigation prepared by a probation officer, the judge flipped through it, stopping at the last page. The final paragraph was the officer's summary, recommending a "lengthy period of incarceration." The judge nodded to the clerk who then read out, "Charging you with manslaughter in the first degree at Danbury on or about December 29, 2006, violation of General Statute section 531-55 (a) (2). How do you plead?"

Panna turned to Attorney Tunnard, who nodded, then Panna uttered, "Guilty."

Judge Ianotti said, "I'm going to read the statute to you. A person is guilty of manslaughter in the first degree, a class B felony, with intent to cause the death of another person. He causes the death of such person under circumstances which do not constitute murder because he committed the act under the influence of extreme emotional disturbance [EED], a mitigating circumstance. As in your case, that fact reduces the charge from murder to manslaughter in the first degree. So, the information your lawyer provided to the state, about your mental state, was beneficial in convincing the state to reduce this from a murder to a manslaughter. Okay?"

Panna said, "Okay."

The judge said, "I'm sure your attorney told you the maximum penalty is up to twenty years in prison and up to a $15,000 fine, or both, right?"

Panna responded, "Right."

"I will see you on November 7th."

———

The middle-of-the-night court runs, mostly of no consequence, that had marked Panna's two years at York came to an end on On November 7, 2008. It was her long-awaited sentencing date—the penalty phase—and any sliver of hope for release had long since evaporated. Stephen Sedensky was still the lead prosecutor. Joining him was Amy Klein, his wingwoman of sorts. Officially she was an advocate for the baby, a guardian ad litem, or GAL. In court proceedings, the GAL represents a child—normally a living child, not a deceased one. This was an odd twist, perhaps a brazen one. When I mentioned it to a few attorneys who themselves had acted as GALs, all responded with a mix of astonishment and curiosity. One, a children's public defender from the Bridgeport district with decades of experience, recoiled with disbelief. "I have to look it up," she said. "I've never heard of that."

Amy Klein, once a prosecutor, was now a personal-injury attorney in the Danbury community, well known in local legal circles. Panna spotted the mid-forties woman, with her briefcase and papers, standing next to the Assistant State's Attorney Colleen Zingaro and thought they looked chummy. "Who is she?" Panna asked her attorney. It was not welcome news that Attorney Klein, reputed to be a dogged adversary, was now part of Sedensky's team.

Klein did, in fact, land the first blow. She had devised an intriguing calculation: Panna should spend a year in prison for each year until her newborn would have reached the age of majority—eighteen years. It was a tidy and seemingly airtight argument—that is, until you plugged in different ages for a victim. (Should a parent get four years for killing a fourteen-year-old?). The formula quickly parted ways with common sense.

The prosecuting team tacked on incidental charges, like failure to report a dead body and risk of injury to a minor, on top of her potential murder conviction, should Panna elect to go to trial. The idea was simple: frighten the young girl. And they did. She took the plea, a win for the state; Sedensky got a conviction with no need to prepare for a trial. With the reduced charge, first-degree manslaughter, the state still pushed for the maximum, a flat twenty (meaning no parole opportunity), ignoring the fact that both parties had agreed on Attorney Klein's magic number of eighteen. The charge-reduction deal was a gambit that barely altered the sentence. It was all fitting: As Attorney General Robert Jackson (later a Supreme Court Justice) stated in 1940, "The prosecutor has more control over life, liberty, and reputation than any person in America. His discretion is tremendous."

At the sentencing hearing, Song, unable to suppress his bouncing legs, or his rage, maintained a stoic face while sitting in his usual spot beside Chan, on a bench in the back of the courtroom. A marshal announced, "All stand for Judge Ianotti." and everyone rose. Song told me, "I see Panna and I feel faint." More than once, I heard him say,

"Every time, it kill me to see my baby like that. Come on. Does she need chains?"

Defense attorney Tunnard requested that the parents be permitted to stand behind Panna. Assistant State's Attorney Zingaro acceded with a nod. Song and Chan made their way up front beside Panna, the closest they had been since the day she was arrested.

Attorney Zingaro stood and summed up the crime, raising her voice for the most salacious aspects of the investigation, and concluding that the cause of death was drowning.

She added, "Although very difficult for the family, I asked counsel for the victim, the GAL, to prepare a statement. She is present."

Judge Ianotti identified Attorney Klein, allowing her to speak.

Klein read her statement, calling this an inexcusable crime and ending with, "It is a very sad situation. But it is one where we need to hold people responsible for actions that hurt the child in this way—by killing it. I consider this an appropriate disposition."

Panna was then allowed to read her statement, four handwritten pages.

First, she thanked the court and apologized to her daughter and to her family. She spoke of the sacrifice of her family, their plight in getting to America, about her unhealthy way of life that led to her crime, her remorse for her daughter. She pledged to work with troubled teenage girls.

"I stand here deeply grateful even though I am undeserving. This is not the end of my world. I have a life to be thankful for."

Panna closed. *Thank you.*

Judge Ianotti asked Attorney Tunnard if the parents wanted to speak. They had very limited English, she said, and it was too emotional for them. She added, "For my client and her family it was a difficult decision for this sentence, knowing she is a very low risk for any future re-offending according to Dr. Lewis, the forensic psychiatrist. We all know the reason she is being sentenced so long. It's for punishment. While I didn't agree with the sentence of eighteen years, we are accepting it because of the risk she could get more had we gone to trial. Based on my client's emotional basis and her psychological status at the time, this was the only disposition we could agree to and we accepted this offer.

"I will not deny right now that someday we may try to modify the sentence based on efforts she will be making to change her life. It's been difficult for her the last two years, but she's accepted what has happened and the consequences, despite the fact she was a child herself when she got pregnant. She was sixteen. She had no one to turn to, and as she told you herself, became a liar in her own world as a way to cope. The school failed her. She couldn't turn to her parents, and she had to lie to her circle of friends, telling them her family knew about this, when in fact they did not. Had she known her family would be the way they are, things might be different."

Attorney Tunnard continued, "I'd ask the sentence be imposed as agreed, yet you should understand that I will be continuing to fight for Miss Krom because in my heart I believe eighteen years is not appropriate for this young girl. I think she could do a lot to change many people's lives if she's outside rather than in prison.

"Thank you, Your Honor."

The judge looked at Panna and said, "Certainly, none of my words are said to minimize the tremendous loss that has occurred here to a young child. I have no doubt Attorney Tunnard will continue to work on your behalf, and I encourage her to do so. That's why, for all of those reasons, I'm going to go along with the agreed recommendation."

The judge continued. "To the charge of manslaughter in the first degree, Miss Krom, you're committed to the custody of the Commissioner of Corrections for a period of eighteen years. Fees and costs are waived based upon that period of incarceration. Good luck."

Panna said, "Thank you."

———

Nine years after the sentencing, I discussed the case with Jack O'Donnell, a New Haven defense attorney. He had approached me some time after a PowerPoint talk I had given at UConn Law School, and he dropped a fascinating nugget: he had been a former law partner of Judge Frank Ianotti. I asked him what Ianotti might have thought of the case.

Looking down at his phone, O'Donnell said, "I'm texting him now."

"Where is he?"

"Retired."

The judge immediately texted back. *This case always bothered me*, he said. A minute later he texted: *I had no latitude in the agreed-upon sentence.*

After a few silent minutes, he texted, *I was stuck.*

"Wow. I'm relieved to hear that," I said.

Before he left, O'Donnell looked at his phone, smiled, and told me, "Oh yeah, he said he's happy someone is helping her."

CHAPTER NINETEEN
YORK LIFE

As a rule, when teenagers first arrive at York, they have a rough go. Panna herself had just come off suicide watch. Seeing the steel bars, the staff in riot gear, and the razor wire, her first instinct was that she would never survive the eighteen years. However, she had a few things going for her. The Krom family had a long history of dealing with peril; they could make do in unlivable spaces; and they never went up against authority. While never exactly bullet-proof, she would grow thick skin, refusing to let the barrage of petty assaults get to her. And she would gather her senses enough to look for what York offered, eventually coming to the realization that she might come out of this mess a stronger woman. First, she had to adapt to the harsh rhythms of life in the general population and find some oxygen while confined to her cell.

A typical non-lockdown day at York goes something like this. Life stirs at 3:00 a.m. with the intercom wake-up for the women making court runs. At 5:30 a heavy metal thunk opens the cell doors and a trickle of women blindly shuffle to breakfast. CO shift change happens at 7:00 a.m. along with count, in which COs stationed around York with a pen and clipboard either spot the women or blurt out their names: "Krom 3 North." Line up for meds starts at 8:00. Structural movement occurs at 8:30, where women go to work, school, and for visits. Lock time on the tiers (in GP, twelve cells) is at 10:00. Lunch begins at 10:30, then count at noon. After count clears—meaning the total facility headcount is verified and the doors pop open—the women go for recreation, groups, and appointments. Lock time is at 2:30. At 3:00 CO shift change occurs with count, clearing at 4:00, and dinner from 4:40 till 5:00. Another count is at 5:15, clearing at 6:00, followed by cell cleaning with no outside movement. For this, women get mops, rags, and detergent from the closets and have thirty minutes to clean their cell. Movement is allowed at 6:30 with tier recreation and the group meetings like Alcoholics Anonymous and Narcotics Anonymous. Lock for count is at 9:00 p.m., all in their cells by 10:00, then the final count. Throughout the night, with their walkie talkies screeching, the COs do "Q thirty-minute rounds," flashing each pair of eyes with high beams or clanging keys on the bars, looking for any sign of life.

The next day starting at 3:00 a.m., it's the same drill. "Groundhog day," as some describe it. "Every morning, you wake up and hope for the best," said one.

Panna was the early bird. She relished the mornings, the stillness when, as she said, "I could hear myself." She had all her things in order by 7:00 a.m., but she had to stay put until movement at 8:30. She never went to the cafeteria. She had quickly lost her appetite once she saw the blind feeding, where the women had no idea who was sliding the food through the slot—not to mention the wall itself, a makeshift barrier of metal scraps soldered together. The eggs were rubbery, the food colorless, and the only utensil a rubbery spork. The cafeteria was the one place to catch a long-lost friend from another part of the facility, but that did not interest her.

Dinner at home with her family was sacred, never rushed. At York, meals were officially twenty minutes, but because of overcrowding, compressed to ten. "Really, it was seven," Panna said, "with a CO hovering over you like a football coach." So, if she did make it there during the month, it was for Taco Tuesday. Otherwise, she and her roomie cooked in. Brunch was a blow-dried bagel in a paper bag, with a fan blowing so the dryer didn't overheat. Otherwise, it was Ready Rice plopped in hot water. Gathering around a stainless-steel counter with a couple of friends on her tier, Panna did her best to make believe she was home.

Panna's cell was six feet across, made of battleship-gray cinder block. The left side had two bunks affixed to the wall. Each cell came furnished —two durable plastic chairs and a polyethylene mattress with an industrial type of filling compressed down to a rock-hard two inches. There were two shelves, but oddly enough, nothing could go on them. She and her cellmate were issued six-cubic-foot boxes to store all their stuff, from dirty clothes, jacket, and underwear to books, toiletries, pictures, legal papers—everything. The box slid under the bed. Glue, tape, paper clips and tacks weren't allowed, so they used toothpaste to hold pictures on the wall. Over her bed was a photo I had passed on to her mom, of Julian Edelman, the New England Patriots receiver—but within days it came down. The one mirror, commissary-issue, had a bubbly plastic sheen. At the foot of most beds sat a clear-shell TV, no speakers, just earphones. Panna said, "Those on the outside picture us like a sorority house with gossipy girls hanging out in your cell all hours of the night. Not quite. Other women aren't allowed in your cell. That's called 'out of place,' a class B violation."

The door, a bomb-proof slab, came with a three-inch double-paned window running half-way down. From the hall, it offered a direct view, give or take an inch, of the aluminum no-lid toilet, killing any privacy. "Guards," one woman explained, "were at liberty to look into your window at any time, which you weren't allowed to cover. You could be doing whatever and unannounced, there they were, a pair of buggy eyes."

Panna hated the light, a flickering fluorescence. And the York air— no circulation. "It was as if it had already been breathed," she said, "Full of stench, spores, urine, sweat and probably TB." A York-approved six-inch fan did almost nothing.

Though to the outsider it might seem insignificant, one improvement was the back window, made of translucent plastic offering a hint of natural ambience. By cell standards it was big, fifteen inches across, enough to soften the fluorescent lights. By the first morning light, Panna read the *News-Times* from Danbury. During lockdowns, she got into good literature—*Anna Karenina, Pride and Prejudice,* and her favorite, *The Great Gatsby*, when in more than one quiet reverie she became Daisy Buchanan.

———

By cordoning off the women, staggering the movements, and reassigning the tiers, York made it almost impossible for girlfriends to see each other. So, they sent kites. It's an antiquated system of messaging, probably going back to the Bastille. A written note is folded into a neat triangle with a first name and tier on the outside, then handed off until it finds its destination. Panna never sent one, never got one. In fact, if a woman she didn't know asked her a random question, or just made small talk, she would act like she didn't hear it. In her eyes, many of them were mad at the world or out to con a softie like her and she didn't want to risk conflict. She never talked about her crime, never asked anyone their business and didn't care to know. She steered clear of card games or even the TV room where "things could combust in seconds." The air had a nonstop swirl of chatter and gossip. Upon hearing something newsy, she assumed it was a lie or at least embellished. As Panna saw it, other women had a way of creating their own reality about their crimes. The younger girls, she said, liked to brag. They would strut or sashay, thinking it was hip to be doing time. The older ones with serious felonies kept quiet.

Money was contraband. A woman's commissary account was her net worth, her currency. If one woman owed another, she would let her select something off her commissary chit. Nothing more than a sheet of paper called the General Population Commissary Order Form, it looked like an old SAT answer sheet with circles for the incarcerated woman to blacken with a pen. At the top, the shopper entered her name, housing unit, bed location, and inmate number. She would put a number beside each item desired: cards, pens, ointments, dictionary, toiletries, mascara, tampons, shower shoes, over-the-counter medicines, even a du-rag. Junk food and candy came in Halloween-sized varieties. Missing was fruit, and that was for a reason: a few apples or peaches, add some sugar, strain it, and after a couple of days of aging, a woman's got wine.

Since Song put $50 in her commissary account every week, Panna became known for her "deep pockets," and nagging questions followed her: "Hey P, you got some..?" Usually it was coffee they wanted, or sugar, or a Maxi pad, but at times it was a staple: soap, teabag, or even a simple hair elastic.

If a woman qualified as indigent, she got a commissary ration, five dollars per month. Panna said, "It was pitiful. Either she stayed filthy or went hungry trying to live off cafeteria food, probably both." Of course, she could always supplement it by working; women were the labor force of the prison. They worked in the kitchen (the worst jobs—smelly, sweaty, heavy lifting), did the cleaning, took care of the library, laundered the prison clothes, did all the grounds work, painted the walls, shoveled snow, disposed of the trash, and cleaned up after the COs. They even arranged their own talent shows. They did everything but the skilled work, like electrical or plumbing. A few were hand-picked for the grounds, jobs that were cherished though they paid close to nothing. For four summers Panna gardened—a chance to get some sun, taste freedom, and see something grow. Once a CO got to know an incarcerated woman and trust her, someone like Panna, she might cut her slack. In turn, the woman made the COs life easier and could make her area shine. A favorite for Panna was to clean up after a VIP meeting to get the leftovers. Panna got flak from a few women about that, but the majority of them didn't care.

Panna's jobs at York included mopping floors, making men's prison t-shirts, gardening, scrubbing, and painting, Some shifts were up to twelve hours or even overnight, but it was worth it to kill the monotony and be outside her cell. Typical pay was 75 cents a day. The rationale was that they were repaying the state for the cost of their imprisonment: a hefty $62,159 per year, the second highest in the country. (The lowest: Alabama at $14,780, according to the Vera Institute.) Sewing sleeves onto t-shirts was her one status job—at $1.60 an hour. But she had mixed feelings about it. With each lost needle—and there were a lot— York locked down until they found it. She had an utter fear of having a needle inadvertently lost in her things. She quit and returned to her janitorial work, taking a big cut.

"Believe it or not, living in prison is expensive," said Panna. "All the prices are controlled by the outside contractors: the phone calls, the price of shoes, hygiene and food products, commissary, medical co-pay, even the spork. They're inflated and competition doesn't exist." She added, "I don't want to think about how much my parents spent on phone calls." (Rough estimate: $15,000).

Every other Thursday before Wally's writing class at 1:30, I'd catch Panna and her best friend, Shannon, sitting like catbirds on a table by the library, timed to perfection for my arrival. Knowing cameras were around, we'd give a quick hi and cut a joke or two while disguising our lips like ventriloquists. I recall one time, in unison, they chimed, "Happy Birthday Doug!" I was not sure how they knew. I frowned and said, "I'm approaching seventy. Wanna trade lives?"

Faith was something Panna had to navigate on her own, as York sanctioned only four mainstream religions. Buddhism was not one, so artifacts of Panna's faith, like Buddha images, statues, amulets, or posters of monks, were considered contraband. In order to go to a service, she registered as Protestant. Nightly, she repeated mantras under her breath on her bunk, timing them with her mom and dad doing the same at home. Rolling down the tier, at that hour, were high-decibel calls to God and pleas for mercy.

———

Women at York learned early on to be wary of the "guards," as they called them, who some considered to be agents of the institution. For the day-in, day-out micro-abuse—"little crap"—they endured, the women had no recourse. They conditioned themselves to avoid talking back or showing any hint of an attitude. Depending on the CO, just rolling your eyes might get a "disobey direct order" ticket, or worse, a cell shakedown. The women figured that most COs had failed their police exam. A few certainly had a checkered past, turnover was high, and occasionally they disappeared, or once in a while were escorted out. The CO "death penalty" would be a York pregnancy.

The day a CO reached twenty years and became eligible for a decent pension, he'd usually pack it in. It was a worn-out joke: the COs claimed that they were doing a life sentence too, one shift at a time.

Some women felt that the female officers, who made up about

twenty percent, were worse, catty and picky. "A pain to deal with," said Panna. "They were meaner, real petty, complaining, like about an elastic on your wrist, a little eyeliner, or your pants were too tight, things a man never noticed."

As for the COs' take, when I asked a small sample of males where they preferred to work, the men's or women's prison, each answered without hesitation: the men's. "They leave you alone," said one.

Arriving as a naïve teen, Panna was warned about officers on the prowl for sexual favors, often using lacy panties or perfume as enticements. She said "To tell the truth, I got more of it from the other incarcerated women than the COs. Any way you look at it, there was stuff going on. From what I heard, closets or vans were favorite spots."

———

Whenever an incarcerated woman sat before the Board of Pardons and Parole (BOPP), the first two items they checked were performance (programs and courses) and tickets. Panna was obsessed with remaining ticket-free, that is, with no disciplinary reports (DRs). Plus she crammed in all the college courses and certificate programs she was allowed. She had a two-inch stack of "Achievement" sheets in her file, for things like Healthy Relationships, Alternatives to Violence, Cosmetology, Sewing, and the popular Judy Dworin Dance class—all run by volunteers. Each came with an attached evaluation sheet and hers, like those for all the cooperative women, were all checked "Excellent." Plus, she did the RAP program. Started in 1979, it was composed of a panel of publicly presentable women who talked to high school students about their crimes. The DOC cherry-picked them: a white, a Black, and a Hispanic, along with her, the Asian, careful to weed out anyone who might plead their case. One of them was in for a manslaughter DUI, another for killing her spouse. Panna, upfront about her crime and her punishment, had the kids crying. She asked them if they had heard of Safe Haven, the program for helping pregnant teens. None had. Some schools sent her the students' feedback. All were moved, very positive. Or almost all. One wrote: "You are a panel of murderers."

As far as health services, first, the good news. The Supreme Court guarantees it for all incarcerated persons. However, the word around York was: unless you were dying, don't go. Before being seen by a clinician, a woman had to clear the well-designed system, which included two layers of deterrence, amounting to months of delays. Also, an admittance to the infirmary earned you a urine drug test, which scared many away, even if they were clean. And if you spent one overnight there, you stood to lose your cell or even your tier assignment. All your stuff would be heaped in a storage room. Finally, if you *were* seen, there was a co-pay, about $4.

Dental had its own reputation. The York women jokingly swore that all the clinic had was a pair of pliers. Complain of a toothache and lose the tooth.

Worse than dental and medical was mental health—not so much the clinic, but the ward. In Panna's case, her crime was reason enough for her to have a court-ordered psychological examination, both upon entry and later. In time, she had three in-depth evaluations. Unfortunately, none were done before she was arrested when they could have been intelligently used as mitigation for her charge. Behavioral problems were widespread at York, while Panna, despite having committed a crime with seemingly far-reaching psychological implications, was one of the healthier women. Perhaps, part of the reason was that she was compliant and never missed a visit in York's mental health clinic.

During the Reagan years, on a per capita basis, Connecticut may have led the nation in boarding up its psychiatric hospitals, old brick facilities with names like State Asylum and Home for the Insane. California's Lanterman-Petris-Short Act of 1967 had set a precedent for ending hospital commitments by the judicial system, specifically eliminating involuntary holds exceeding seventy-two hours. The result was the psychotics being released to the streets and a spike in the number of homeless, along with their criminal behavior. New neuroleptic treatments, like Thorazine, failed to meet expectations. So the quick solution was more prisons—during the 70s and 80s Connecticut increased its bed capacity by roughly a factor of five. By 2006, a US Department of

Justice study indicated that nationwide 56 per cent of people in state prisons had mental illness. According to the Marshall Project numbers, the women were higher than the men, 68 percent vs. 41 percent.

At York, evidence of this under-treated population was on display each morning at 8:00 a.m. when the tiers emptied and the hallways were packed—for med call. The women found it easier to be seen by a psych clinician than a medical one, the rationale being that cancer or heart failure gets less press than a suicide. An unavoidable spillover of this pharmaceutical bounty was a flood of pills—not just the old sedatives and newer antipsychotics, but others that were crushed and sniffed, like Wellbutrin, Neurontin, Detrol and Suboxone. They created their own traffic in the hallways.

The in-patient behavioral health unit was a different story. Early in her sentence, Panna had one short stay there. She said, "In mental, it was permanent lockdown, with nowhere to sit but on a bare floor in an ice-cold cell. You get nothing, no TV, radio, blankets, shoelaces, no bra, no panties, nothing——just a paper gown. Not even plastic utensils. You ate with your hands." Coffee, tea, and chocolate were forbidden, the theory being that caffeine could trigger a flare-up. In the morning, she was allowed to walk around, but only in tight circles, which counted as her exercise hour. In the evening, without the luxury of a one-on-one consultation, she sat in a ring with others. "In group," she said, "our so-called comrade picked a word of the day, something like 'trust,' and we'd all beat it to death." Panna, after some painful years of coping, is now able to find humor in it, adding, "Mental was a prison within a prison. You don't want to go there. You'll leave crazier than when you went in."

PART FIVE
CAMBODIA

CHAPTER TWENTY
PEUR

I spent many hours with the Kroms. Mostly it was in their living room, then mine, at times at the Pad Thai Restaurant, or the Danbury Reservoir, listening and taking notes, sometimes taping, then transcribing. Truman Capote, author of the true-crime classic, *In Cold Blood,* considered these methods intrusive, affecting the natural flow of his subjects' story. He trained himself to memorize long interviews, boasting a ninety percent accuracy. That wasn't an option for me, but over time I got better. I did steal a handy tool from the biographer Robert Caro who interviewed thousands of people for his monumental biographies on Robert Moses and LBJ. I peppered my notes with the letters "SU," reminding myself: Shut Up and listen.

I went to Danbury schools and Cambodian festivals with the Kroms, and to temples and funerals. I met most of their relatives, some in other states. My wife Connie and I worked together to configure their family tree, trying to get their names right. This process was, at times, comical. For instance, after a few years with Song Krom, I came upon his name on a document: Song Lrom. And Chan, late in the game, revealed that Chan Krom wasn't her real name—they misspelled it in one of the camps. Her first name was Chai and her last name was one I had seen and wondered about: Prum. In this book, I use both.

———

The first evening I sat down with the Kroms, I felt I had Panna's story in a tidy nutshell: nice girl, born and raised in Danbury, the unusual crime, and imprisonment. Within hours, I realized the family history was like a touch-me-not: as soon as it was broached, it exploded with wrenching tales. Though well-travelled and well-read, I was embarrassed that I had given so little thought to the refugee crisis, the mass of stateless humanity in our world (United Nations estimate: three percent of the global population).

The Kroms' recall for details of their childhoods, their lives in the Cambodian jungle, was encyclopedic and virtually photographic. What's in this chapter came out of extensive interviews with them with only modest supplemental research on my part. I wanted their oral history and personal interpretations, above all.

After the Asia phase of their lives—beginning the moment they stepped on a plane in the Philippines, through their time in Connecticut, and in particular, Panna's childhood—their memory was inexplicably lacking. This frustrated me. For instance, they were uncertain as to their stopovers in the Pacific or how long they spent in San Francisco, or the first place they lived in upon arrival in the US. It was a house in Connecticut—was it in Hartford? They weren't sure. No photos, nor any paper trail, existed. Nevertheless, feeling duty-bound to help me (to free Panna), they were scrupulously open and honest.

When I finished this chapter and typed it up, I slipped it to my confidante in the York writing class, Chasity, who then passed it onto Panna on her tier. While reading it, Panna was brought to tears and told Chasity that she had no idea what her parents had gone through. They had never talked about it.

———

I spread out a map of Cambodia on the living room floor. Song and Chan lit up like kids on Christmas morning. The sprawling city, Battambang, was easy to spot, and from there we located their nearby home villages, Dahan and Sisophon.

Battambang province lies in northwestern Cambodia, on Thailand's contentious eastern border, crossed by the lazy Sangkae River that empties into the massive Tonle Sap Lake. As a stopover between Bangkok and Phnom Penh, it has long been a hub of commercial activity, not to mention Cambodia's most fertile rice-producing province. After oppressive heat in the dry season in March and April, the summer brings drenching monsoons, flooding the rice paddies.

The Krom family (Song's) had seven children and the Prum family (Chan's) had six children. Two aspects of this region dominated their lives: the rice, for it was the reason their parents came from Thailand and it was how they stayed alive; and the Khmer Rouge, because it was why they left—or how they died.

The two families had settled in rural areas, their huts beside the paddies. Nearby was the modern and vibrant city of Battambang, with the paved roads, French architecture, diesel trucks and taxis, schools, temples, hospitals, and shops, the array of languages and dialects and jobs drawing the countryside people from all over the province. For Song's family, because they were penniless, it was an unwelcoming place. And it was too far for either Song's or Chan's family, who traveled by foot. Chan said, "We never went. What are we going to do there?"

Both of Chan and Song's extended families, huge in number and fanning out over the jungle regions of Thailand and Cambodia, had strong bonds, hardened by suffering and scrapes with death. In the 1960s and 70s, before the Khmer Rouge, each day was a test to make it to the next morning. After the KR took over in 1975, the lucky ones managed to get out of Cambodia, but for a decade had to navigate forced moves into and out of camps, while being nameless, stateless, then declared refugees.

Song began his life in Basoon, a collection of huts outside Sisophon in the west, closer to Thailand than Chan's family. Chan lived even deeper into the more southern jungle of the Battambang region. Her village, Dahan, was, according to her, farther away from the city. The Khorat language they both spoke came with their families from Thailand, taking its name from a town there. It was a poor man's dialect, a quick reminder to other Thai that they were peasants. More urbane

Thai, like those in Bangkok, had little tolerance for it or claimed not to understand it.

The hike between the Song's and Chan's villages, along a well-traveled dirt path connecting them, took a full day. It was a busy trail full of boys on their water buffalo, a few men on old bikes, monks in pairs, and women balancing fruit or clothing on their heads. The children, also loaded down, some naked, kept up from behind. Families made their livelihood pulling carts of whatever might sell at the market. Going way back to their fathers' mutual friendship in old Thailand, the two families knew each other well, spoke in that rural tongue, and shared the same struggles. On holidays, it was worth the hike to see each other. Sitting around, eating, and watching a fire gave the men a chance to roll cigarettes and talk, and pass around homemade rice wine. For the kids, it was a break from work in the paddies. The moms congregated around the stoves to talk.

Song and Chan knew each other as children, they said, but they denied that there was any spark of romance. Any hint of that behavior in children would be verboten.

Everything, Chan told me, was about getting food into their bellies. She said a boy never came home without something in his hand to eat: fish, fruit, spiders, mushrooms, anything, even tarantulas and rice rats.

Home was a thatched hut, one big room, made almost exclusively of bamboo. Bamboo, they told me, was everywhere, the shoots spreading and popping up to form thick groves—weed-like and hard to stop. It was strong, light, and waterproof, yet you could bend it, sharpen it, decorate it, even eat it. The villagers watched it grow on a daily basis and used it to make not only huts but also ladders, furniture, tools, pipes, and weapons. Bamboo went into a trap that caught hedgehogs, squirrels, deer, and eels. Because of the monsoon floods, huts had to be lifted onto stilts by numerous men. Although the hut walls were woven from grass and the roof of matted field straw, the frame and floor were bamboo. However, bamboo came with one big caution—the blossom. It wasn't much—no more than a cluster of hanging green strips. And it occurs only once, after a span of maybe a hundred years. But that's when the bamboo dies. It told the farmers the soil was bad and starvation was coming—a curse.

In the center of every hut was a stove. Made from the river mud, it was a block of clay formed by hand and dried in the sun until rock-hard. Clay supports formed the burner grates, strong enough to hold heavy pots of water. Because local wood chopped by axe and machete was the fuel, the surrounding land was stripped bare of trees. In Thailand, but not Cambodia, they made charcoal, by cooking wood in closed drums; it burned longer and hotter. With no refrigeration, they kept very few perishables. Ice was a luxury, found only in the city, and in dreams.

One corner of the hut was devoted to religion. They prayed and burned incense, sending messages skyward to Buddha. Song said that that smell, which filled each hut, was a status symbol. The Buddha was usually a statue, made of anything from high grade marble brought from India to cheap stone, but it could also be a hanging fabric or a picture on tattered paper. Every home had one, the undisturbed center-piece of their world. If it was marble, it glistened, because of its ritual daily cleaning, strictly by a man. Eventually all those precious Buddhas became targets for the butt of an AK-47 wielded by a kid soldier in the Khmer Rouge, which sought to wipe out all religion.

Beds—simply floor pads like the walls—were made from the high, grass-like reeds called *kak* found in the marshes; it was the same grass that for three days hid the four Prum girls, Panna's mom and aunts, from the Khmer Rouge. The reeds were cut, stripped of flowers, and sun-dried to a stiffer dull green, then the women weaved them into thick wavy mats that had a welcome give. Every bed was covered with a blanket and had a pillow, which was stuffed with the seeds of the cotton trees, fluffy like dandelions having exploded during the summer from rupturing pods. An absolute must, though for some unaffordable, was mosquito netting. They draped each adult bed. The children, no matter how many, huddled under another. Each net, well cared for and constantly mended, had to be bug-proof and last forever as the mosqui-toes carried malaria and dengue (known as breakbone fever). Although they lived only about ten days, the mosquitoes could penetrate even the thick hide of the cow sleeping under the hut. To protect the cow, every night Song had to make a small smoky fire with green wood next to it.

At night, most huts had a single flickering fire coming from a central shelf. Dinner would be ruined without the soft yellow flame. Its fuel, kerosene, was precious. Song's family stored theirs in a fish sauce bottle; the Prums kept theirs in a dented condensed milk can. The kerosene level was a sort of bank account. Song said, "You always know exactly how much there was." If you couldn't afford it, the next best thing was an acrid, smoky cow grease. For kerosene refills, Song hiked five or six miles. On his return, he would sometimes tie a string around the bottle, swinging it as he walked, attracting villagers willing to bargain.

Villages had schools, but the elder Kroms and Prums had never gone, and regrettably, their kids didn't go either. That decision wasn't cruel or even ignorant—they had no choice. Chan's older sister did go for a short time, but had to leave to help out. Going back a few centuries, in the traditional Cambodian education system, only boys attended the *wats* where they spent their youth with the monks learning the hundreds of Buddhist chants in *pali,* a dead language from the subcontinent. Sometime in the early 1900s, Cambodia's colonial French masters replaced this with a European model of teachers and various grade levels in a steep three-tiered system. The plan was for each village to have an elementary school. Both Chan and Song remember theirs, a hut. It had a blackboard on the front wall and a short row of chairs and tables. They were afraid to enter it. To go you had to pay. For peasants like the Kroms and the Prums, school was for the rich. Money, if they had any, was for kerosene, salt, or medicine, in that order—but not reading. Nor could their family sacrifice a pair of hands in the rice paddies.

Song remembers those early weekday mornings. By sunrise he would be knee-deep in the rice paddies with his cow and plow when the children from a larger village passed by on their way to the school hut. As soon as he heard the chatter approaching up the road, like a swamp croc he slid out of the paddy and squatted behind a mound, his legs caked with mud, hoping he wouldn't be spotted. With his heart pumping, he spied. The children sauntered by, as if it was nothing for them, wearing fresh clothes and real leather shoes. Under their arms were books. The boys wore khaki pants, the girls had dark blue skirts, and everyone had crisp white shirts and carried something he could never get over: backpacks. Sometimes they spotted him and a few pointed, but never teased; their parents had warned them not to.

Song described to me how he slapped the ground with his stick, over and over, arguing to himself and feeling angry—not with anyone in particular, just angry. He would never do what they were doing: walk to school, have homework, talk about kings and wars, and carry a backpack. He had never held a book. "Missing out" was a feeling in his gut that never went away.

"There's nothing you can do about it," said Chan. "That's what poor means. No matter what you do, you will always be poor." She added, "I *hate* being poor. I hate *everything* about it. I hate not having shoes. I don't even have flip-flop in the village. I hate not going to school, eating bugs, drinking dirty water. Even now, when I go to somebody's garden, I don't want to pick anything. I don't want to live like that."

The village had no books. The only print Song saw was on the newspaper wrappings from the market. There was no pen or paper. Neither Song nor Chan had ever read a real book. Years later, in their apartment in Danbury, the only reading material I saw was a couple of flimsy palm-sized paperbacks, formatted like comic books with pictures. In the village, these were highly valued items. Song told me he had one and cherished it, kept it tucked under his bed, at night pretending to read it over and over, year after year. Not until he reached the Philippines, after leaving Thailand, did an illiterate Song get hold of a regular book. He taught himself to read Thai, he told me, in only six months.

———

Each village had a town doctor, a shaman, called *mau pa*. When an ailing villager came to him, he inspected the palms, the eyes, and the skin to determine which of the many spirits might have caused the illness and tried to appease that spirit. His bag included herbs, bamboo leaves, dried jackfruit leaves, carved beads, mushrooms, and lemongrass leaves. He shaved the roots and put them in a water elixir or made a poultice of wild herb seeds.

When sick, the first thing you'd do, they said, was try your own remedy. But if that didn't work, you would call the *mau pa*.

I asked, "What do you mean, call?"

"Someone would run to his hut," Song said. "And you boil water.

But sometimes you don't want him, because he cost money. He usually gave you a shot. He only had one needle, which he poured the boiling water over. Chan's nephew got a shot in one arm and today the arm is paralyzed and barely of any use."

Everyone in the village knew that, with enough time, infections largely heal on their own. "Just let it be," said Song, "it gets better." Song allowed any cut to heal on its own, even if it had pus and swelling. Much like the days before penicillin, the shaman had no antibiotics. What he did was urinate on the cuts.

Urine, in fact, had several uses. Aside from the shaman peeing on his patients, it was an antidote for leeches and was widely used to fertilize crops. Farmers collected it from their families, let it sit in a jar for two days, diluted it, and then poured it over their crops.

———

The river represented life and was their main source of water. It was also where you sometimes saw dead bodies—usually cows, but occasionally people. A daily chore for Song and Chan was to haul water back to the village. They didn't have carts, only the *dong re,* a simply designed strong bamboo pole with twine on each end holding baskets. You placed it across the shoulders to balance the baskets. Flexible, it bounced as you hustled along keeping the knees bent and in rhythm.

Chan said, "Yes, me and my sisters, we carry water every day. It's why I'm so short." A great line.

When I asked if children were a burden or a help, she said, "Nobody plans. Most just happen. They are a mouth to feed. But by eight or nine they cook, help in the field, get wood, do the cow, the rice."

In the village, the reality of death came early in life. Chan said her oldest sister, the one she never knew, had died as a baby. "She was three months and just stopped crying. That was it. It just happens. We had three die as a baby." The causes of the deaths were never known. She continued. "I didn't really know my mom. I was so small. I was closer to my dad. You die. It happens to a lot. Many drown. Bad infection. Snake bite. We don't know anything. If fever, we know. But if it's a big thing then we don't know."

Villagers are cremated at the time of death: shrouded in a blanket and burned over sticks. By the ninetieth day, there's a ceremony in which the body (ashes) is blessed and sent heavenward. "There are four spirits," said Chan, "called *winya*." The first remains with the body and is cremated with it. The second stays at the place of death, remaining dead, often in the hut. The third comes back to the loved one, like at home. Around seven days the family can see it or feel it. And the last goes on to heaven or hell, depending on what kind of life they led. "The monk, the man with the shaved head and the orange robe," said Song, "he is the representative who can lead the right path for the spirit to get to the light, heaven."

Chan's mother had six children, that is, six who lived. Three didn't. Song's mother had nine, but two died. He said simply, "We're not sure why."

———

A few times I heard Song mention Peur, so I asked him, "Who was Peur?"

Peur was his best friend. "Me and Peur, we hunt together, frogs, snakes, mouse, rat. We fish. He live maybe one mile away. One day we take the water buffalo together to work in the rice fields. After finished, Peur take care of the buffalo. He took it beside the rice paddy to eat the grass around the paddy. Maybe six or seven people there. Peur stand beside it. I don't know why. The buffalo, he just really shake his head and the horn hook Peur in the stomach. The buffalo shook him. In and out of his stomach. We took him and put our shirts on his stomach. We carry him to barn. We don't know what to do. Peur he just talking. Say he hungry. Chatting. Then his eyes roll back. His intestines coming out. We are long way from village. We build stack of wood, wrap him in blanket, put him on top, and burn. No monk is around. One parent try to do chant. We wait until his ashes and spread them at rice paddy."

CHAPTER TWENTY-ONE
SUWAN

Cambodia occupies the middle of the Indochina peninsula with Thailand and Laos to the north and Vietnam to the east. In the early 1970s, a band of communist guerrillas called the Khmer Rouge started roving the rural regions of Cambodia. The country had become a battleground. On one side, the US backed a government headed by Lon Nol and on the other, the Vietnamese assisted the communists. Massive secret US bombings over Cambodia aided Lon Nol by halting the flow of arms to the local Viet Cong, who were South Vietnamese supporting the communists of North Vietnam. With fear of the bombings and a promise of peace by the Khmer Rouge forces, many peasants joined them. By 1975, that guerrilla army, with its newly installed prime minister, Pol Pot, had captured the capital, Phnom Penh, evacuated it, and taken absolute control of Cambodia. During the four years that they held power, they orchestrated a sweeping genocide, turning the country into a graveyard for almost two million Cambodians. This was the Cambodia that Song and Chan grew up in.

———

Chan never knew her grandparents, only that they were farmers. No tales were handed down. Her family never saw their history as a bank of stories to be cherished and told to their descendants. Perhaps they viewed it as shameful and believed no lessons could be drawn out of their lives of desperation—besides, none of Chan's elders were left. There was little to recall about her own parents. They came from Thailand, but she wasn't sure from what part. She had no photos, letters or mementos. There were no graves or ashes, just her faint memory; after all, she was a little girl. Still, she and her siblings continued to pray for their parents to protect them.

———

Chan said, "Doug, we are all that's left."

She was sitting on the couch in their Bethel apartment between two of her older, very private, sisters (who remain nameless). Song sat next to me. For well over a year, I kept hearing Song and Chan speak their names. I had arranged this meeting and felt it was a stroke of luck to have the three of them together in one room. Missing was her brother, Saht, and the two older sisters, Pung and Paht. The three additional siblings died as babies and had no names. And her mother and father— they were gone.

All the sisters are hard-working, had attended Danbury High School, same as Panna, some twenty-five years before her. That, in fact, had been the beginning and end of their schooling. By November of their first year, they were gone. Chan was pregnant, one was discovered to be over twenty and the other was bullied out—being pelted with pizza and tennis balls.

The two had no more than elementary English and able to write only their names and addresses. During my many interviews with Chan, I had heard enough to know that her whole family possessed a story that I was pretty certain had never been told. Now they would talk. In fact, they were willing and appreciative, for they understood that I was there to help Panna. When I asked Chan, she said that Panna and her cousins understood to never ask their mothers about Cambodia, telling me it was something they had remained mute about. That was a delicate way of conveying their private suffering. I knew from my readings that assaults and child murders had occurred on a large scale; Chan had previously hinted about something that Cambodian women "were not proud of." The tag *blind ladies* was in the literature, specifically coined for Cambodian refugee women. Maybe it was an attempt at folklore, or ridicule, but it was a real entity, a form of suppression. In neurology we call it functional blindness or conversion disorder, a mechanism sometimes intended to protect oneself from a hidden, deep-seated conflict.

The three sat together, collectively shy. Each appeared to be in her young fifties and each was graced with a certain sparkle—soft smiles, beautiful teeth, and glowing eyes, fit, healthy, and neatly dressed. It utterly defied any hint of what I already knew: child labor, prior primitive living, or having endured a historical tragedy. It was a draining experience for me to observe their reserve while digesting the story they calmly retold. By late that afternoon, I arrived at my private declaration: They were the most charming sisters in the state of Connecticut.

Song wasted no time. "Doug, you have to see this.," He instructed them in Thai and each boldly lifted her blouse part-way to reveal a disturbing array of scars. I could see that they were wounds that, in the parlance of field surgeons, had secondarily closed—were never sutured. Song, like a field guide, pointed to one, then another of the scattered scars, each about two inches long. Chan had one on her forehead, which I hadn't taken note of before, one on the back of her neck and another on the rib cage. The others had one on her belly and the worst, a matchbook-sized one on her right hip, which Song knew had had maggots. And one had a scar on the chest, which moved in and out like a bellows when she breathed, and several randomly fanning out on her back. "Bayonets," said Song. "You believe it?" I was astounded how their emotion was contained as they revealed their scars.

On that distant afternoon in the rice paddies, when the Khmer Rouge boys stood over them repeatedly plunging the blades in and out, they were just pre-teens. Instead of wailing, they played dead. That was why the three were here today.

———

Chan's parents left Thailand before she was born. Driven by hunger, they headed east toward Cambodia. Poor Thai families streamed along the same well-worn roads for what the word-of-mouth told them they would find: work and food. They crossed the border with no fanfare, as there was no guard or checkpoint, bringing their children, a cow if lucky, and whatever bare essentials they could carry—certainly no papers. Eventually they settled on a clearing deep in the jungle; being close to a river was a must. The men gathered bamboo and put up shelters. They called the tiny collection of huts Dahan, borrowing the name of one of their elders.

They were peasants, which in the Battambang region meant that they worked the rice paddies. Having been farmers already, they knew all about growing peanuts, potatoes, tobacco, and bananas—but here it was rice. Paddies were nothing like farms. The work was backbreaking, requiring the movement of tons of mud, constant stooping, and being suctioned into the muck up to your thighs, along with bug bites, cuts, and leeches. The steamy sun was suffocating; their only protection was a flimsy conical matted hat (*koup*). The only so-called relief came in midsummer with the drenching monsoon rains. While they worked, the women kept their babies swathed on their backs until they were big enough to share the load, scattering seeds or planting seedlings. By four, they were rank-and-file laborers, already embarked on their career in the paddies. Children, like Chan and her sisters, had no dreams of being anything or anywhere else. Pay amounted to a few coins or plastic bags of rice.

There was never news in their Cambodian village. On occasion the girls heard a radio playing, usually rock music. Nobody read newspapers. Philosophical or political debate was not part of the elders' chat with their homemade wine. To them Vietnam was a country, not a war. Breaking news about the conflict, which was slowly consuming their country, poured out of Washington, Hanoi and Phnom Penh, but never reached them—only bullets, bombs and rumors.

Chan said, "One day the Khmer Rouge, *Kmin Dhang* we say, came into Dahan. At first, we see them, just boys, they wear all black, red scarves, hats, carried big rifles. No one warn us. We never heard of no war. We don't know politic. They come at night to talk to the old men.

They want us to go with them. We don't know what they are. They want us to join, even the little girls like us. At night, the older men in our village talk to themselves and decide. They told them no. Nobody want to." She hesitated and said, "It is final. We tell them no."

"They try to wash our brains," added Chan's sister. "They walk through our house with a bag and take anything, watches, necklace, even our Buddha. We sit on the floor and watch. They break things. But we don't have these things they are looking for. Many are small boys, some only thirteen or fourteen. Even eight."

Song explained how, in order to show his fitness to join the Khmer Rouge, a boy followed orders by shooting his own parents. And if asked, a villager had to tell them they would rather be with the Khmer Rouge. "Nothing," he said, "came in front of the Khmer Rouge, no family, no Buddha, nothing."

In a collective voice, with Song and Chan interpreting and injecting commentary, the Prum sisters told me their story of escape.

———

A small village sat directly across the river from Dahan. During the period of escalating conflict, Chan's family heard gunfire, and saw people, just shadows in the dark, leaving that village. Once the sisters saw them being led away by Khmer Rouge soldiers, they knew they were next. Their choice was clear: escape. Her sister said, "We are five girls, one oldest brother, and our mom and dad. The first time we try to escape, but they see us and we came back. We are in our hut with the army, the good army, who are around us. KR everywhere and we have no chance. Our army is small, has no more bullets, empty guns. Finally, one day they're gone."

Every night the Khmer Rouge shot at their huts and took away two to three screaming neighbors who they never saw again.

One sister said, "One night we are there, hiding under hut, and my dad whispers, 'We got to go to Thailand.' We pack our stuff."

What followed was a tally of executions of their family that reminded me of what's been commented on many times before: man's utter failure as a compassionate being.

Before sunrise, without a sound, the sisters' family held hands, and with heads down, ran. In no time, the Khmer Rouge surrounded them. Their father fell to his knees begging for them to spare his family. They kicked him and told him to get up. As he stood, they tied his hands behind his back, taking him off. One said, "My father—he know he is going to die. He look at us, not cry. He say to Paht, my older sister, 'Don't ever leave your sisters.' *P'yoon* [sister], his last word." They never saw him again.

Another said, "Paht, she take care of us."

"But she's not here," I said.

"Paht. We lose Paht," said one sister. "That happen later. But we sisters, four, were still together."

"Then who else was missing?" I asked. "What about Pung, the oldest?"

Chan said, "She was shot, but we don't see it. For no reason. Like that. First, she shot in leg and have trouble walking. Then she stop. Say, no more."

"She stopped? That's it? You left her there?"

"Yes, that was it. She refuse to move."

"Did she have children?" I asked.

Chan said, "Yes, she had two—no three. One died when she born. And the other two die on lap of the sisters. Khmer Rouge stab with bayonet in front of us in village."

"We see this happen to Pung, then we march," said one. "We go, my mother, three sisters and myself."

Chan said, "Mother, she started having pain in her belly. She bent over like this," signaling with her hand. "We tell Mom, 'Please get up!' We pulled her arm. We drag her. 'Mom, Mom, please, get up!' A boy kick her and yelled at her to get up. She give up. I think because of my father. The boy stand over her and calls her a name. I remember, he was skinny boy. He thinks she's pretending. On her knees, she looked right at him. The soldier pointed his gun and shot her one, two, three times."

One said, "I think why he shot her, she looked right in his face. Not afraid. We all grabbing our heads and closing our eyes. We were waiting for the bullet."

"What was her name, your mother?" I asked.

"Like me," said Chan. "Chan."

Song reminded them of their cousin. She had told them, "Leave me here. I'll die here."

Song said she had a bullet wound across her belly.

Chan said, "She don't want to go, just be left alone. She wasn't afraid. But her brother carry her anyway. While he carry her, she die. Leave her by paddy."

Along the way, Chan spotted a shirt. "I know that shirt," she said. Her brother had worn it every day. "He was down in a ditch. I never see his face. But I know. It is Saht. He is dead. We are going to end up like that. I just know it."

The soldiers led the four girls along the rice paddies. Then, told to line up and get down, they squatted. "They give us meal," said one.

"Like the last supper," said Chan. "Banana leaves with rice, make you believe they save us." After that, the Khmer Rouge, going down the line, stabbed numerous girls, one by one, each body silently sliding into the paddy.

"They used boys to stab us. Over and over, fifteen times. Here. Here. Here." They pointed at their bodies. "They used two hands with all their strength."

"When the lady next to me is stabbed, I go out and fall back," said one. She stopped a minute and then continued, "Me and my three sisters were passed for dead. But they stab us anyway, this and this. My sisters talk to me. They faint also. We are all stabbed and bleeding. Chan, the littlest, was the last one."

When the boys left, the girls hid in the bushes, where they stayed for three days. Chan said, "We eat anything we can catch, crickets, toads, centipedes, mice, scorpions, worms. We are afraid to move, but were told we have to go to Thailand, like Daddy said. She push us, push, and make us. If we had stayed we die for sure."

Traveling only at night, they crawled through the brush. The first night they spotted a pile of wood burning in a clearing and people saying prayers; these people were left alone because they were old. Still afraid to come out, the sisters smelled the incense and food coming through the trees. It was dark, with the firelight flickering and the sound of snapping wood over funeral chants. Chan said, "Through the leaves we see. It was *our* funeral."

Holding hands, with only scraps of clothes on their bodies, they made their way through the jungle. They followed the dikes, staying away from roads. They found peppers to eat but also saw dead bodies. An army man had advised them on how to avoid mines, telling them to look for big leaves placed on them used as a warning, and to try to walk on the bodies.

Frequent sounds from the Khmer Rouge came through the woods. Marching and chanting, over and over: "The brave children of *Angka Leu*."

"*Angka Leu?* What's that?" I asked.

"It mean the rules, sort of. The Khmer Rouge," said Song.

"Like the law," added Chan.

Chan said, "After seven days, first, we see a base. Finally, an army man, who live in our village. He recognized me and Paht and told them, "I know your daddy. He is my friend." He took the girls to a Thai military base hospital not far away, where they got their wounds cleaned and stayed for a month.

I said to the sisters, "You must miss your mother." They nodded. "And as for your dad," I said. "it was his decision to leave the village. He chose a new life for you."

"He know," said Song. "He give his life."

"Your mom's name was Chan. What about your dad? I didn't catch his name."

"My dad?" said Chan. "He was Suwan."

———

On the way home, I was deep in thought about the sisters and their stoicism. I recalled that in Panna's psych assessment, they did a Harvard Questionnaire subscale for PTSD for which she scored clinically positive—the causes identified as the genocidal trauma of her parents as well as the subsequent death of her daughter. However, she had never heard this Cambodian story. The sisters' charm and what seemed ease in telling their stories belied the armor they had adopted. The consequences of their trauma had been unknowingly passed on to Panna and her cousins. Part of the Cambodian story has been to adapt in order to negate the psychic pain, something vital for their survival. Subconsciously, high schooler Panna was already well-prepared with a steely exterior, equipped to deny her pregnancy, handle the cruel comments, battle on, and reveal nothing.

CHAPTER TWENTY-TWO

POL POT

I asked Chan and her sisters, "The name Pol Pot."

There was a hesitation.

"What does it mean to you?"

They looked at each other. No immediate reaction. Chan, usually the first one to speak up, said, "We know him. But we don't read. We don't know politic. We know, but we don't know. You see?"

Song said, "We know he killed our family."

I explained, "Pol Pot almost destroyed Cambodia."

"We know that. We never think of him. He's gone."

Even before I knew the Kroms, Pol Pot held a certain mysterious curiosity for me. His name had a catchy and iconic ring to it, like Che or Marx. To the uninformed—that is, most people—he never seemed to be in the same stratum of tyrants as Hitler and Stalin—but he was. I gave a talk about Panna and the Kroms at Yale's Cambodian Genocide Program and Song and Chan came. When I asked them to stand at the end, the audience applauded. We met Ben Kiernan, the Whitney Griswold History Professor at Yale, who had authored two books on Pol Pot. The four of us had lunch at nearby Clarks Diner. Kiernan, an Australian, conversed with them in Cambodian. Impressed with their story, he sent Panna one of his books and helped me in my research on

Pol Pot, the dictator who stood at a historical apex in the lives of Song and Chan. Kiernan willingly reviewed this chapter.

———

This private man, Pol Pot, who never ran for office and had little in the way of a public face, became what Cambodia had been missing: a historical draftsman, a dreamer, and he came up with a grand design for its revival. Although he was the architect as such, there was never an actual blueprint, only results. At his height, deeply hidden in the jungle and paralyzed with paranoia, this unlikely man drew out the map for Cambodia's path to utopia, quite simply called *Democratic Kampuchea* (Outsiders used the term *Year Zero*.). The methods, stolen from Russia and China, were mostly across-the-board purging and evacuation of its people. While the rest of the world was shut out, Pol Pot led his soldiers to become the most absolute of murdering regimes in history. During this four-year bloodbath, in two tiny jungle villages near the Thai border, lived two children. They were Panna's parents, Song and Chan. Struggle, hunger, and now the likelihood of murder was the fabric of their youth.

———

Pol Pot. Khmer Rouge. Comrade Deuch (war criminal Kang Kek lew). All chic, catchy, curious names. Each one dripping in innocent Cambodian blood. All gone now, like vapor. No country in history had undergone such a mindless sweeping elimination of its own people like Cambodia in the years 1975 through 1979. No other country was quite so silent on answers or as devoid of justice. Adding to the tragedy, except for Deuch (who served a life sentence and died in 2020), not one of the murderers ever admitted going to bed—never mind prison—with even a pang of guilt. Stare at the haunting photos from the S-21 torture chambers. This was a book with no ink.

As for Pol Pot, the country's major twentieth century historical figure, there was almost nothing on him—no musings, no writings, books, papers, or probing interviews; there were only scarce photos in grainy film. He left no *Mein Kampf*. There was no body on display and no grave. Just one fuzzy photo of him under age thirty exists; he's in narrow-waisted pants and shirt with wind-tousled hair. He had an unseen psychotic wife and a long-disappeared daughter. It's hard to comprehend how the mixture of the influences of his childhood, his religion, his education, and his mysterious personality in the setting of those revolutionary times, would lead to what happened. The lights went out. When the lights flicked back on, one-fifth of the Cambodian population was gone.

———

Saloth Sâr, Pol Pot's real name, was born into a middle-class family in 1925 with eight brothers and sisters. His father, Loth, owned twenty acres of rice paddies, a considerable amount. So Saloth Sâr never lived with the agrarian poverty he later claimed was the key issue demanding his extremist solution. He was raised on folk tales of the Khmer people, the main ethnic group in Cambodia—legends that elevated tragedy, rewarding it as a virtue. Another lesson was that villainy was praised as long as it succeeded, and trickery was admired. Nowhere in his lexicon was there room for compassion. During his year in a monastery in Phnom Penh he memorized the tenets of Theravada Buddhism, which taught that merit was not to be expected in *this* life, but will be apportioned in a future existence.

At nine, his father sent him to Phnom Penh, the Cambodian capital, for a better education in a private school; it was a place into which he never fit. Called *Ecole Miche*, it had a French curriculum. Sâr was, at best, a mediocre student, often stumbling and required to repeat some crucial exams.

Almost every Cambodian from all points in this desperately poor country made it their life's journey to stand in the immense shadow cast over Phnom Penh by the Angkor Wat, the grand temple. Whenever that happens, they say one can feel the history that surrounds the colossal structure and begin to comprehend the splendid stories told of twelfth-century Cambodia. Tiny Cambodia, because of that temple, was the glory of the world. Every Cambodian grows up knowing by heart about that grandeur, when their king was revered beyond anything else, like a god. He constructed Angkor Wat to be the greatest religious site in the world. At first it was a Hindu temple, then Buddhist, eventually becoming the king's own mausoleum.

Angkor's ancient god-kings had ruled its vast Hindu kingdom from Burma to Malaya and half of modern Thailand, plus most of Laos and Vietnam. In the twelfth century, it was an agrarian society, over which Angkor Wat towered. Certainly, as Sâr stood under the magnificent structure, he saw that Kampuchea, the indigenous name for Cambodia, had long relinquished its splendor and was now merely one more puppet under the French empire in Southeast Asia, alongside Vietnam and Laos. Sâr compared the grandeur of the temple to what he had seen in Phnom Penh; he denounced it and all other cities as evil. In the past Cambodia had slave labor, dams, dikes, and rice that paid for all the glory—as they said then: "Rice is steel." Now he saw those things as only for subsistence. So, Angkor, in the mind of all Cambodians, had become a constant reminder of their failure to reclaim those heights. What he was witnessing would eventually drive him into an obsession for his grand vision: Cambodia as utopia.

———

At the French school, Saloth Sâr mingled with brighter minds. Revolution was the talk. He was a listener, absorbing the political dialogue and harangues of the day. Opposition to French rule was strong and this had great influence on him. In 1949 he was selected, despite mediocre scholarship, for further study in Paris. He boarded the *SS Jamaique*, a troop ship, with a stop in Djibouti, then Marseilles. Skipping that city, with his good friend, Mey Mann, they took an overnight train to Paris, a seminal adventure for the two boys. They claimed they never once talked politics. Mann was, in fact, the first one to remark on the power of "Saloth's famous smile."

In the City of Lights, Saloth Sâr lived in a third-floor walkup behind the Pantheon, on Rue Amyot. This was the Latin Quarter, the Left Bank, the intellectual hub of the world and, for any fertile mind, one of the great world addresses. The various colleges of the Sorbonne—

science, law, architecture—were steps away, as were book vendors along the Seine. Across on the Right Bank he could head up through the Tuileries and the Champs-Elysées to the Arc de Triomphe, along the way slipping into the Louvre to view a Van Gogh or the genius of Da Vinci. Or he could head a few blocks in the other direction to the Jardin de Luxembourg where he could sit on one of the steel chairs by the fountain and watch the most cultured women in the world stroll by. He had to have stood under the Cathedral of Notre Dame and the Eiffel Tower, where anyone would be in a state of breathlessness. Paris was the last and best chance Cambodia had to sway his demonic fixation on that primeval yesteryear toward a most wondrous array of humanity and aesthetics.

Paris was buzzing with revolutionary talk. Intellectuals carried worn-out copies of *Das Kapital*. Saloth Sâr read these but struggled, getting too mired in the philosophy. Discussions of communism, a new ideology, redirected his mind. It was the discovery of the Terror (harsh measures against the enemies of the Revolution) in France that finally brought him into the conversations. He admired the French Revolution for ridding the country of the monarchy.

He stopped going to the Champs-Elysées or even to the Right Bank, preferring a favorite corner bistro. Perhaps this was the first sign of a man destined to retreat, sometime later into the jungle. To the intelligentsia, he remained simply a pedestrian carpenter apprentice with a middle school certificate.

Sâr had a newfound purpose in life with his interpretation of the Revolution. Then he came upon the work of Stalin, another paranoid despot—but someone who appealed to him. The dense volumes of Marx were too much for him, but he found Stalin's essay *Marxism and the National Question* easier to understand. Perhaps it was the parts about the state using a military means for repression and purging. This Marxism he interpreted through the prism of Cambodian class distinctions. Stalin became his conduit to evil. Stalin was a quick lesson in how the party grows stronger by cleansing itself. Sâr would plagiarize the Russian's playbook to devise his own scorched-earth policy.

Combining Stalin's grim prescription for maintaining purity in a revolutionary party with Mao's guide on revolutionary practice, he had his grand scheme. He parted ways with those two leaders when it came to dependence on the industrial proletariat. Cambodia had no industry, only the peasantry. They were his Bolsheviks. He later saw struggle as not good versus evil, but *srok* and *brai*—farmland and forest. He viewed the Cambodian people as soulless instruments and used the ox as a model for them.

Once back in Cambodia, Sâr shifted his attention to the jungle, where he felt the power dwelled. He lived there under near starvation, suffering relapses of malaria. For a period of nine years, he never left his headquarters, wandering out only on the back of an elephant. Surrounding him were his *Montagnards*, fanatically loyal hill people, who were unsullied by Cambodian Buddhist village life. Hermetically reclusive, even in group photos he was almost unnoticeable, off to the side.

———

In 1962 Sâr was selected to be the leader of the Khmer Communist Party, with its loyal followers, the Khmer Rouge. A convincing speaker, they designated him Brother #1. His rhetoric was all about overthrowing, stirring up a revolution in the slums of Phnom Penh. All of his followers were to do like him and leave the city. But being a master of deception, he disappeared. Few knew he was in the jungle near Vietnam where he sought out the simple agrarian life in the village with his converted tribesmen. All this and the outside world still had never heard of Saloth Sâr.

Secretly Saloth Sâr had already twice visited China, where he viewed firsthand the Cultural Revolution and how it expunged intellectuals. Inspired in this way, Mao had convinced him he could return and do the same, even better.

Around this time American power was growing in Vietnam.

Nixon bombed the Viet Cong bases in Cambodia in 1969, near Sâr. The US assisted the effort to eliminate the communists. It was Cambodia's failed civil confrontation and the international conflict that spread into the country from the Vietnam War that allowed Pol Pot to rise to power. That's when the lights turned out in Cambodia. No one knew and no one had heard of him.

In 1970 he said, "From now on I will call myself Pol." Later he added Pot as it was the custom to add a euphonic monosyllable. Pol Pot continued to be a man of modest means who concealed himself in the jungles. Fed by his paranoia, he operated under aliases. One of his rare quotes was, "If you preserve secrecy, half the battle is already won." While in the jungle he laid down the principles for the future Khmer Rouge regime and planned for radical surgery: abolish money, law, the courts, newspapers, religion, the postal system, any creativity, individual rights, and eliminate the bourgeoisie and artists. The future of Cambodia lay in the hands of the agrarians, as it did eight hundred years ago with the Angkor kings, but in his calculating eyes, even more glorious. Cambodia was cleansed, the earth scorched, and killing fields filled with the bodies of all the intellectuals and urbanites.

Peace came to Vietnam in 1973. But Cambodia broke with Vietnam and the US pulled out. Sihanouk, the monarch who had been deposed in 1970, returned, but Pol Pot was the real leader. It didn't matter that he was hidden. The world had abandoned Cambodia. Cambodia under Pol Pot was renamed Democratic Kampuchea.

———

Angkar is a word that meant a lot to the Cambodians. Chan and Song said it was "the temple." It was the symbol of greatness in Cambodia. Ever since the 13th century Cambodia had been in a steady state of collapse. During the Khmer Rouge, Angkar took on another widely understood meaning: "the organization." It stood for the ideal, the way it used to be—Utopia. As Song and Chan said: the temple. But to the villager it was double-edged, for it also meant authority, the absolute. It brought out fear and led to death. It was Angkar that ordered factories burned, people to be led to the killing fields, anyone speaking French executed, monks shot.

It was Angkar that marched into Chan's village at night, randomly shooting the huts and leading villagers to their execution. It was Angkar that offered Chan's father a choice: join the Khmer Rouge or die. And die he and half of her family did, all except the four sisters.

The Khmer Rouge marched into Phnom Penh and ordered it to be emptied by April 17, 1975. Everyone was commandeered out of the city. People left; they had no food. They carried the wounded, oxen pulled carts with chickens, people were on bikes and motorbikes, arms were loaded with all they could carry. During the ensuing war, rice was dropped to the city dwellers by American airlift. The capital now became a ghost town.

In 1978, Pol Pot made a calculated mistake, thinking of the Vietnamese as enemies and attacking them—and his army was defeated. While the Khmer Rouge government collapsed, Pol Pot lingered in the jungles.

With the disintegration of the regime, Cambodia was able to open up. The killing fields all over the countryside, littered with skulls, were discovered.

By the late 1990's the Khmer Rouge was down to perhaps 40,000 troops, with Pol Pot still out of sight in the jungle of Anlong Veng district, the most northernmost part of Cambodia. He was tried for treason but never punished. Consumed by paranoia, one by one he had his close officers shot.

In the end Pol Pot was sentenced to life imprisonment. He remained unrepentant and never served one day.

The last picture of him—staged—shows a gray-haired man hobbled by a stroke being helped to walk. "I have nothing to apologize for," he proclaimed. The Khmer Rouge may have decided to hand him over to an international tribunal to stand another trial. But the night before, he died in his sleep and his body was burned on a pile of rubbish and tires.

Eighteen months after Pol Pot's death in 1998, and after thirty years of war, peace returned to Cambodia. The last of his guerrillas laid down their weapons.

But if you went through the rural areas of Cambodia, life as Song and Chan knew it was virtually the same, unchanged from before and after the Khmer Rouge.

I asked Song and Chan, "Do you remember when Pol Pot died?" Chan said, "We know he gone. That's all."

CHAPTER TWENTY-THREE
BATAAN

During the Cambodian Civil War of the 1970s, the Thai people held a dim view of the Cambodians, their neighbors to the south, once they were fleeing over their border by the thousands. To them, they were poor rice farmers, less educated, and after having lost so much family, deeply traumatized and depressed. The Thai military confined them to labor camps and limited their food supplies, worsening their starvation. Chan and her sisters had made the trek through the Cambodian jungle while Song and his ten family members had arrived; just as the Khmer Rouge were starting their campaign. The families ended up in the camps together. Being Thai by blood and fluent in the local dialect, they thought they would avoid the camps, that relatives would take them in. But they were wrong; Song's uncle and Chan's relatives turned them away. Over those ensuing seven years in Thailand, as described previously, they were in and out of the camps. They survived on the margins, treated as outcasts, living off handouts of rice from paddies they built and harvested.

In one camp, Song started noticing something disturbing just outside the gate. As he explained it, "Some Cambodians refused to get on this bus. The Thai hit them with the butt of the rifle. I know where they go, to the cliffs. Never come back." The way he told it was rather offhanded, making me wonder: Cliffs? Actual cliffs? If so, what happened there? Or was this just a camp rumor? He said it didn't stop; soldiers were herding unsuspecting Cambodians onto the buses. With growing concern, he protected his family, having them remain in their tent, out of sight of the army.

Those events were part of larger patterns that attracted international attention. The pro-Vietnamese government of Cambodia charged Thailand's military with atrocities. The Thai forces were reported to have pushed thousands of Cambodian migrants over the border back into the war zone, often deliberately marching them across minefields. Even worse was what Song had witnessed—the packed buses. The peasants boarded the buses, told they were going to America.

Then in 1979, an event in northern Thailand got worldwide press coverage. Forty-two thousand Cambodians were taken in buses to Preah Vihear, a mountain village on the Thailand-Cambodian border. Abruptly stopping the buses, Thai soldiers fired into the air, chasing the passengers off the bus and up a ridge, and finally pushing them over the crest. Families with children helplessly slid down a cliff into the minefields below.

One of the survivors, Pov Thai, who later became a Dallas police officer, told a reporter of one incident in particular. A mother carrying her baby stepped on a mine. Hearing a click, she knew if she moved, it would explode. She froze and screamed for someone to just take her baby. People stood by and watched; no one came. She kept screaming. After minutes, a man did. As he came forward, and in her excitement, her foot moved and the three blew up.

Similar accounts eventually stirred the watchdogs for displaced peoples. Established in 1950, the United Nations High Commission for Refugees (UNHCR) protected their rights and reduced the barriers for asylum. Thailand's topography made border crossing easy for the war refugees. The UNHCR prevailed upon the Thai to not abandon their humanitarian obligation. They provided support by setting up processing facilities in their camps. Additional centers, needed to teach the refugees about modern life, were erected in three remote locales: Galang in Indonesia, Phanat Nikhom in Thailand, and Bataan in the Philippines. They served as temporary stops for the refugees, before they were sent to a preselected home in a secondary asylum country: the US, Canada, Australia, or France. In conference rooms in faraway Geneva, Swiss diplomats were sketching out these cross-continental freedom trails–little did Song and Chan realize that their lives were in the balance.

On designated dates, Cambodian refugees in the Thai camps were given directives to leave, then packed into the unpressurized cargo bins of twin-prop planes. Chan and Song and one sister, still together, got on one plane and were instructed on blowing on their noses to pop their ears, and completed the first leg to the Philippine Refugee Processing Center (PRPC).

The PRPC was a facility on the Bataan Peninsula consisting of neat rows of Quonset huts set deep in a lush valley of mahogany and banana trees. Reassuring for the war-weary, only an hour to the north was Subic Bay, the Singapore-sized US naval base.

Thailand, eager to rid itself of its illegal aliens, rapidly ran into a shortage of aircraft, and in desperation, turned to the American military. The navy downgraded ships and deployed them for what the sailors called "civilian diaper runs." In the chaos of everyone rushing for the exits, an older sister, having delivered a baby in the camps and still nursing her, had been separated from her family. She was assigned to one of the ships, a former ordnance transporter. Her bed, next to the engine room, was a steel grate over the oil bilge. Her three sisters, by now settled at the PRPC, grew more despondent each passing day with no sign of her. Ships arrived and thousands came ashore, but no sis. They feared the worst. Rumors didn't help—her boat sank or sharks ate them, as Song recalled. In reality, her ship ran into a tropical cyclone and nearly all the live cargo, confined below deck, became seasick. The ship had to be diverted to the Subic Naval sick bay, where all the passengers disembarked on stretchers.

The PRPC gave the new arrivals a taste of town life in the West: it had schools, libraries, electric lights, refrigerators, soccer fields, showers and outhouses, a market, a hospital and a temple. Song's family shared a wood hut, which was bare but clean, and after testing negative for TB, they were cleared for classes. They picked up a smattering of English in one and sat through mandatory cultural and work-orientation classes, while the children were shuffled off to the more structured ABC class-rooms. The women, including Chan and her three sisters, tending to the babies and home duties, often got no class time. Being caught in a political no-man's-land and referred to only by numbers were minor matters —the mood was upbeat. Also, word got out around camp: they would never again see a rice paddy or the Khmer Rouge.

———

During his six months in the Philippines, fourteen-year-old Song was like a sponge, soaking up all he could. Sitting in a classroom was a thrill. He recalled the days of seeing kids in his village headed to school in their uniforms. Borrowing his cousin's khaki pants and white shirt with the name stitched on the pocket, he was able to sneak into Upper English. In the mandatory culture class, he memorized each slide that popped up on the wall. Childlike cartoons depicted the dos and don'ts. How to turn on a light, open a door, and flush a toilet. A phone rang and they all crowded around, in disbelief when a woman's voice came out of the plastic. Slides showed a friendly policeman, a firetruck, a stoplight, snowfall, ice on a pond, and a church. They were told not to spit, pee outside, cut down trees, take roadkill, or touch the red alarms. They learned that shaking hands would not cause pregnancy.

Out of a scattering of boys, a Filipino plucked an eager Song out and took him in, instructing him about watch repair. Song teamed with the old shirtless man out of the back of his jeepney (an old American WWII jeep re-purposed to be a taxi) with signs plastered on the windows, *Relo*. Song started with the stems, crystals, batteries, and bands. Within weeks, he was on to the movements, the inner gears. A decade later in a downtown Manhattan boutique, he refurbished Rolexes and Bulgaris. Delicate metalwork became his calling; now he's soldering complex circuit boards.

———

Hearing a loudspeaker announcement, one of the volunteers hurried Song and his family over to stake out their spot in the line for asylum seekers. At the UNHCR table with all the officials in their powder blue vests, Song gave his name but didn't know his birthdate; his family used only days of the week. The official jotted down December 6, 1965.

Chan told me, "When they put our names in English, they sound strange. In Cambodia mine was Paun. They change it to Chai but he wrote Chan, same as my mother's. My family still calls me Chai."

Song said, "Song was easy."

"At the table, they give us a choice," recalled Chan. "We can go to Canada, United States, or... I don't remember the others. They say it so fast. Just like that. I show them a letter we have from our uncle."

The official looked at it and said, "Okay, this is your sponsor. US."

He checked "USA" on the immigration paper, initialed it, slid it back and said, "Danbury."

They gave you a passport? I asked.

They didn't. But their names were on a manifest. It was a list that included their birthdates, an address, their signature and their photo. At the top was a stamp they recognized, that of the United States Government. That manifest got them on a plane headed over the Pacific. They were no longer stateless.

———

Chan said, "Before coming to the US, I am thinking, it is all concrete and steel, machines and robots. In the airplane, when I look down, I see trees all over. It surprised me." Neither of them recollected much beyond that, not of the long flights over the ocean, or the stopovers, likely Guam, Wake Island or Hawaii, then San Francisco.

I asked if it was on this journey, maybe somewhere over the Pacific, that their romance budded. They both smiled and didn't say.

Danbury, Connecticut was their resettlement destination, because that's where Uncle Pong, the sponsor for both families, lived. From what I could piece together out of the bits they told me they flew to Hartford in 1980. For two months they lived in a house designated for refugees, probably on the rough north side of the city, any details of which Song is at a loss to describe. It was November, dark and nasty, and they thought street gangs were waiting for them. Afraid to flush the toilet, they slipped out the back door only for a quick pee. Apparently, food was dropped off. Song's brother, who was never bothered by his year spent in a ruby mine shaft in western Thailand, described the general atmosphere: "We were scared." They feared that creating any speck of trouble would put them back on a plane. In the house, they basically remained huddled in a room with their mattresses, using a candle for needed light.

———

Left behind in the Philippines was Chan's oldest sister. Paht. Bequeathed the role of head of the family by their father as he was led away for his execution, she had led her three siblings through the Cambodian jungle to safety. She died in the Philippines. Chan, grasping for reasons why, told me, "We think maybe food poisoning. Or maybe allergy. The next day her body swelled and smelled bad. We had no ceremony. They cremated Phat. No monk. No blessing."

No one else was able to offer any other ideas as to why the thirty-year-old mother of two suddenly died. That troubled me, not only because it was unresolved but also because she, like her father, who was shot in a rice paddy, were heroes, then simply vanished, all but forgotten.

I suspect that the Krom and Prum families survived in part due to the notion that they don't dwell on their fate, much less question it, but move on. Grief may give way to sweet memories, but such heavy thoughts, in abundance, become burdens. In my years of taking histories from in-patients on the neurology service, I discovered that people over ninety who were happy and healthy denied being nostalgic. That fits. Buddhist teachings, I would come to learn, embrace the present.

PART SIX
THE NUTMEG STATE

CHAPTER TWENTY-FOUR
BETHEL

Song and Chan's long journey from war-torn Cambodia finally ended in 1980 in a place they could call home: Danbury. A mid-sized city located on the western border of Connecticut, it was once world famous for hats. Styles changed, the hat factories disappeared, and the city broadened production to an array of merchandise. Song and Chan were part of the surge of immigrants eager for work.

Sponsored by Uncle Pong, the Kroms joined other families from the old country. Song and Chan, only teens and expecting a child, dropped out of school after a little more than a year, then married in a traditional ceremony in Uncle Pong's living room. Panna was born in the living room of an apartment on May Street, a few blocks away.

By 2003, Song and Chan had steady work. Panna was getting big and was keeping up with the American fads. Family ties remained strong; several of their elders still lived with them. Song even had a high-end racing bike and competed in several criteriums.

Pooling their money with others in the family, they purchased a three-bedroom Cape-style house, yellow with white trim, which sat on a corner lot on Arch Street, a twenty-minute walk to the high school. They loved it, not at all bothered that ten people were squeezed into the three bedrooms and there was only one bathroom. For many Southeast

Asians, having spent years in one-room bamboo huts, cramped living spaces were part of the fabric of family life. In fact, being alone was something they never experienced. Song was always out in the yard, trimming bushes, mowing the grass, raking leaves, and cooking on the fire pit. On school days, Song was up long before the kids, biking to the train station, then catching some sleep on the Metro North to Manhattan. Life wasn't bad.

Then in 2005, two businessmen showed up on their front porch, white guys in shirts and ties. The news was not good: the bank now owned the house and they had three weeks to vacate. Song was devastated and to this day is at a loss trying to explain what happened. When I suggested that they must have missed mortgage payment notices (just as they missed the school notices about Panna), he said simply, "I don't know."

The Kroms' next move later that year would be to the tiny apartment on Fifth Avenue.

By 2007, after what had occurred with Panna at that fateful address and now with her being away at York, Song and Chan decided to get out of Danbury. They liked it in nearby Bethel; it was a village, a rural setting, yet close enough to commute and see family.

They largely felt a need to get away from the other Asians. I had figured, wrongly, that the Southeast Asian community would rally to support them and even suggested we get the word out about Panna via the temples. But Chan warned me, "When your daughter is in prison for 'murder,' people love to ask questions you don't want to answer." That aside, even everyday questions, they told me, could be uncomfortable: "Why are you driving that SUV?" or "How come you have a green card?" Plus, as soon as you need them, added Song, they disappear. What happened in Thailand during the war—being abandoned by their family and left in the camps—still pains them. "Many we know call themselves Cambodian," they told me.

Bethel was a refuge; a place where they knew no one. That meant no more needling questions, no more phony excuses. Song and Chan wanted to be unseen, to stay home, pray, go for walks—like the saying, when you imprison someone, you imprison their family. They were hesitant to let Panna know they had moved. When it finally slipped out, Panna blamed herself, because Danbury was home.

After a quick search, Song and Chan found a place in a complex called Oak Woods Estates. At night, they heard crickets and were able to see the stars. The next morning, they called the real estate agent and told her, "We'll take it."

"But I haven't shown it to you!" she cried. They told her it was okay and minutes later were in her office putting down the cash deposit and signing a year's lease. What they didn't tell her was that the night before, they stood on the small grassy space between the parking lot and the building, lit sticks of incense and prayed, so the good spirits would protect their new home. They did admit to me that they had waited until all the lights were off, because they didn't want to "look funny." Once they got the key from the agent, before setting foot inside, they had Chan's great-uncle, the fortune teller Chhoeun, do a walk-through and bless it.

When I asked if they ever got his blessing for the apartment on Fifth Avenue, they admitted—with obvious regret—no, they never did.

The apartment complex sat at the end of a winding drive, perched on a gentle slope, just down from Bethel High, home of the Wildcats. (Locals were quick to let you know that Meg Ryan went there.) After moving in, their ritual was at sunset to hike hand-in-hand through the woods to the athletic fields. They slowly did laps on the track, preferring not to see any young girls—painful reminders of Panna's missed year at Danbury High.

———

The move had no bearing on their jobs in Danbury, a city with a constant supply of the Asian and Hispanic: they were cheap and reliable, non-union, had big families, and had no means to pick up and go. The factories accommodated them. Missing visas, birth certificates or green cards, and broken English or even illiteracy were not problems for human resources.

The first jobs Chan and Song got were at the Danbury *News-Times*, the same paper that would one day splash a photo of a distraught Chan emerging from the courthouse on its front page. As freshly printed papers rolled off the conveyor belt, Song collected them and inserted coupons. "But we were let go," he said. "Too young. That's what they told us."

It was in her second year at Danbury High that seventeen-year-old Chan became pregnant, just as her daughter would be a generation later. She quit, had her baby, then took a job at Wentworth Laboratories. She said, "In those days, jobs were everywhere." Wentworth manufactured something called water probes, which were used for testing semiconductor circuits. Chan explained, "I had to make this tiny thing. Oh, it's so small, like a hair, you can't breathe on it." Focusing through a microscope, she inserted a filament of titanium through a tiny wafer. She went on, "I put a tape on it with a tweezer, put it in an oven, then in water to make it freeze. After that, I pass it to someone else and get another." While she was at work, a neighbor, a Laotian, watched her toddler, at a rate of $25 a week.

In 2005, Chan found work at Hologic, the top international manufacturer of mammogram machines. Her routine was to start with a cart, select her parts, maybe fifty in all, and return to her station. Seated at a long table and using an array of small tools, she assembled the pieces to make the device that slid up and down, eventually clamping down on the breast, repeating this same ritual every twenty minutes. She told me, "I do it blind." A row of workers sat inches apart, doing the same thing. It was easy for all to see that Chan's productivity was the highest. That gave her a sense of accomplishment, a first for her.

Since music and earphones were prohibited, chatter was constant, in a mix of tongues. All were women, Latina, Puerto Rican, Black, and a few Cambodian or Laotian. Many struggled with their weight, their sugar, and bad joints. Few had husbands, though most had kids, not always their own, and took care of their moms. They shared family stories, often about early deaths, alcohol, and incarcerations. Tales about their losses and bad choices were tinged with humor. For Chan, having a daughter at York would have been hard to hide—but was okay. A large African-American woman sitting closest to her was the voice Chan wasn't; she spoke the truths Chan had kept to herself about the cops and courts. Chan told me, "She knew everything about Panna. 'You know why Panna get so many years?'" she said, pinching the dark skin on her arm.

These ladies understood that good people get forced to live out their poor choices or forced choices. They didn't judge, micro-analyze, or cast blame. To them, all sisters, whether they rode the city bus or drove a Mercedes, were "poor dears" and deserved a second chance.

Cell phones were prohibited on the factory floor, but Chan was allowed to keep hers, stashed in a drawer next to her. When she heard her ringtone—Merle Haggard—she slipped away to a bathroom stall for the full DOC-allotted fifteen minutes. In return for that privilege, she never took her two scheduled breaks or even sat at lunch with the others. Calls came at any time. She told me, "I know the boss, why it don't bother him. His older brother, he killed his father. He tell me, 'he still my brother.'" Panna sent him a thank-you letter.

———

Now settled in Bethel, every morning before leaving for work, Song kissed his finger and placed it on the faded photo of four-year-old Panna. After dropping Chan off, he drove to his workplace, Imperial, a job he felt lucky to have. After the Manhattan watch company folded, a place where he had worked for twenty years, it took him six months to find another job. At one point he walked the streets of the East Side, refusing to go home with nothing. For one interview, near Jones Beach on Long Island, he took a train. The work paid seven-fifty an hour. He told me, "It cost me more to get there."

When an agency asked for a résumé, he gave them one which said little more than two years at Danbury High School and watch repair. I asked if he mentioned his languages on it. He told me no, why?

"You speak Thai, Kourhat, Laotian, Cambodian, some French, a smattering of Tagalog, English, and who knows what else? If you had applied to Harvard, they would have accepted you," I said. He and Chan liked that.

One day, when he was desperate, Imperial Metal Finishing called. Could he solder? they asked, something he had never done. He told them yes. The next day he showed up, nervous they would ask him a technical question, make him read, fill out a form, or worse, hand him a soldering iron. But he knew the supervisor there—a break. He got the job, which paid a dollar above minimum wage.

Each morning at Imperial he quietly took his station. Most of his co-workers were from Laos. The place was Swiss-like: obsessively well-ordered and white-glove clean. Standards were strict, with warning signs posted everywhere. His counter, an eight-by-four-foot stainless-steel table, gleamed. Seated in a metal swivel chair, he waited for a runner to drop off a blueprint, like the ones for an electrical panel, along with a plastic crate full of the material he needed: wires, solder, clamps, etc. He couldn't read any of the text, but he could decipher the technical specs, and pulled the right wire types called for, able to pinpoint where each solder went. He laid out a dizzying array of plans according to an almost indecipherable diagram of tiny circuit connections. Using a soldering gun, a lead-free spool of solder, and his giant magnifying glass, he went to work.

Song's career goes back to his being a street vendor in the Philippines, putting batteries in watches. Since that time, he has honed his skill on fine metalwork: watches, circuit boards, and soldering. Everyone knew he was good, even though he complained his eyes were going bad. A quick glance by the quality control guys told them which soldering belonged to Song. "Looks corporate," one told me. Song liked it when they saved the tough jobs for him, those that challenged him for days. At the end of every year he got a score. When I learned that his last one was a ninety-five, I told him that sounded pretty good. He shrugged, indicating that he had no clue how the scoring worked.

When Chan and Song got home from work, the routine was simple. Song put together the meal while Chan prayed. He would peer around the corner and catch her sitting on the floor, her legs under her to one side, the female way, with three sticks of incense burning. Her hands represented the eight petals of the lotus when it bloomed, and her thumbs were for her lost mother and father.

Every night they cooked long-grain rice. Rice was part of their blood, Song explained. "You see there are three kinds of rice: long, medium, and short grain. In Cambodia, all we eat was the short grain. That's all they gave us. It was damaged, broken. But now we can eat the long grain." He smiled, as if it was an overdue victory. They made a further distinction: they only eat jasmine rice from Thailand, and only from the Asian market on Osborne Street. Whenever a fresh harvest arrived, it was a local event.

Song explained, "See, everybody, like in the grocery, say they make jasmine. But it's not. This is it." He poured some from his bag into his palm and, like a vintner describing pinot noir grapes, said, "You grab it in your hand and smell it. It is so sweet; you won't believe it." He fingered a few grains, poured them into my hand, and said, "See how long it is." I agreed, the grains were long. "I tell you when the next shipment come. You see." One month later my wife and I discovered a twenty-pound bag of Thai jasmine rice sitting on our porch.

Panna missed her dad making her favorite meals. I had discovered a letter she wrote to her parents in which she described one of them. "Dad's hands," she wrote, "that went through so much torture can magically come up with a meal for a king." She told how Song selected fresh shrimp, then he and Panna peeled the shells off. He got fresh lemongrass from her sister's garden. The stems were tough and when snapped smelled wonderful. He diced it into tiny pieces. Lemon leaves came next, which he rubbed between his fingers until a great aroma spilled out. He added turmeric, fresh ground garlic, red chili pepper, onion, ginger root that he had sliced, and large grain sea salt, then put them all in a big wooden mortar and pestle. Here was where the muscle came in, as he ground it for a long time. Then he added olive oil and wheat flour and deep-fried the shrimp. Topped with parsley, they were a delicacy. That was the meal waiting for Panna when she got out of York.

"The more people say about her, even if it is bad, the more I love her," Chan told me. "Every step we take is about Panna," she said. "We used to go to birthday parties out of respect. Now we only send a gift. People at work say stupid things. I get angry so I get quiet. When I am quiet, they know—don't talk to me! There are people who say to me, look at her, go to school, get pregnant. All the time we hear it. Like she's a whore. That's why we are here in Bethel."

I told them. "When Panna gets out, people will forgive her. Deep down, we all know that could have been anybody's daughter. Even the prosecutor's."

Song smiled and said, "Yes! Thank you."

———

One evening when I was leaving the apartment, I noticed at the bottom of the stairs, a dented rolling walker with a numbered tag affixed to it. Song told me it belonged to a woman on his floor. An older woman? I asked. No, he said, she was maybe in her thirties. He said, "She had something wrong, could barely walk." I mentioned that it seemed odd that she was on the top floor, making it kind of tough for her to get out. That comment reminded Song about a fire.

Late one chilly night, the fire alarms went off and all the tenants left their apartments, congregating in the parking area in front. As Song stood there, he could see smoke coming from the disabled woman's apartment. He ran back up and opened the door. Smoke billowed out. Putting a wet shirt over his face and waving his arms, he went in. The place was filled with smoke, but he stayed low, ducking into every room. He couldn't find her. Seeing the flames, he went back to his apartment, filled a bucket numerous times, and doused it out.

The woman had apparently gotten out okay without being noticed. Fire trucks and police arrived.

I asked, "What did they do?"

"They take me to the station and ask me questions."

"Tell me they didn't arrest you."

"It was okay." He added, "They give me a ride back. And the people cheer."

CHAPTER TWENTY-FIVE
THE CAMBODIAN DAUGHTER

Chan's cousin, nicknamed Bo, 43 and married, lives on a small farm in rural Connecticut. Born in Thailand, her family had moved to Cambodia, and later escaped back to Thailand just as the war was starting. She spent her childhood in refugee camps before settling in an apartment in Danbury. By then she was thirteen and entering the eighth grade. Not counting a few weeks in school in one of the camps, which she said was just a tent with some toys, it was her first classroom experience.

"I wasn't ready," she said. "When I got to high school, I couldn't believe what I saw. The kids had money, they were loud and they were big. Big hair, cars, boobs, even their laughs. Guys were all over the girls and smoke filled the bathrooms. Teachers just ignored it all." She said, "My first courses were ESL, math, reading, ESL everything. Mexicans and Puerto Ricans hung out in the back, faking it. They understood. I felt like a dummy, totally lost. But I worked like a dog. Did okay." She was one of the few in the Krom circle from that period who didn't drop out. Her three brothers, her sister, and the sisters-in-law, all just a few years ahead of her, didn't fare so well. Too far behind to ever catch up, they got teased, got F's, got in fights, and just quit going. Today, thirty years later, burdened with supporting a large family, they still struggle at reading.

Bo described a particular aspect of life as a kid in the Cambodian villages. Up through the teen years, the sexes never mixed. Village boys were not allowed anywhere near the girls. She told me, "It was known as *bamream,* a taboo I guess you call it. And when we got to the US, it came with us. Spin the Bottle would have been Russian Roulette. A boy could hold hands with another boy; that was okay. But not a girl."

Song added, "If we see a boy and girl holding hands, the boy, he have to marry that girl. Even if they have to wait," meaning until thirteen or fourteen. Just being seen with a boy tainted the girl and brought shame to her dad. A lot was at stake.

Chan said, "A father, his most valuable possession was his daughter's virginity."

Song and Chan explained how a boy's father would spot a girl and if he liked what he saw, would make his claim for her, even if she was only ten. He would negotiate with the girl's father to have her saved for his son. With this discussion between the fathers, a deal was struck. From that point on, it was common knowledge that that girl was taken. The last to know was the girl. Of course, the flip side of the deal was that the girl's parents must approve of the boy. Chan said, "Sometimes the boy, they see he don't do anything, and they say no."

"Yeah, he don't like to work," added Song.

"He's a bum," I said and they laughed.

Parents carefully protected their girls, even from education, thinking they might write a love letter to a man before her marriage could be arranged. When she reached the right age, the girl would be married in a ceremony in the boy's hut, an all-day affair with a monk, music, and everyone bringing food. The boy's father had to pay the other father a hefty price for having brought up the girl, not really a dowry—preferably cash, but it might be rice or maybe a new roof.

"Did Panna know about this tradition?" I asked.

"Yes, she know," said Song.

Bo said, "All Cambodian girls know. It's something we live with."

Song said, "Panna know. But also, she need to go to school."

Chan said, "You see, we never go to school. So we expect Panna to go. This was very important to us. She gets good grades always. Always, always."

Song added, "I look at the card. I see Honor Roll every time, and I am so happy. I tell Panna don't worry about the boys."

I mentioned the obvious to them: she had had a boyfriend; she carried on a double life.

Song said, "We know this now. We are not angry."

Chan said, "See, we learn a lot when Jennifer [Attorney Tunnard] talk to us. She spend so much time with Panna and us. She tell us, 'You *have* to accept what Panna say. *Anything* she say, you have to accept this.' So we say yes. We love her. We know we do things wrong for her. We tell Jennifer it was okay, *anything* she say. We just want our baby back. Now Panna say to us, 'Mommy, Daddy, I tell you everything. I hide nothing.'" Chan made a point to look over at Song and say, "He know he cannot get angry."

Song admitted, "I know Panna was afraid of me. I know I do this to her."

———

I asked Bo, "These taboos you mentioned—*bamream*. I'm curious. You think it was part of what happened with Panna?"

She said, "We got the call that Sunday morning when they found the baby in the closet. I said, 'Oh my god!' We dropped everything, and called them. The second I heard about the baby, I knew exactly what Panna went through."

"You knew? Really?"

"Oh, yeah."

Bo told me that when she was young the boy-girl taboo never bothered her. Her circle of friends in Danbury was nearly all Cambodian. They spoke the language and stayed out of the mainstream. She never hung out with the white girls, much less the boys, or went to football games, parties, or learned to drive. Nor did she care to. But soon teenage Bo started listening to the lyrics on the radio, caught onto the girls' gossip about boys, and thought about the clothes they wore and the way they did their hair and nails—it looked cool, sexy. More and more, she could see it coming, a head-on collision. Her beliefs made less sense, and the stuff she was seeing that at first looked strange and scary really wasn't. She said she was carrying a "kernel of fear," but had to keep it her secret. Someday, something would happen.

That day came when she met Akra.

She and her cousin, both rising seniors at the high school, took the day off to go to Cape Cod for a schoolmate's June wedding. It was their very first getaway, a chance to do something touristy—see the beaches, stroll the streets and window shop. By that time, seventeen-year-old Bo was turning a lot of heads. While she was getting an ice cream, a guy stopped his car in the middle of the street and beeped. Bo pivoted and smiled, even though she later denied it, saying "I'm not sure I really saw him." This guy jumped out, ran up to her, and with an unabashed smile said, "Hi. Where are you going?"

She looked at him. "Why?"

He was gamey, muscled, and tattooed, but clean and confident, and she liked his whole thing. "He told me his name was Akra. That's Cambodian. I knew by his look. He stuck out his arm and told me to write my number. That was cool, so I did." She wrote her name and number on his muscle and he darted back to his double-parked car. Before he did anything, he looked at the number, took a deep breath, and smiled. For her, it was daring, crazy. She had never been on a date. In fact, she had never flirted, been asked out, or even been attracted to a boy. "I said to myself, 'This guy can do anything.'"

Akra didn't bother with the obligatory waiting period. That night he called. But before he put a finger on the phone, he knew the rules. Her name was Cambodian. If the father picked up, hang up. Lie low, never show up, don't write. Before long, they had devised a complicated system of evasion. It involved warning rings before calling, key phrases if the "enemy" was nearby, and a detailed timetable based on the parents' whereabouts. For late-night calls, they simply timed it right and silenced the ringer.

The intrigue and distance only raised the temperature. Akra, who lived in Holyoke, outside of Springfield, skipped school to go see her. For him, as he put it, "It was no biggie. I wasn't doing so well and missed days all the time." But for Bo it *was* a big deal. Her good grades came by way of gritty work, always being the first one in class and sitting in the front row, taking notes, and never skipping class or homework. Her girl cousins ahead of her had left a trail of school failure; they had gotten married and pregnant or simply disappeared.

Bo and Akra became battle-weary from living double lives. One day Akra devised a plan, simple and bold. He was up early and on the road to Danbury. Like any normal day, Bo got on her school bus, but with a change of clothes in her pack. At the school, as soon as she stepped off, she made a breathless 180, bee-lined to the back of the gym building, and got into an idling black Civic. At the wheel was Akra.

She slid down and the two motored off. The town was all theirs. The first stop was Friendly's for a chocolate-sundae breakfast. Then it was off to the mall to pick out something precious but undetectable by a rummaging mom. After that, a noontime movie. She said, "I pulled down my hat and acted like a secret agent. The town has Asians, who have eyes and love to blab."

"And if you got caught?" I asked.

"Oh my god, if one person saw me, my dad would know in two minutes and it'd be over in three minutes."

With each rendez-vous, she got bolder. And Dad grilled her. "I knew I'd get it when I got home, but I went anyway," she said. "I remember being gone for two hours and would get the back of his hand when I returned. But I never said a word. The Cambodian girls get beat but we shut up and still go out."

She told me, "One day I said, 'Enough!'" She was nineteen, working at a deli, taking community college courses in accounting, and like her parents, going nowhere. She was too smart for this, she thought. She went home, packed her bag and got on a train. In a note left for her parents, she said she was leaving and would call. She had $75 in her pocket. Akra picked her up at the station in Springfield and took her to a relative's house, where she stayed a few weeks. Before long they moved in with his family.

Her dad, so typical, was furious and refused to talk to her, though she did have communication with her mom.

Bo's dad had a plan of his own for her, which was constantly made clear: go to school, get good grades, and no boys. When the time came, he said, a man would arrive at the door and declare to the parents, "I love your daughter and want your permission to marry her." With a laugh, Bo told me, "My dad actually thought that would happen. Of course, he never stuck around." He eventually left his family and made it to Viet Nam, supposedly to study religion.

Eventually, he resumed speaking to her and everything was okay. He told her to come home and to get married. She did, with a Buddhist ceremony in the living room. She told me, "Now my dad's old, somewhere back in Thailand, I guess. We never hear anything. Just go by the rumors."

———

Davi was Panna's main hangout buddy in high school; she was two years older, their families were friends. When I met her, Davi worked in marketing analysis at a big security device company in Stamford. During the hectic period of Panna's arrest, she stayed in contact with her and offered support. At times, she deciphered the day-to-day legal nightmare for the family. She was a bit of an academic trailblazer, though Panna, a bright star in her own right, was finding her own way.

Davi, just like Bo, had to do the near-impossible as a teen—navigate an ever-widening cultural chasm.

When she was sixteen and a Danbury High sophomore, she was at a family game night gathering at her uncle's split-level house. Afterward the kids had a sleepover, all piling in the downstairs TV room, nothing unusual. After they fell asleep, it looked like the aftermath of a battle. Bodies were haphazardly scattered on the couch, cushions and in sleeping bags. A boy named Vibol, a regular drop-in and Davi's sort-of-secret flirt, arrived later. He saw everyone crashed and sprawled on the floor and picked a spot, conveniently next to her. By morning, a school day, the younger kids were up and gone. Davi and Vibol, the last two, slept through the commotion, only now a few very lethal inches apart. The scandal was spotted by a father. Davi chimed, "We never touched. I'm not that dumb."

In Cambodian villages this transgression was a sin—a big one. By ancestral decree, Davi and Vibol had to marry. Both, being bright and ambitious, had had other ideas, like being normal American teens, partying, and heading off to college or even overseas. When the wedding day arrived, Davi's stomach was so knotted she ended up in the Danbury Hospital emergency room with a panic attack. They calmed her with Valium and an anti-emetic and discharged her. Turns out, Vibol had been in the same ER hours before her and had gotten the same cocktail.

Despite those delay tactics, the dreaded ceremony took place. In the uncle's living room, before an elder monk, they recited their vows and were declared husband and wife. There were chants to Buddha, along with hoopla and heaps of food.

Three months later Davi was pregnant. "Yeah, he couldn't stand me, but he wasn't going to pass up that opportunity," she said. Three months after that, Vibol was gone. Since they were never legally married, it was a simple parting of ways. Her son finished high school and began a job driving trucks to Asian markets. Though she has moved on, Vibol stayed back. He and his kid are best buddies, hanging out in video arcades. If you were to tell the regulars that they were father and son, they'd say, "No way!"

After telling me that story, Davi admitted, "So you see, I was a close-call Panna. I didn't get pregnant. If I had, before our wedding, and that could have easily happened, then all hell would have been unleashed. I would have had nowhere to turn. I, more than anyone anywhere, understood Panna's problem."

"Panna knew this whole thing what you went through?" I asked.

"Oh yeah, she knew. She was there."

CHAPTER TWENTY-SIX

CHHOEUN

Chan, sighed, paused, then asked me, "Doug, you believe in fortune teller?"

"No," I told her. "I mean, I've never gone to one. Why?"

She said, "I need to tell you about my grandfather."

"Grandfather?" Both of her parents died when she was eight.

"That's what we say. He was my father's uncle. His name is Chhoeun. He is really old, can't walk anymore. We always get together at my sister house, for long time."

"He's a fortune teller?" I said.

Song replied, "Yes. In Thailand, we call it *mor dambra*. Everyone goes to them."

"How does it work?"

Song said, "They talk to you, see what you want. Ask many questions before he tell you. The first thing he needs is your exact birthday, the year, month, but especially the day of the week. He study the skin, hair, palm, eyes, and he listen. He even look at the lines on your hands; see if you have 'leak' between your fingers when they are together." He held his hand up and showed me a little gap of light between his fingers. "They tell you about the future and you just wait for it to happen. Or maybe tell you what to do."

Chan said, "See, we don't believe one hundred percent. Two fortune tellers can tell you the opposite things. But Chhoeun, we believe him."

During Panna's early years at York, they frequently went to Chhoeun. "We take with us candle, incense, and some money to give," said Chan. "He don't want it. He is always careful with us because we are so hurt. So he never say much, only tell us how to pray, go to temple, meditate. So, what he tell us, really nothing, like it was hopeless." She explained how Chhoeun had her drop incense from overhead and based on where it landed, he would give her advice. One time he told her that a woman lawyer would not be strong enough. Panna needed a man lawyer. But they had Jennifer Tunnard and were deep in debt with her.

Song told me, "His house was behind the high school. All the time, I saw him walking. I stopped to ask if he want a ride, but he always say no. He spoke no English. But he love boxing and could understand everything when he watch it."

It was Chhoeun, who, as a monk on Christmas Day in 1982, had married Song and Chan, both just teens, in Uncle Pong's living room. All their relatives were called to witness, including, by way of incense, the dead ancestors. Chan's parents weren't alive to give her away or offer the traditional money to Song's family.

Each time Song and Chan moved, Chhoeun was called to bless the new place. Through a relative, sometime later, they found out that Chhoeun said that the little house on Arch Street that Song and his brother purchased—and foreclosed—was not a good buy. She was too afraid and never told the Kroms.

"Did Panna know him?" I asked.

Song said, "Oh, she know him good, since she was baby."

Chan told me, "Before we meet you, one day I was with my grandfather, Chhoeun. He ask about my daughter. He never do this before." Chan continued, "I say to him, she fine, she fine, she go to school. I don't say too much. We never say much about Panna. But I don't know why he ask."

Song looked at Chan, and said, "Do you want to tell him?"

"Tell me what?" I asked.

Chan spoke Thai to Song, and then said, "Something happen then, Doug. It was Thanksgiving, at my sister's house. We finish eating and

Chhoeun look at me and smile. I ask him why you smile? He was very weak. He say, 'This year there will be a *movement* on Panna.'"

"Movement? What do you mean?" I asked.

Chan said, "I don't know an English word. Something big. See, we can barely hear him. He say somebody come into her life. I say, 'Who is it, a woman?'"

Song added, "Because we believe maybe Jennifer, her lawyer."

Chan went on. "But he say a man. He say that he have white skin. He not tall, not short. He tell us that someone step up in Panna life, do something. He don't know what it is, good or bad?"

Song said, "He say not five feet, not six feet. We think five-seven, five-eight. At first we think Steve, my boss, because his skin is real white, but he is real tall, over six feet."

Chan pulled at her skin and said, "The white skin, to us was a big deal. We don't know anybody like this." This meant someone not in their family or even their community. She said, "Chhoeun tell us, 'I hope I don't die before this happen, so you believe me.'"

She continued, "One day, maybe one month after that, Panna call us, excited, and say, 'You know Wally, the man who sign the card?' I say yes. She say, 'A man in his class ask me if he could do something for me.' She asked me, 'Mommy, should I?' I tell her, Panna, it is up to you. If you want it. She told me, 'Yes, I want to do it.' She said she would give him our number to call. I believe we never get the call. In a million year. I never believe it. I ask her what color his skin. She say white. And how tall? She tell me, 'Not too tall. Why?'"

Song leaned forward and said, "Then Doug, you called."

———

I wanted to know where Chhoeun was. I was dying of curiosity to see him.

Song said, "Now he's in his nineties. His mind disappeared. Before, Thai, Cambodians from all over come to him seeking advice. They came from Danbury, out west, Canada, Thailand, and even France. On Saturdays, a line of Asian people circled around his house and stretched down the block. People asked him everything: what day to have a wedding, about taking a job or buying a car. The most common question was: Should I marry her (or him)? They even asked what days were best to go to the casino. If someone had a hornet in their house, Chhoeun would come over to rid the house of the bad omen. If a house had a tree root going toward it, this was a warning to the owner of problems ahead, and they sought his blessing."

Song and Chan took me to Chhoeun's house, a white clapboard in a tidy middle-class Danbury neighborhood. A neighbor, someone Chan knew, a close friend of Chhoeun's, named Thyda, let us in. She and Chan hugged. She was a handsome woman with a welcoming smile, probably in her late forties. She had been attacked by the Khmer Rouge. And had gone through the same path as Chan: escaping Cambodia, camps in Thailand and stopovers on the way to the US. When I asked her if she had similar wounds, she said, "No, different," followed by silence. I took it to mean something unmentionable.

Arriving in Danbury, Thyda entered school at eighteen but fractured her hip in an accident and after three years left with no diploma, but eventually went back and became a legal assistant.

Chhoeun no longer lived at this house. She said that he needed nursing care. She knew his story and told me how he grew up in Cambodia, one of twelve children. Only two of them made it out. Chhoeun had been a farmer, a government worker, and mayor of his village. Many evenings he was gone for hours to study fortune telling with his brother, who was very practiced in this. Since the brother had a house, the Khmer Rouge thought he also had money. This was a reason to kill him. He had his wife and kids leave, telling them, "I am a man, I know what to do." The Khmer Rouge shot him, leaving his body on his front steps.

In 1980, after years in the refugee camps, Chhoeun, with his wife and two children, relocated to Newtown, Connecticut. A quiet American couple, both teachers, took them in and went on to sponsor sixteen more families. Chhoeun's first job was in a nursery, before secluding himself to resume his studies in fortune telling.

Chhoeun's body of work sat in the house's library: an impressive fifteen neatly stacked leather-bound books, full of Chhoeun's precise Thai calligraphy. One cover was in old Chinese script, which my wife translated. It referred to the modern period of Cambodian history, from 1893 to 1993, the years closely overlapping his lifetime. Interspersed throughout the pages were zodiacs, calendars, tables, graphs, and formulas. Some appeared to be intricate decision-tree diagrams. Fortune telling, according to these texts, was an arcane practice—high art, blended with hard science and geometry.

Over a cup of tea, Thyda revealed to me that she herself had heard about the bad omen for the Kroms' apartment, where Panna's crime occurred. She told me, "I knew Chan and I was scared to say anything to them. I didn't even know what it was. I feel bad now."

She had even been there at the house during the Thanksgiving dinner in which they heard Chhoeun's pronouncement to the Kroms. She corroborated the story, repeating the same details the Kroms had told me about a white man, not so tall or short, who would appear in their lives. When I first heard it from Song and Chan, I was skeptical. I was relieved to hear her repeat it.

———

That evening, when I returned with Song and Chan to their apartment in Bethel, Chan said, "We want you to have something." She looked at Song and spoke Thai, while he walked over to the Buddha corner of the room. He paused, closed his eyes, and held his hands together, as his lips silently prayed. Then he gently lifted the statue with an olive-green cloth under it and presented it to me. "This is for you."

I gasped, for it was a special Buddha. It was some fifteen pounds of gleaming marble with swirls of green and brown, the very one I had photographed on one of my visits. Buddha was seated, meditating over lotus petals, with his hands in his lap, right over left. I had learned that that position symbolized purity and divine birth.

Chan pointed out how the balls of the feet point to the heavens. She said, "We wanted to give you something, but don't know what."

I couldn't take their most prized possession. But obviously, this was well thought out. Buddha, according to their plan, was to continue their mission in my home.

Song said, "This one is blessed by a monk at a temple in Bristol."

"I will cherish it," I said.

Chan instructed me, "You must keep his head high, not low. Always make sure he has water. That is important. Keep it clean. And it should be the man who cleans him. Only man. I mean a woman can lightly touch, that is all right, but not the head. But it is okay after she have, what do you call it, later in life? Menopause. Yes, that's it, menopause." She added, "Until then, she is not pure. Something about when Buddha gets away from his wife to be a good monk and he can't touch anything from a woman until her change in life. You can talk to him; help us in our journey to get Panna. But make sure he *always* have water."

I drove home that night, Buddha propped up in the seat next to me, wrapped in my jacket with the seat belt, through Newtown, down winding Route 34 onto Roosevelt Drive, softly hugging each curve of the Housatonic River, past Derby, Woodbridge, and Hamden, to North Haven. I gently cradled my Buddha inside, placing him in a central location, on the mantel over the fireplace. He would easily keep an eye on everything. His head was near even with mine. Under the base, I put a *mola*, a Kuna Indian handmade embroidery from the San Blas Islands off Panama. I retrieved a teacup with Chinese script about fishes, filled it with filtered water, sprinkled a few flower petals in it, and set it beside the statue.

I knew little about Buddhism. I am not religious. But as I gazed at the beautiful statue, I felt bonded with the Kroms in their quest.

————

Months later, I told Song and Chan that I must meet Chhoeun. It was important; I had to see him in flesh and blood. They told me he was very ill now, not able to meet or even talk, was moved to a nursing home. Some weeks after that, I reminded them again. This went on one or two more times. Finally I called, and with an urgency in my voice, said, "I'm coming up tonight. We're going to find Chhoeun. Wherever he is."

They were puzzled at my insistence. I explained to Song, "I'm afraid I'll never see him."

That cold February night, Song, Chan and I drove to Danbury Hospital. At the front desk we asked for Chhoeun Bunleut and got our visitors passes to see him. He was in a private room on the twelfth floor. His nephew, Prak, and Chan's sisters were there. Chhoeun, lying in bed, was a miniature man, skeletal thin with wispy gray hair and protruding ears, reminiscent of Gollum from Lord of the Rings. With each gulp of air, his head softly swayed back and forth. Song leaned in closely and with a forceful voice informed him in Thai that I was here. Chhoeun's eyes found me and remained focused on my face. Song turned to me and said, "He understand. He know." Chhoeun uttered nothing. I noticed his eyes fixed and widening upon seeing me.

Uncle Pong, his best friend, the one who had sponsored the Kroms in the late 70s, had died a few months before. Both were pillars in the extended Krom family, patriarchs who had led their families safely out of Cambodia and staked this spot in western Connecticut for their new home. For the Kroms, Chhoeun's passing would mark the end of their long journey to the new world—and fulfill his duty to the family.

Outside the room, perhaps drawing too much on my years of work in hospital ICU's, I told Song that I thought that Chhoeun had only a few days. I hoped that might help them say goodbye.

Two days later, while at work, I got a text from Chan, something out of the ordinary for her to do. *Hi Doug. I want to let you know my grandpa pass away last night.*

———

That Saturday, I drove to Danbury for the funeral. It was early March, still chilly, but cloudless. I expected it to be at a temple, but it was held at the Cornell Memorial Funeral Home, on White Street, right across from the Three Brothers Diner where Panna was arrested seven years before; a spot for which Song told me, "I still close my eyes." The parking lot quickly filled with Thai and Cambodians, getting out of cars from as far away as Virginia and Georgia. Everyone was dressed in black. In total, there were some 150 people. I was the only white guy. No one seemed to take notice of me.

Inside, Chhoeun lay in a casket. He was dressed in a dark suit, his hands across his stomach. The mourners, forming a long line, streamed by, each one laying a thin stick, tied with an oxeye daisy, onto his chest.

Many whispered to him. Chan's sister remained a few minutes longer than anybody. I watched her clasp his hand and caress his chest and face —for she had seen him almost every day from the time she was a baby in her Cambodian village.

The director of the Danbury temple, a man in a dark suit with a gray subcontinent beard, gave a sermon, which Song translated for me, about how Chhoeun had escaped Cambodia, was a monk, and became a master of fortune telling, a name sought out by other fortune seekers around the world.

Monks in their saffron robes lined the front, chanting in the sacred Pali dialect. Everyone repeated the words with them. Song pointed to one of them. It was Chhoeun's nephew, Prak, whom I met in the hospital, only now he had a shaved scalp. Song explained that he could become a monk solely for this occasion. To fulfill the conversion, he cut his hair, even his eyebrows, and he wore no underwear. In three days, his conversion would be over. Song told me, "He have to go back to work."

Immediately following the ceremony, a procession of cars drove to a plain cinderblock building located on farmland in nearby Oxford. On this short trip in the car, I noticed Song drinking, rapidly emptying two or three nips while he was driving. After we stopped, I walked with Song to the building, telling him, "Song, I saw you drinking in the car."

He replied, "I know. It's wrong. I feel so much stress."

"Song, if you ever get pulled over and you're arrested, Panna's not getting out."

"I stop. Thank you."

Chhoeun's body was inside the building, lying in a state of repose in the open casket. Outside were some young men, milling around in small groups, looking put out in their black suits, speaking Cambodian, passing around cigarettes, kicking pebbles. The women, in faux-fur coats and high heels, headed straight in to avoid the chill. Inside, it was disorderly. The people weren't in a line, but crowded close to the casket. More daisies were tossed wildly in the air beside the body while the monks chanted.

A man in a suit emerged, holding a coconut over Chhoeun's head. With one dramatic swipe of a machete, the shell split open in his hand, letting the juice splash over Chhoeun's face. Song explained that this was for a final cleansing as he entered heaven. Two men let the lid drop and rolled the casket to the steel door of the furnace. As the door opened, you could hear flames roar inside and feel the blast of heat. Everyone was quiet. They propped the lid up a few inches, but when it didn't fit into the furnace opening, they lowered it, pushed the casket in, and, using long sticks, propped the lid up again, giving a final push. The gray steel door banged shut.

Over by the wall, Prak and his sister, Sorya, stood side by side, and were shown the green button on the wall between them that would further ignite the furnace. They looked at each other, then pressed it.

CHAPTER TWENTY-SEVEN
THE LAKE

Song came into the kitchen, startling me. I turned and said, "Hey. You're always talking about the lake. Is it far?"

"Ten minutes."

"Can we go?"

"Now?" He looked at Chan.

She said, "Go, go. Dinner will be ready when you get back."

He said, "Why not? Plenty of light."

We hopped in his car for the quick ride to the East and West Branches of the Reservoir, both part of a vast water supply for the Danbury area, graded AA, fit for drinking. Summer or winter, the pair of lakes had been the sanctuary for Song and Chan and Panna. It was a place for contemplation, where they were one-on-one with nature—their shelter from being ignored or belittled. He had told me, "I fish. We don't talk. Listen to nothing."

Halfway there, he pulled into a gas station and dashed in for a six-pack. We were like two boys with fake IDs. When he got back to the car, a bag of Sam Adams tucked under his arm, I pointed to the next car over, an SUV filling up, and said, "Did you see the girl?"

He said, "No, what girl?" At that moment she came out of the store.

I watched his eyes follow her. She looked Southeast Asian, almost a carbon copy of Panna, hair exactly the same.

Song said, "Oh, she look like Panna."

"I thought so. Maybe I should just shut up."

"No, no, it's okay. This is why we don't go out. I will think about this girl." She pulled away and Song said, "I think she Vietnam."

On the way, Song mentioned how the day before he picked up a BB gun at a tag sale and used it to hit a few sparrows, which he dressed and cooked for dinner. I said, "I had no idea you could get a BB gun nowadays." Sometimes, he told me, he uses a slingshot. One time, cops in New Milford, using binoculars, spotted him under a bridge hitting pigeons with marbles. Amused I suppose, they gave him a warning, their parting words being, "Next time buddy, stay in Danbury."

While on one wavy road, Song chimed, "I even get roadkill."

"You get what?"

"Yeah, if I see it fresh or get hit, I go by it, turn around and pick it up. Just clean off the messy part and it's good."

"And you cook it?"

"Sure."

"This goes way back when you had to survive." I was going to respin this. Plus, I was thinking, please Song, don't tell me which animals.

"Yeah, to me it's really nature. Sometime I get deer. I call the cops. Make sure it's okay. I have no license."

"They say okay?"

"Yeah."

When we got to the lake, he lifted the tailgate and showed me his army surplus satchel, a kind of grab bag. "I've got rice, lemon, matches, knife, string..."

I guessed that he could do quite well with nothing more than what was in that bag.

I asked, "What happened to your hand?" He had a fresh open gash on the thumb.

He held it up like a trophy. "I hunt crab this weekend, in Stratford. Blues, you know those?" He held out his hands, measuring six, eight inches.

"Crabs?"

"Yeah, big suckers."

I asked how he catches them. "I have a light, like this," he explained, flicking a six-inch penlight. "Works underwater." He whispered, "I go behind it, real slow, then ease my foot on it and go down and grab it."

"Underwater? Let me guess. No goggles, no shoes or gloves."

"Yeah, yeah, just bare hand. And this one, he grab me." Song laughed. "But I got him. Two dozen more."

It didn't take long to figure out Song was still eking out a living off the land, or easily could, even in genteel, well-paved Connecticut full of squirrels and sparrows.

The hike to the lake was short. His rucksack was small and frayed. On the back was a faded "Jason." Ahead was a sparkling blue stretch of water backed by a pastel of yellow-orange woods. As we walked, he showed me how when he first arrived in the US, he'd pinch leaves on bushes so he could find his way back. Song knew every twig and weed, how strong it was, what it smelled like, if it was cookable or edible. He pointed at a rock and told me, "That's Panna's favorite. We come here all the time. She like to fish. She's good." Panna loved to camp, while her brother, more of a techie, hated the woods. He added, "I come to this lake because it clean. The other lakes smelly, people swimming, see garbage. I don't like it."

"Gee, Song," I said, "I remember you telling me about drinking from the river with dead cows and animal poop floating by. Right?"

"No more. I want it clean now." He dropped the sack, saw the name on the back and said, "I need to take that off."

Standing on an outcrop with his fishing rod, he flicked his wrist, whipping the line a few times. With a soft arc, it plopped into the water. "Watch it bob," he whispered. Ten seconds later it did. He told me, "I let him play. When it go down, we got him." On cue, the bob went underwater, Song snapped the line and reeled in a six-inch sunfish. He took the hook out and tossed it back. "He's lucky."

It reminded me of what he had told me about village life: We eat anything that moves.

I was relieved to discover the one exception, the turtle. It was unlucky to kill one.

On the trail he grabbed a thin ten-foot maple and bent it to the ground, trimmed the twigs, set up a Y device out of small branches, rigged a sort of trigger, and laid a twine noose on the trail. He said, "You come back and find animal in the noose, maybe kicking."

"Like what?"

"Boar, rabbit, squirrel, even small deer, all kinds."

"Wow, boar? Can't imagine a boar." I pointed at the trail ahead and told him I used to race on trails like this. For twenty years I did that, all over Connecticut and Massachusetts, even Vermont.

He said, "Crazy. Bet you were good."

"Not bad," I said. "Now I can't run across the street." It impressed him. I suspect the idea of running twenty miles in the woods for no reason.

Song casually pulled up a random weed, pinched out some liquid, and allowed it to drop on our tongues. "Sweet?" he said. It was. He pointed to the land around us and said, "Before sunrise, I get mushrooms."

"To eat?"

"Of course, what else?"

"Most are poisonous, at least that's what every American kid is told," I said.

"Not these," he said. I was thinking how our mothers had us convinced of an agonizing death if we ate one. "I know the good ones. The only thing I hate are snakes."

"Really, snakes? All you see are garter snakes. Totally harmless."

"I know, frog snakes. But I still hate them. Won't touch them. But if I do," he quickly added with a wry smile, "I cook them."

The sun was low. I took a silhouette picture of Song with the orange October background over peaceful water. "We'll send it to Panna," I said. We sat on rocks and took two beers out of the satchel. He told me again how this was Panna's favorite spot.

Looking at his watch, I asked, "Song, did you make that?"

"No, I just fix it."

"Let me see that." I looked at the band. "Is that Tagalog?"

"Yes, it mean morning. How do you know?"

"I can't read it, just recognize it. I lived in the Philippines."

Song said I had spent hundreds of hours asking about their lives, but they knew little about me. A couple of times, he and Chan stopped to ask me questions. I had balked. But now Song insisted: Why are you so interested in us? Where are you from, Doug?

———

I was born in Detroit. At the time, Dad was working in a steel factory, though his mind was always on flying. After enlisting in the Air Force and passing a selection board review, he spent a year in a flight program in Mississippi and got commissioned. While that was going on, we waited in Mount Olive, North Carolina, where my brother Den and I began elementary school. Our little duplex was just blocks from Granddad and where Dad grew up.

Dad got his orders and was gone. For me, one day I was playing marbles with my buddies; the next day, I told them I was going to Japan. Days before we left, an Air Mail letter arrived. It was Dad's; he had been there for weeks in training. His letters always had a "high command" feel about them. Mom read them to me and Den, always just before bed. Dad liked to slip in a page from Graham Greene, injecting a little military intrigue. Like in this one: he mistakenly landed his T-bird at a Japanese airbase and soldiers surrounded his cockpit pointing their rifles. His envelopes were always plastered with stamps from far-flung military outposts: Thule, Yigo, Don Muang, Bien Hoa; now Yokota. Remote assignments that lent an intimacy, as if it could be a final communiqué. This one ended with a storybook-like challenge: *Spojons* (that's what he called me and Den), *When you get to Yokohama, look for me on the dock.* He closed by stating his love, something I never heard at home.

Mom was not a worldly woman; she was smallish, plain-faced, with loose farm girl hair. Growing up in dot-on-the-map Allen, Nebraska, after high school she had found temp work as a typist. But now, starting in North Carolina, she and Den and I rode buses to Raleigh and on to Chicago, then got on the Northern Pacific Railway, which took us through Wisconsin, North Dakota, Montana and Idaho, all the way to Seattle. There, we boarded the USS General Mann, a 600-foot Navy troop transport vessel. Den and I, being the only kids, didn't have a lot to do. He took his spot on the bunk with his books. I found mine; it was up on the main deck where the sailors kind of took care of me. The Pacific waves swelled; flying fish playfully skimmed its surface with us. I took measure of how endless and indifferent the ocean was, hypnotized by its black depth, the white caps, and its might to toy with our rugged mass of steel. Buffeting winds with its salt spray residue pummeled me and my mind took flight—something that persists to this day.

On day eleven, the captain of the *Mann* came over the PA: Tokyo Bay. We scrambled to the taffrail to spot Japan. First, we saw Mt. Fuji, which looked like a painting. I yelled, "Hey Den, Den, look!" Den was imperturbable. You could sense that, even at seven, his rightful place would be in a boardroom, not in a Bulgarian hostel, never to be bug-bitten like me. We passed through an inlet and Yokohama burst into view. Rows of tankers, barges, cranes, then a line of docks—finally Dad's dock.

It took forever, but, aha, there he was, waving away. Dad was a skinny thing, maybe 120 pounds, a "drink of water," as his own dad would say. He was decked out in his crisp Air Force blues with his garrison cap nudged down between his eyes and the brassy second lieu-tenant bars, which I know he polished, sparkling on each shoulder. Little did I realize that that moment—Dad's arm flailing above his head, bursting with pride—would be the one defining image I'd return to. Most of the time he was stony silent and steely-gazed, a thinker, I suppose. I was forever trying to figure that out.

This was 1950's Japan and our world was now flipped. The unique faces, the calligraphy like scattered Tinker Toys, the bowing gestures, and the street aromas—all new. Dad had already figured out a lot and gave us a quick lesson on key phrases, like How are you? He gave Den and me an abacus. Mine sits on my office window. We took a train to Aomori Prefecture, the province at the northern tip of Honshu. This was now home, he said. It was a village called Misawa, outside the gate of his air base. These are a few things I can never forget: our house had *tatami* mat floors, sliding doors made of paper, called *washi*. Den and I peppered them with baseballs. We wore funny *tabi* socks that fit into the *geta*, the wooden clogs that we laughingly clomped around on. And weirdly, I still carry guilt from the rock I threw. It landed on the shaved head of a Japanese kid. He ran over and kicked me. I stood and took it. An airman at the gate saw it and told me, next time run to the base—he can't touch you. I thought, Wait, I'm in his country; I'm wrong.

———

My high school years, although they began in Schertz, Texas, were mostly spent on Luzon, another World War II island, quite different from Honshu—tropical, with banana trees and typhoons, not the pagodas and earthquakes. News in the "PI," as we called the Philippines, came from the day-and-a-half old news in the *Stars & Stripes*, the military paper. TV and radio were basically full of interference. We lived a couple of hours north of Manila, in a town called Angeles. It was noisy, packed with street vendors and wartime jeepneys decorated with tassels and Kool Aid colors. Filipina women in thick makeup and tight silk dresses strolled outside the Clark Air Base gate. Wherever we went, the words *"bigan, bigan"* followed us, a Tagalog slang for "friend." The way we got around was by hopping on and off the jeepneys for five centavos, that's like two pennies. To the west was a towering presence, Mt. Pinatubo, a volcano rumored to be active. Due to the street crime, our houses came with iron bars on the windows and cinder block walls, strewn on top with broken glass. Tiny Negritos with rifles manned the street corners. It resembled martial law, but it wasn't. No one got hurt. Petty stuff, they mostly wanted our watches and laundry off the line.

Den and I spent two years at Wagner, Clark's once proud open-air high school. It's no longer around today, because in 1991 it was buried in ash by Pinatubo, the largest eruption since Krakatoa in the 1880s. All that remains are a few online Wagner yearbooks. There's Den, top of his class, captain of teams, and me, hard to find, somewhere in the middle.

Such were the perils of troubled, dictator-enraptured PI, which still clings to the hope that mythic General MacArthur would return—and save them again. For us, that desperation had an allure. They loved the Americans and we loved the isolation. I was in no hurry to go back stateside.

I told Song that when our tour was over, the students group-hugged on the tarmac. Our little four-prop job skipped across the Pacific islands like they were stepping stones (Wake, Guam, Hawaii) before touching down in San Francisco. Exactly like he and his family would do some twelve years later. "Except," I told him, "during our takeoff, we cried. Bet you guys cheered."

———

Song asked about my daughter. He had met her one time. "What about her? How old is she?" he asked.

"Suki? She's Panna's age," I said. For her story, as I told him, we go back to El Salvador, I believe 1989. We were a dozen or so ragtag medical workers on a mission for Healing the Children. Picturesque El Salvador, despite its lush vegetative-thick mountains with low-hung clouds, was hardly a jungle getaway—a sad place, hot and sweaty, beaten into dusty poverty and ruled by roving murderous gangs.

Patient number one for day two was Rosa Isabella. She was an eight-year-old cutie sent by an orphanage. She had disfiguring kerosene burns with contraction scars on her face and down her neck. I had done the pre-op, then scrubbed in on her surgery. On the operating table, while we were draping her—her heart stopped. How does that happen in a healthy little girl? While awash in tears and near hysterics, the team tried until pure exhaustion, but could not revive her. It was an anesthesia blunder—an OR tech, a teenager, gave her a muscle blocker, unaware that she had to be intubated. Lifeless Rosa Isabella was wrapped in a shroud and unceremoniously driven away in a jeep. The monumental chill around little Rosa symbolized the infuriating hopelessness of El Salvador—the Savior.

The case the following morning was seven-year-old Nancy, with an identical injury. It was something we saw a lot, from tipped-over stoves in the huts. Her mother was understandably apprehensive and we put a hold on the operation. I eventually made arrangements to bring her to the US to have the same scar-release surgery done in our hospital, St. Raphael's (fees waived). As part of her clearance and visa, I had to register as her foster parent. It proved to be the missing piece in my flighty ideas about adopting a child, specifically, an orphan. I was unsure about fatherhood—this would test that.

During Nancy's summer stay in Connecticut, my Spanish-speaking friends rallied and we did handoffs, creating an integrated family for Nancy. By September, her neck was looking pretty good and with a flood of goodbye smiles from the team, we got Nancy onto an escorted flight, donated by American Airlines, back to her mom in Santa Ana.

Feeling like maybe I passed that exam, I put in a call to a Seattle adoption agency. They had never handled one for someone like me—approaching fifty, male, and single—but were eager to try.

Within weeks, they located an orphan, a girl named Hua Jin. She was in southern China and had been passed over by others, now four and a half. They sent me three photos. I asked two questions: Can she run? Yes. Can she sing? Yes. Okay. Those simple items told me her mind and body were working. As part of an eight-family adoption group, I was handed little (now named) Suki at her orphanage in Fuyang. First thing she did was eat my apple and hand me the stem.

Alas, she could barely walk and didn't speak a word. But Suki wasn't developmentally delayed; all of her precious life had been spent in a bare room, but for a few toys. If, at that moment, someone would have asked me, "Do you know what you're doing?" I would have replied, "Yeah, I got this." Within two days, she said, "fish" and "rock." Turns out, like me, she was a scrapper. Over some fifteen years we retraced many of my favorite routes, logging in forty-nine countries. Orphanages became our go-to targets. I recall one in a high-crime section of the Honduran capital, Tegucigalpa, called El Hogar de Esperanza, and another in the windswept moonscape of Tierra de Fuego, homes all but forgotten that considered us VIPs. The saintly women served me hot tea and Suki played ball games with the adorable kids.

In college, Suki got a Spanish award and set seven swimming records. Now a young woman, she lives within walking distance, in a house she fixed up, bopping over whenever I'm in a fix-it jam. She donates her hair to Wigs for Kids and she still has the travel bug; only now it's with her work colleagues and more in the resort mode. Acapulco, not Cuba.

———

Back to Dad. By sometime in the mid-80s, he had some 7000 flying hours under his belt. I have a photo of him in his flight suit and aviators, hands on hips, as squadron commander of the Black Sheep, whose watch was the South China Sea. A veteran of three wars. He was done, except for one final act. In 1985, The Pentagon called, informing him that they were repatriating Col. John Kwortnik, an MIA who went down over North Vietnam in 1966. The colonel, then a captain and Dad's co-pilot, was last spotted parachuting after his plane was hit. Along with Kwortnik's wife, Jimmie, Dad escorted his remains from San Francisco to Arlington National Cemetery. After the burial ceremony with all the guns, flags, and salutes, Dad returned home to Florida, put all his medals and ribbons in a cigar box and we never mentioned flying again. For a few years he quietly repaired motor boats. Then he became a regular in the Merritt Island fishing bars. Toward the end, he simply sat on a lounge chair in the garage, with a refrigerator of beer within reach and AM country tunes blaring on a pocket transistor. Dad had checked out. Den and I tried to get Mom to leave him, but she wouldn't do it. She was a soldier—you don't do that. We'd find out too late that Dad had taken his name off the Arlington Cemetery register.

I wondered then and I still do today: What did Dad take with him? And is this my fate?

As a kid in Japan, the moment I had reached our village, Misawa, my recurring role as an outsider began. I was okay with that: inserting myself as the odd fit, a bit like that drifter, Hal, in the 1953 William Inge play, *Picnic*. After several go-arounds, I thirsted for more—that elixir of expectation, disorientation, loneliness and ephemeral romance. Bleak at times, yes, yet with intoxicating moments.

Hiking across four continents with only a carry-on knapsack entailed a lot of border controls, "no vacancy" signs, crashing on overnight trains and bothering locals—all at a relentless pace, constantly on the edge. But everything ends. The first real hurt was my legs. I had been a marathoner, something that came in handy, for instance when you can't find the Loch Ness or when you want to top out Mt. Agua in Antigua. Into my late forties, then my fifties, I was losing precious steps. They weren't simply bad days. At my level, running was an art form. My racing flats were now hiking boots. It wasn't long after that that the psychic weight was too much; I had to stop. My days as a fresh-faced gust of wind were past.

So, for Cliff (that's my dad), it was the wings; for me, it was the wheels. He was done; I still had things to do.

———

When Wally heard me express interest in Panna's story, he wondered aloud, "What's driving you?" My head was full of noise. It would take me years to recognize the dots on the deck of the *General Mann* were the same as those in the Kroms' living room. When I first stepped into the Krom apartment, I found myself in a familiar role: the stranger in the midst of an untapped mix of mystery and challenge. When Song firmly gripped my hand, I knew: They trusted me. I was home.

Drawing a deep breath, I apologized to Song. It was okay, he told me, and patted my shoulder. "I was born into middle class America," I told him. "We never had to struggle. I tempted chaos, going to all ends of the world, some pretty places, you know, like Paris, and some heart-breaking ones. I was oblivious to the plight of many. When I heard your story, it made me go back, rethink about what I had been missing. You guys took a grip on me."

He smiled.

"So, you see," I went on to explain, "a lot of good deeds are really disguises for someone's hidden pain to resolve a personal conflict or deeply-seated need."

He looked puzzled.

I told him, "Song, it's all about me."

He laughed.

———

I mentioned to Song, "In the woods, you come to life."

He said, "I tell you, Doug. I see *Survivor* on TV and I say, wow, if my English were good. I tell you, all those things they do—make a lean-to, fish, hunt, trap, catch water, make a fire. I can do those. I make a hut no time. It won't leak, even have a floor."

"How about making a fire with sticks?"

"Oh easy, even if raining. I do this all the time."

"Song, how is work?" I changed the subject.

"You mean work work?" He laughed.

"Yeah. Not like in Cambodia, right?"

He told me, "In Cambodia you had no power. No money, no papers, nothing. When you are poor you are nothing. In the mud. A man in uniform, he have total power over you. You will crawl. You can't look at him." He paused. "I still don't."

"What? I don't get it," I said.

"When the bossman he come by, I bow and I don't look at him in the face. I have to go through this every day."

"You mean even today? Look him in the eye. You can't do that? Be proud?"

"Oh no, never. For us to look in the eye means disrespect. No, no, you can't do that."

"Wow, for us avoiding contact means you're afraid, not confident." I asked him, "Did this ever bother Panna?"

"I tell her. She upset, tell me not to. She say, 'Daddy, you have respect.' But daddy has to do this. I tell her. If I get fired, we lose apartment."

I asked Song, "Does it make you angry, these guys, the boss?"

"Before, yes. But, I'm okay. They treat me good."

"Sounds like you just want to avoid any hassles."

Song laughed and patted me on the back. "Yeah, Doug. I want to keep my job."

With that pat, I felt less like any kind of advisor and more like we were on par. He needed me; at first it was as a way to get Panna out of prison, but now to understand—and respect—his world.

We packed up and drove the five minutes to the West End Lake. The sun was gone and there were no cars. We hiked through lush ankle-deep grass to a steep hill. "I call this Killer Hill," he said. The air had an October crispness. At the top he pointed to a concrete kind of pier and said, "Panna love to come here. Sit there and watch me fish. For hours."

The water was turning dark, still sparkling. In weeks the leaves would be gone. We walked along the short ridge. There was a backdrop of yellow and purple wildflowers. "I pick the flowers for our Buddha."

As we drove home, Song suddenly turned somber and told me, "I did something wrong today."

"What do you mean?"

"I got my mind where I needed a break. So, I am sitting alone, thinking."

"You're talking about at work, your soldering work?"

"Yeah, work. Slow day. I look at the drawing right in front of me. I say, 'Oh, shit.' I have five amp and ten amp and I see I put five on ten and ten on five. It is a big mistake."

I was thinking of how Song had told me how he is so expert at what he does. I see his hands and they are like magic. They can do anything; the things he fixes. I'm angry hearing this. Way back, some Filipino in a roadside stand had him change watch batteries and he's used his hands ever since, rebuilding watches, laying out tiny circuits, soldering intricate wires. He was twice as fast as the others. Deciphering a schematic blueprint was another language he knew, circumventing the English, German, or whatever; the more complex, the better.

He continued. "They put that unit in machine. Already sent out, gone. I get depressed all day. I sit down and think about it. Finally I tell the boss."

"What did he say? I mean, mistakes happen."

"I know they happen. But three strikes and you're out. I could tell by the look on his face."

"What look? Three mistakes? What do you mean three?"

"Yes, and I have one already."

"In ten years? One? That's like a world record."

"It doesn't matter. I do twenty, thirty circuits a day. Yes, I make mistake. It happen. The inspector miss it too."

"The QC guy? That's more his mistake than yours."

"Doesn't matter. I tell you. It doesn't matter."

"But the people who got it didn't report it, is that right?"

"Not yet. Plus, it's embarrassing. The supervisor, he want to find something wrong. People like suffering in others. I'm so tight right now. I don't talk to nobody."

"People love watching others get kicked. You're the dog."

"Yeah. That's me. All my life."

"The Germans even have a word for this, taking pleasure in someone else's pain. You know Song, it's the same with Panna, watching her suffer. Society thrives on it. Glad it's not them. And they don't want the full story. They don't believe in second chances—unless it's them." He smiled, nodded, and pointed his finger at me.

I recalled right after meeting Song and Chan, reading up on Buddhism. It said there were four rules and suffering was the first one. "Suffering is a big deal for you guys."

"Yeah, it's big." Song continued, "I can't tell Chan. She get depressed. We work very hard to get the rent going, find a place to stay. If I lose job, we must stay on sister's couch."

"Chan's sister?"

"Yes. Before, we have enough. We could go out. Now we have car payment, rent, bills, and go see Panna. That is all."

We were halfway home. I remembered him telling me how just the York phone bills were crushing them. And that was before the lawyers. Seven years out and they are sliding down a mountain of debt. He called ahead to tell Chan we'd be home. He looked at me, broke into a smile, and said, "You like quail?"

———

We arrived at the apartment parking lot. He killed the engine. It was dark, the chill seeping into the car. Song and I sat there with only the bluish light from one streetlamp, when he broke the silence. "Hey, there's a few more beers."

I said, "Let's split one."

He reached in the back seat and pulled out a bottle. In a blink he set the cap on the rocker panel and in a pop, snapped it off. He poured half in a Styrofoam cup and handed me the bottle. We tapped them. "Cheers."

I told him, "I'm pretty deep into your story. Committed to seeing it to a proper end." He put his hands in the prayer position and closed his eyes.

I said, "Proper means seeing Panna walk out of York. I *will* be there and I don't want to be eighty when that happens." It was quiet for a minute.

"Can I ask you something?"

He nodded.

"It's something that's been on my mind. I don't mean to upset you."

"It's okay."

"When you found the baby, or Chan did. I know you called all your family. I mean, everyone was there. You guys talked about what to do, right?"

"Yeah, we talk."

"All right, let me ask you this. How many babies died in your family? In Cambodia."

"Me? We have two died."

"And Chan's family? I think she said three." He agreed. "What did you do with those babies? Their bodies."

"We cremate."

"So, here's my point. You had seen dead babies before, right? And knew what to do?"

"Oh, a lot."

"That day, did you guys talk about options?"

"We talk. We ask ourselves, do we call police or not?"

"So you called."

"We call because they said they help us."

"It was the right thing to do, you thought."

"Yes, that's what we think."

"Was.."

He cut me off. "I know what you mean. I should have pray and have a ceremony for the baby. I was wrong. If I do that Panna never go to prison. It was my decision. No one tried to stop me."

"You can argue both sides. It was ethics versus morals. The point is, you did the right thing and made the call. The cops and DA should have respected your family's integrity and gone soft on Panna."

He sat silently, nodding in agreement. "Thank you. I think about this a lot," he said. "It was stupid. Panna pay for it. I do so many things wrong. I should be there, not her."

"It'll work out for the better. You'll see. There's good karma, right?"

He laughed. There was silence.

I said, "I'm hungry. Let's go."

You could smell dinner before we opened the apartment door. Chan was sitting, legs folded under her, on the couch with a small DVD player. In her lap were grocery coupons. I peered at the screen and asked what she was watching. "It Thai movie," she said.

She got up and brought out dinner on plates, quail with rice and soy. I inspected the grains as they had taught me, to make sure they were long grain and not damaged and not short and sticky.

"It's jasmine, real jasmine," I announced. They liked that.

I was still thinking about what he told me about respect. "Song, when we talked about the boss coming by, you mentioned your head."

"Yes, I bow, always, and I say *sawadee*. Sir, good morning boss. Don't say name."

"And you said this bothers Panna, that you do this to someone you don't know?"

"It does. We do it to policeman. Even ticket-taker at movie."

Chan added, "And we have to bow when he walk by. Make sure to stay lower."

"What do you mean lower?" I stopped eating.

Song said, "The head must be lower."

"You mean your head is lower than his?" They nodded.

"I know you do that for Buddha. But for these guys, like at work or some plumber or banker?"

"Always." I looked at Chan and they were smiling at my reaction. Song said, "We do it to you."

"Come on. Me?"

"Yes, when you are here, don't you see I am always lower? You see me crouch down when I go by," said Song. They were both laughing. I wasn't sure if he was kidding.

He was sitting on the floor. I considered what was just said. He was right. "Song, you've never sat at my level. That's on purpose?"

They laughed again.

"Song, you still do this?" I said. "It's thirty years that you've been here."

He said, "I still do."

Chan, always one for edifying, said, "In our country it is a *big* thing."

"And the hands?" I asked, pulling mine together.

They both showed their hands in the prayer position. Chan said, "The girls' hands are lower." She showed them near the chest. "And the boys' higher, like this." Her hands were up near the forehead.

As we resumed eating, I took stock of the apartment, with a quick panoramic view. "And the blanket on the floor?" I asked casually. One corner of the living room space was occupied by a thick cotton sort of quilt. I pictured Chan's nightly meditation there. "For praying?"

"Oh, we sleep there."

Suddenly I took account of something that I already knew but which never registered: that this place had one bedroom. And it was for other family. "You sleep here?" I pointed at the blanket.

"Yes."

"So, this is your bedroom?" I saw no clothes, no closet.

"Yes."

After all these years in their *zawan*, the Khmer word for heaven, the Kroms were still sleeping in a common room, still on the floor.

"You guys are something."

PART SEVEN
NEONATICIDE CASES

CHAPTER TWENTY-EIGHT

THE SWIMMER

W hen I began working on Panna's case, about all I had was
one number, her sentence—18 years—which seemed long.
I mentioned it to a pair of rather grizzled retired detectives.
They both agreed, saying something along the lines of, "Oh, that's
fucking crazy. For that?"

There had been an earlier neonaticide case in Connecticut. In a
column in the *Hartford Courant,* journalist Rick Green mentioned it.
Addressing Panna's sentence, he said, "We can all agree that Krom
should be punished for her crime, but sending a teenage girl to jail for
eighteen years is what I can't get over." He referred to another case
involving a girl from Cheshire, Connecticut charged with the same
crime. The similarities to Panna's were striking: single, seventeen-year-
old high school student, hidden pregnancy, newborn homicide at home.
Except her sentence—it was a fraction of Panna's.

I tried tracking down that case, but without a name, I stood no
chance. I sent Rick Green an email and got no response. I canvassed
various people from Cheshire, the next town over from mine, but they
didn't know her. My daughter, Suki, swam against Cheshire, and we
knew the Cheshire swim families. They had no memory of it, which
told me that it must be old. The police station needed information I

didn't have: her name, plus the date and address. The Cheshire High School principal's office, understandably, was dismissive, telling me they would never release that kind of information.

In the Cheshire town library, I went through newspaper microfiche crime files and scanned the obituaries. I even looked at the yearbooks—maybe I would see a girl "showing." Losing sight of my mission, I browsed the library's crime section, all of two shelves. *Murder in Connecticut* by Michael Benson caught my attention. I shook my head, as this could only be about one story: the horrific Cheshire home-invasion triple murder. Thumbing through it, I recognized that it was mostly extracted from the extensive news accounts—that is, he pasted in the work of other journalists. The only original reporting appeared to be the author's eyewitness account from rubbernecking as he drove back and forth past the taped-off crime scene.

Benson had expertly honed his craft with a stable of books, quick-turnaround murder stories, books like *Nightmare in Rochester*. I was curious about his sources. His bibliography, as expected, listed very little beyond the news services. But one source in particular kept reappearing: *Myrecordjournal.com*. I pulled it up and noticed it had news and classi-fieds from central Connecticut, which included Cheshire. I subscribed and did a search, putting in Panna's name. Nothing. Keywords about her crime. Still nothing.

However, when I played with other specific words—Cheshire, newborn, student, death, arrest—some articles popped up. At last, I had a name:

Julia Gee.

I also got the other key items: the date and address. Obtaining police documents was critical for each case. The quality varied: some were attentive to details, while many were written at a fifth-grade level, disor-ganized with tedious redundancy. They redacted a name or address, but then enough clues could be spotted elsewhere. Nevertheless, for me, Panna's report was the big one. When I requested it, I received a worri-some letter from the Danbury Legal Counsel office requesting my iden-tity and my reason for wanting the report. I talked to my boss and responded, on letterhead stationery, that I worked at Yale New Haven Hospital in Neurology (true) and was doing a study on the psychological profiles on women who committed "neonaticide" (also true). To my surprise, it was accepted, as was my $50, which I realized made for an easy cash flow for police departments (one cost me $80). Of all the documents and interviews I went through for this investigation; nothing matched the moment when Panna's 100-page police report landed on my desk.

The Cheshire Police Department told me that since the Julia Gee case was a murder, something rare in Cheshire, the detectives had called in the Major Crime Squad; they directed me to the Connecticut State Police in nearby Middletown. The CSP records department asked me why I wanted it. I said I was doing research at Yale New Haven Hospital and showed my badge. I gladly paid the $15 fee and they cheerfully handed me a copy. It occurred to me that this was a public document and I didn't need to prove who I was.

With high anticipation, I wanted to compare the "facts" of police reports with what I had been told by others and had read in the press. But in particular I wanted to see how cases were handled differently.

The Cheshire newborn murder investigation started not in a bathroom, or even a home, but in a town dump—and not Cheshire's.

———

At the trash-to-energy plant in Wallingford, the next town over from Cheshire, on the morning of Friday, November 24, 1995, Don Pagano was sitting in a pay-loader where the trash comes in, as a truck was dumping its load into bay number five on the tipping floor. The dump truck had to backup and push four or five times. Pagano's job was to load the trash into the incinerator. Another worker, Gary Kafka, was piling, which means stacking the trash into the bay. As the dump truck finished and was pulling out, Pagano spotted something that looked like a doll on the fifteen-foot pile. While he was loading the incinerators, the doll stuck in his mind. To get a better look, he back-bladed the pile, something he normally wouldn't do. What he saw was more like a baby, not a doll. He got out and leaned in as closely as he could. He motioned to Kafka to stop.

It was a newborn. It had a penis and an umbilical cord, which had been cut. Pagano immediately called Mike Melanson, his supervisor, to come over. Other guys had overheard the call on their radios and wandered over as well. They asked what was going on but Pagano didn't tell them. Melanson arrived and they all watched him inspect the dead baby with its two-inch blackened umbilical cord. To him the baby had a good color—it wasn't blue—and did not appear to have been dead long. Below the arm by the stomach area was a laceration. He patched in a call to the plant manager at the New Haven Trash Station and described the finding. The manager told him to shut down the plant and call the police. After describing it on the 9-1-1 call, he put on a pair of gloves, went over, and lightly poked the baby, he later told police, to make absolutely sure it was dead. The body was positioned halfway out of a green plastic bag. To him, although the body was not rigid, there was no question it was dead. Melanson figured it had to have been from one of two trucks. The one he really suspected was from Cheshire, a dump truck of Sharon Bozzuto's.

At noon that day, Sharon Bozzuto made her regular stop at Nardelli's Lunch in Waterbury. Two other drivers sat down at her table. They asked if she had heard the news: a dead baby in the Wallingford plant. She hurriedly finished lunch and picked up one more load before heading back to Wallingford. Mike Melanson told her about the baby, figuring it came off her trailer. Police were already there and she described her day to them: getting loaded up with 18.71 tons of refuse from trash trucks in Cheshire and dumping it all in Wallingford. She told them she never saw anything unusual. The trash she got came off the pickup garbage truck of Matthew Legasse, who had done his usual morning route in Cheshire. The police located Legasse. He told them he saw absolutely nothing suspicious.

Police strung up yellow crime scene tape around bay number five in Wallingford and examined the contents of the green plastic bag which held the baby. Inside were bed pads, medical bandages, swabs, and latex surgical gloves. Also, there was a credit card, cut with scissors. It had a name on it: Bernice Gee. In the rubbish surrounding the victim was also a letter. The address was 25 Ridge Road in Cheshire. The same address checked out for the credit card.

Located in central Connecticut, Cheshire is considered a township for those seeking status, upscale and bucolic, with nice homes on big lots and highly desired schools. Cheshire High School is known for competitive academics and high-caliber sports teams, sending their stars into the Ivies and major leagues.

Detectives arrived at the four-bedroom colonial at 25 Ridge Road, which was set back and shaded with fully grown oak and pine trees. They informed the owners, Bernice and Ed Gee, that on November 24 a dead baby was found in the town trash and materials tied to it were traced to their address. They specified the items: Depends, Nitro Pads, surgical gloves, a prescription bottle for Anona Sands with this address, and a Shawmut Bank Card with Bernice Gee's name on it. Bernice told them that Anona was her invalid mother; she lived upstairs. She said that the items sounded like those used for her care. The police asked, did anyone else live in the house? They said all the kids were gone except for Julia, their seventeen-year-old daughter, a senior at Cheshire High School. The detectives asked to speak with her.

With her parents in the room, the detectives asked Julia if she had been pregnant. She told them no, she had not. Police continued the same line of questioning, but she continued to deny knowing about any birth or anything about a baby. She did offer the names of three of her classmates whom she believed were pregnant.

The following day at Cheshire High School, a counselor told the detectives she only knew of one girl in the school who was near full term: Julia Gee. Mandatory reporting was not required.

The following day two detectives showed up at the Gee home, now with search-and-seizure warrants executed for both the residence and Cheshire High School. At the house, several items turned up matching those found adjacent to the victim's body.

In the high school, police interviewed the school nurse, Evelyn Ricci. They discovered that, months earlier, one of the swimmers had spread a rumor that Julia was pregnant even though she was continuing to swim on the team and she had passed the physical. At the request of the swimming coach, Ed Aston, Nurse Ricci had met with Julia. She informed Julia that she appeared pregnant, but Julia denied everything. When asked about her sexual relations, Julia admitted to having had sex one time but insisted she was not pregnant. The nurse suggested Julia see her doctor and that she and her boyfriend visit a family planning center. Julia agreed, but she never did either of those things, nor did she ever take a home pregnancy test.

The detectives interviewed Julia's parents, friends of hers, a boyfriend and a neighborhood boy who admitted to having had sex with her.

I was most interested in reading the interview of the mother and father, Bernice and Ed. What was their explanation for what was obvious? The police had limited their conversation to questions about the items in the trash, the invalid mother, and taking out of the garbage. Nothing about their pregnant daughter. Julia's mother, Bernice, was a pediatric nurse.

———

In Farmington, on November 26, 1995, medical examiner Dr. Thomas Gilchrist performed the postmortem exam. Detective Theodore Kraus was there as a witness. The baby, "unidentified male," was later named Joshua Paul Gee. Dr. Gilchrist noted multiple lacerations and contusions to the facial area. After inspecting the lungs, he determined the baby had been alive at birth. He dictated that the umbilical cord was, with reasonable medical certainty, cut after death. He further stated there was no evidence of disease or other medical problems which would have led to the death. On the death certificate, in clear block letters he entered for cause of death: ASPHYXIA, and for manner of death: HOMICIDE.

Later that day, after getting the call from the medical examiner, the Cheshire detectives returned to the Ridge Road residence. They informed the Gees, "Things have changed. We're dealing with a homicide." Julia Gee was taken to the police station and interviewed again. They informed her that several sources said she had been pregnant. Even with the police convinced that she had recently given birth, she denied it. After her parents were asked to step out, she continued to deny it.

The police requested that she submit to a physical examination by a female physician at the Veteran's Memorial Medical Center. Julia agreed.

Dr. Susan Sgambati, a gynecologist, did a pelvic examination on Julia Gee. She found the breasts to be engorged and lactating, the vaginal canal had signs of trauma including a third-degree perineal tear, the uterus enlarged, and striae on the abdomen—all consistent with a delivery two to five days prior.

With Julia's parents waiting outside, Dr. Sgambati explained her findings. Julia admitted to the doctor that she had given birth. The detectives were called in and she repeated the confession.

———

At the police station, Julia willingly described the days around the birth.

In her statement, she described her sexual history starting her freshman year—a boy in her class, one in the neighborhood, and two brothers in a nearby town. Late summer before her senior year, she realized she was pregnant. The neighbor boy was assumed to be the father, but she never told him. Months later she felt the kicks but told no one. Counselors and teachers at school told her she looked pregnant, but she denied it and they seemed to accept that. She feared that her parents would send her to a home for unwed mothers.

Tuesday, two days before Thanksgiving, Julia had severe pains in her abdomen radiating to her back. She woke her mom but was told to go back to bed. The following day, November 22, her cramps were bad and she stayed home. As the pain got worse, she made many trips to the bathroom, finally feeling the urge to push. When she did, a head seemed to protrude. A baby slid out and into the water, then the placenta discharged and fell into the water. Julia reached down and lifted the baby, still attached by the umbilical cord. She testified that the baby's head was never submerged. Lifting it up by the feet, she spanked it on the buttocks to get it to breathe. It never took a breath, moved, or cried, she said. She then placed the limp baby with its attached placenta on the counter. After running down to the kitchen for a plastic grocery bag, she gently laid the baby face up in the bag. She was clear to the police: the baby never moved.

Julia wiped down the bathroom. Stopping at the top of the stairs to make sure no one else was home, she carried the plastic bag down to the garage. In a trash can, she discovered another dark green bag. She put her bag inside it, tied the green bag, pushed it to the bottom, tossed other stuff over it, then tightly attached the lid.

At 2:30 p.m. her mom came home from her work at Hartford Hospital. Julia went downstairs and talked to her. She confessed, "I never told my mom about the baby."

The following morning, Thanksgiving, she slipped into the garage to peek in the trash can. The green plastic bag was still there, undisturbed. Later, her father drove her to a school powder puff football game. The report made no mention of a family dinner that day.

Early Friday morning, Julia peered out her bedroom window and saw her dad drag the trashcan and other bags to the curbside. She watched the garbage man lift the trash can and empty it into the back of the truck and toss the can to the side. Confident that her secret was safe, that night she went to the Cheshire High football game. A few days later, she found out from the police that she made one slip: putting her bag in the green bag. Though it seemed like a doubly safe move, the items in the green bag led to her prosecution.

Based on the autopsy results and the written confession, on December 13, 1995, a warrant was issued for the arrest of Julia Gee. The charge was manslaughter in the first degree in the asphyxiation of her newborn. First-degree manslaughter, as it was explained to Julia and her family, meant recklessly but not intentionally causing a death. The affidavit for the arrest warrant, which included twenty evidential parts, was sealed by Judge William Hadden. That meant that, unlike in Panna's case, the media had no access to the warrant.

Two days later, with her mom and her attorney, Kevin Hecht, an ex-cop, at her side, Julia Gee surrendered to the Cheshire Police Department. She signed the warrant and initialed each point of her Miranda rights. Authorities considered her a low flight risk. She was released with the court setting a bond consisting of only a written promise to appear before the Superior Court in Meriden, Connecticut on January 2, 1996, at 10:00 a.m.

Cheshire High School issued an automatic ten-day suspension. Her friends took the news well and were still hanging out with her.

Attorney Hecht told me that in June of that year, he and his client got hit with a bombshell. The Prom Mom story out of New Jersey was all over the news. In the middle of her prom, Melissa Drexler, an eighteen-year-old student, delivered a baby in the gym bathroom. She severed the cord with the edge of a sanitary-napkin dispenser, wrapped the body in garbage bags and threw it in the trash can. Then she returned to the dance floor. A janitor, who told authorities about the blood in the restroom, had found the heavy bag and discovered the baby. The teenager was sentenced to fifteen years in prison.

The Drexler news torpedoed their strategy. Attorney Hecht said that it made for an "excruciating discussion I had to have with a seventeen-year-old girl." It was her decision: go to trial and risk a sentence of fifteen years or do a plea for second-degree manslaughter with much less time? He added, "She would have been a lousy witness." On August 30, 1997, Julia Gee negotiated a plea under the Alford doctrine, in which a defendant claims innocence but concedes that the prosecution has overwhelming evidence (enough to get a conviction), and received a one-and-a-half-year prison sentence with five years' probation. Judge Robert Devlin stated it was one of his hardest decisions but he had to send a message to other pregnant teenagers.

Later that year, Julia Gee entered York Correctional Institute to begin her sentence. She was quietly released after serving seven months. Years later, a CO told Panna that there had been another girl there with a similar crime, but that was all she heard.

————

In the Cheshire High School yearbooks for 1995 and 1996, Julia Gee can be seen. But for her graduation year there were no pictures of her— senior picture or with her swim team. She was at York.

Those pictures from her sophomore and junior years are small and grainy. To the right is the swim team picture, with her in it, and the team's record: eleven wins, no losses. It was in the middle of a streak of dual meet victories that started in 1986 and would continue for twenty-six years, 281-0, the longest such streak for any US high school team, any sport.

Julia's attorney, Kevin Hecht, said he had heard that she attended college, but had not been in contact with her and no longer had her legal documents.

I didn't find her on Facebook but did find her brother, Randy. He lived in Rhode Island and had two kids. My wife, Connie, sent him a friend request and he accepted her. We were able to see pictures of Julia. She's in her early forties, married with two kids, living in Bristol, Rhode Island.

An hour later Randy messaged Connie, "Do I know you?" We carefully thought out a reply. Connie explained we were working on a case like Julia's and wanted to reach her for help or ideas on it. He wrote back that he did not have contact with Julia and we could try to friend her. We stopped there.

CHAPTER TWENTY-NINE
DAVID PAUL

Song, Chan, Connie, and I met for lunch at Pad Thai on one of our regular Saturday afternoons. As soon as we got seated, the Thai waitress, who by now knew us and our backstory, brought a couple Singha beers for me and Song. Everyone was smiling and relaxed; it was always the high point of our week.

In a serious tone, I announced to the Kroms, "I found another case —just like Panna's. It was one I had heard about. But I finally got the papers I needed and have the facts."

They both looked puzzled. Song said, "Another girl?"

"Yeah. High school girl, like Panna, seventeen, who got into trouble. Same deal with her baby. Even a family of four like you guys."

"Baby died?" asked Song, sitting up straighter, no longer smiling. I nodded.

Chan said, "And what happen with her?"

"She went to York."

"She at York?" said Chan.

"No, not anymore." I had picked up my glass but held off drinking and said, "This part may be hard to hear."

"What do you mean?" said Song.

"She got a fifteen-month sentence." They froze. "Actually, she left after seven months."

Raising his voice, Song said, "And went home?"

"Yeah."

"Seven months," he said. Tears formed in his eyes. "Doug, you kidding me?"

"No, I wish I was."

Chan said, "She rich?"

With a strained smile, I said, "She's from Cheshire. Not poor, well off, but not exactly rich. She had a lawyer. Look, I know all this hurts. I waited to tell you. Even thought about not telling you. But I can't do that. This is the kind of stuff we're going to find. But listen, in an odd way, it may help Panna."

"How? How it going to help Panna?" asked Chan.

"I'll get to that. This happened almost ten years ago. When you tell Panna."

"Tell Panna?" interrupted Song.

"Yeah, when you see her, tonight. You'll need to tell her."

"I can't tell her that," said Song.

"You have to," I said. "Everyone has to know everything. There's going to be some bumps in the road and we have to deal with them. Like I said, it might help."

"How?"

"The short sentence. Problem is, it's just one case and that won't be enough to sway a parole board. I need more."

"And you think that will help her?" said Chan.

"Yeah, if I can find them."

"Can you?" asked Song.

"I think so. Listen, there's also a chance we find one with a longer sentence. I've seen cases where they got life. Life. That would kill it for her."

———

That evening, they told Panna about the Cheshire girl and her sentence. She sat there stunned. For at least a minute she didn't say a word, just looked blank with her head resting on her hands. She nodded and told them that she understood. At the end of the visit, as her parents were getting up, with tears in her eyes, Panna said, "So this girl walked out of here after seven months." She paused. "Mom, I'm starting my eighth year."

———

The Cheshire case energized me. I would discover that with each new case I found, it often made reference to another. Neonaticide was the term. It was coined in the seventies by Professor Philip J. Resnick, a Case Western Reserve University forensic psychiatrist, referring to babies killed within the first twenty-four hours of life, virtually always by the mother. He published landmark papers that uncovered a unique set of psychological stressors involved with those young mothers. Many of them were isolated and displayed a familiar pattern of naïveté; culture often played a role. It was their first pregnancy, they hid it, and during delivery they were alone, in a dissociated state. In fact, Resnick found that the most common motive for neonaticide was the social stigma of pregnancy. All of these factors were applicable to Panna; in fact, she was a textbook case.

No jurisdiction in the US has a separate statute for neonaticide, infanticide, (a legal term for killing a baby less than a year in age), or pedicide (up to the age of majority), making those homicides indistinguishable in the eyes of the law. When I attempted to tabulate child murder cases in Connecticut, establishing the child's exact age required arduous, and not always successful, research. The US legislators had yet to apply the work of Resnick and others so that mothers who committed neonaticide could be handled separately, evaluated psychologically, and potentially offered compassionate sentences—or counseling with no prison time, as in some countries. England has an infanticide statute that places a teenage offender in the juvenile court, where the purpose is rehabilitative, as opposed to the adult court, where it is punitive. Their young women neonaticide offenders are not sent to prison. Applied to Panna's case, the justice system would not question her committing the act, but explore why, and, if appropriate, use that in her mitigation. Journalist and Yale Law School fellow Emily Bazelon wrote in *The New York Times Magazine*, July 4, 2021: "When science makes it harder to prove guilt, police officers, prosecutors, and judges may see it as an impediment. They keep doing their jobs, much as they always have."

Numbers for neonaticide crimes were not easily traceable in Connecticut. I know; this is what I spent years attempting to do. I was told by a New York medical health officer that they register the ages of their homicides through their medical examiner's office. I called our ME office in Farmington and asked if they kept a record of newborn deaths. All criminal case corpses, and infants, pass through their facility for autopsy, so logging the age seemed like an easy and obvious thing to do. Their response was curt: "No." They provided no elaboration.

I stumbled upon an even darker side to this tragedy. I have no idea how it was studied or quantified, but according to estimates out of France, for every known neonaticide case, two to three times as many were not known. In other words, live birth babies were being disposed of and never recorded, reported, or discovered. I reviewed my list of cases. Based on the way they were disposed of, by odds virtually all should have escaped detection. Interestingly, my short list of young women includes all levels of socioeconomic status. I suspect few researchers have any desire to explore, or expose, this shameful demographic statistic.

I had met Jennifer Tunnard, who had been Panna's defense attorney, in the winter of 2012. At that time, she was open to working with me on Panna's behalf, but soon stopped responding. By February, I had a conversation with Song and Chan, who discussed the matter with Panna. We would look for another lawyer. I sent Tunnard an email stating our decision and within minutes she called me. Her caseload was overwhelming, she said, and suggested that finding another attorney might be wise: she even broached the idea of seeking a public defender.

By April 2013, I was exhausted from my efforts to attract other defense attorneys. I had called, sent emails with attached documents, even dropped off Panna's file to several, hoping to generate a twinge of interest in her case. I never got beyond a few questions asked. I had saved one name for last: Vicki Hutchinson. She had been Panna's first attorney. She knew the case. From the court documents I read, she came across as tough and aggressive. I was concerned that she had long ago washed her hands of the case and had no desire to revisit it, or quite possibly was owed money. The family reminded me that back in 2007, their self-appointed legal expert, Song's boss, Steve Ogden, squabbled with her, leading to her departure, and then they retained Tunnard.

I told Song and Chan, "Remember Vicki? I'm calling her," unsure of how they would respond. Chan fired back, "We like Vicki."

Attorney Hutchinson emailed a quick reply, telling me that the case was no longer hers but belonged to Jennifer Tunnard. I responded that Tunnard had dropped out and was okay with another attorney taking over. Hutchinson agreed to see me.

Just before my appointment with her, I set up a time to talk with University of Santa Clara Law professor Michelle Oberman, who, with Cheryl Miller at Wright State University, had co-authored the definitive book on neonaticide, *When Mothers Kill*. During our conversation, Oberman, who afforded me seemingly unlimited time for discussion, asked, "Why don't you do a clemency?" I barely knew the term. She told me that some years before she had been an expert witness in the successful commutation (lowering of a sentence) for Rebecca Hopfer, a teen in Ohio who got fifteen-to-life for suffocating her newborn. After serving eleven years, Rebecca was released. My spark of optimism was quickly doused with cold water when Oberman added, "It took us two efforts. And I should warn you: You'll need publicity. We had *48 Hours*."

According to the website for the Connecticut Board of Pardons and Paroles (BOPP) at the time, by the simple numerical criteria—having served more than four years of a sentence greater than eight—Panna qualified for clemency. But what was it? How often was it granted? What criteria were they looking for?

I asked several private defense attorneys, but none were familiar with clemency. Few lawyers in Connecticut knew about it—after all, it didn't pay, was a lot of work, and the clients could be untrustworthy. Plus, it was rarely successful.

That May, I met Vicki Hutchinson in her Danbury office. I was uneasy—the idea of me pitching a clemency strategy to a seasoned defense attorney had a certain folly about it. We took our seats at a round table in her conference room. I had on a rarely worn sports jacket and best shoes. My notes in front of me were neatly organized in a two-page outline. Hutchinson, in her conservative attire, was sparse on words but had an air of confidence—and listened. She asked me, "So, what do you have?" The hard facts in my argument were scant, almost embarrassingly so: the Cheshire case with its fifteen-month sentence, law professor Oberman's advice to explore clemency, and the BOPP numbers indicating Panna's current eligibility. I added that I had a lead or two on more cases, plus I was gathering names for support. She asked me, "Like who?"

"A few people have agreed to write letters, some of them big names in their fields. Even a couple of formerly incarcerated women who knew her," I said. "The story is an easy sell. She's done well. And I'm in an academic community where it's easy to find liberals with impressive titles."

Hutchinson sat still, didn't say much except, "uh huh." She was humble and gave me room.

"Panna's injustice, with her family's history, is a sympathetic story," I added. "She and her family are likable." I sounded desperate; I was.

"Did she have a psychiatric eval?"

"Yeah, showed what the psychologist called 'extreme emotional distress.'"

"EED. Normally, that'd be enough to defend a case like this, a young kid, but only if you went to trial. Listen, it's all good," she said and paused. "But what you have right now doesn't make a strong case. In a pure legal sense, you know. We will need something more, maybe another case or two. Not even sure if that will do it."

"Like I said, I have a couple leads." No reaction. I felt I was losing her. I asked, "Don't you just love taking on the system?"

Then Hutchinson, with her impact-resistant exterior, cracked a smile. She said, "I do. I do." She added, "Well, I'm near retirement. And I do have some free time coming up." She thought for a minute, flipped the two-page clemency application back and forth, then said, "All right. This looks doable. See what you can do—I'll leave it up to you. Let's keep in touch."

After seven years away, Vicki Hutchinson was back. Days later she emailed that she had bumped into Jennifer Tunnard at the courthouse. They talked, and Tunnard handed over Panna's files with no issues. A week after that, her office called me; they had a copy of the files ready for me to pick up. I drove up that afternoon. They were neatly packed in a tote bag.

On Saturday, Chan and Song let Panna know, "We got Vicki back." Panna was thrilled.

———

My task of finding more cases would entail legwork and creativity: calls to lawyers and judges, sending certified letters, going to town libraries for local books, paging through yearbooks, sifting newspaper microfiche, requesting reports from various police departments, questioning the incarcerated and some veteran nurses, contacting reporters, going to the LOB in Hartford, and even knocking on neighborhood doors—stuff I kind of liked doing. However, most were false leads and dead ends. News coverage for "baby killer" crimes was usually local, or non-existent; most escaped detection. Unless the mother was wealthy or in college, neither the internet nor statewide newspapers picked up on it. Adding to my frustration, the press was loose with its labels; a "newborn" might be a baby weeks or months old.

At the medical center where I worked, some older ICU nurses were certain of a case or two. One recalled a patient she had who told her that she "left her dead newborn at an I-95 rest stop bathroom in Milford." There was only one stop—I checked it out. The Milford Police Department and town library had nothing on that one. Did it happen? Yeah, probably.

The nation's collective memory regarding neonaticide was formed largely by a pair of cases that occurred within an eight-month period in 1996-7, one in New Jersey, the other in Delaware. Two teenage mothers disposed of their newborn babies in the trash, then went on as if nothing happened. One was the "Prom Mom," Melissa Drexler, and the other was a University of Delaware student, Amy Grossberg, who, after throwing her baby in a dumpster, joined her conspiring boyfriend in a motel. Cover stories in the national media depicted them in the most demonic way. Public attention on them, however, faded quickly. Their judges felt they deserved mercy. Few realize that both women were released from prison after only two to three years and have gone on to lead untroubled lives.

There were nights when my wife found me missing from my side of the bed. It might be 3:00 a.m. and I would have dashed off with a brilliant idea. Our dining room looked like a basement file room. In neatly ordered stacks, I had police reports, psychological summaries, newspaper articles, research papers on neonaticide, letters of support. Song, taking stock of my drive, came over to our house a few times to power-wash the deck, trim some trees, and replace the glass on our deck table.

By dribs and drabs, one discovery led to another and I hit my stride.

————

Meriden is a mid-sized manufacturing city a half-hour south of Hartford. Because of one mysterious case, it became the state's emotional nerve center for any abandoned baby. For over three decades, the Baby David Paul homicide case remained open. Other towns had neonaticide or infanticide cases, some that remained unsolved, grew "cold," and faded from memory—but not Meriden. They embraced little David Paul and refused to let him be forgotten, in fact, celebrated his short life each year on the anniversary of his body's discovery.

In the early morning of January 2, 1988, a woman walking on the side of a road spotted a baby in a parking lot. The boy was wrapped in a pink blanket; he was propped up by a tree where he could be seen; but he froze. Police called in the FBI and together they worked the case for decades, never finding the mother. They referred to the Bible in naming the boy David Paul. Every two or three years the lead detective handed it off to a fresh set of eyes.

I showed up the morning following New Year's Day 2013, in the falling snow and biting wind for the annual graveside ceremony. Channel 8 News was there. I chatted with the detectives, and because of my obvious interest, was invited by the Meriden Chief of Police to pore through the investigative files to see if I could come up with any new leads. They gave me a private room, three cardboard boxes full of paper-work and photos, and all the time I needed. There had been only one really viable suspect: neighbors had spotted a woman, pregnant, then not pregnant, but with no baby. Eventually, her DNA cleared her. After that, the only practical hope was that the mother, now probably over fifty, would voluntarily come forward and allow the Meriden police to close the books.

I had no illusions that I would spot something that hundreds before me had overlooked. Instead, I used the opportunity to write a two-page letter to the department, telling them what I had learned about neonati-cide in Connecticut and the unseen plight of the desperate mothers. I don't know how they took that: I never heard back.

A break finally came in January 2020. Tracing the baby's DNA through GEDmatch, an online company that compares autosomal DNA data files from different testing companies (like 23andMe and Ancestry.com), the mother was tracked down. Standing before a row of reporters exactly thirty-two years after that dreadful day, she told them, "I was twenty-six and single. My life was a mess. I left the baby, thinking someone would find him. I have been waiting for the police to knock on my door." She was remorseful, convincingly so. The twenty-year statute of limitations was up; she was not charged.

———

More neonaticide cases followed.

Twelve years before David Paul, there was a tragedy at an exclusive girls boarding school. Miss Porter's School, in Farmington, though tiny, had a top-heavy alumni list: to wit, Jacqueline Bouvier Kennedy and Gloria Vanderbilt. In November 1976, a student pulled out a trash bag from under a bed in a Victorian house dormitory. Inside was a suffo-cated baby. There was little question as to who the mother was. All fall, a fourteen-year-old freshman had been walking around campus in maternity clothes. One day the story was making national news. The next day it disappeared. The girl was back home. No one was charged, no name was released. The Farmington Police today claim there are no files on this case and they have no recall of it.

In 2002, a seventeen-year-old Stamford High student and her boyfriend buried their newborn in his backyard. This one made *The New York Times*. After the girl's family retained a Park Avenue lawyer, no charge was made, no names released. Around that same time, Stamford had another case. This time it was a woman who cleaned houses in order to support her three children in Honduras, one of them on dialysis. Having no insurance or legal papers, she became distraught when she found out she was pregnant and killed her newborn. Once she was in custody and with no money to wire home, her twelve-year-old on dialysis died. Her name is Angelina and she got a seventeen-year sentence. For a while, she and Panna shared a tier. Panna found her to be quiet and sweet, and said she never bothered anyone.

A few towns over, in a city park in Fairfield, the body of a newborn was found in 1986. The wounds on the body had the hallmarks of a Caribbean religious cult called *palo*, in a kind of ritualistic murder. Police were uncertain if it was a hoax. It has remained a cold case with no leads.

And in 1998, a twenty-two-year-old East Hartford mother of a three-year-old, whose apartment looked like a drug den, hid her pregnancy, delivered in the bathroom, and threw the baby in the trash—all so her boyfriend wouldn't see it. Unaware of this, the boyfriend tossed the bag of trash over the fence into the neighbor's yard, where their dog discovered the baby. After twelve and a half years at York, she was released, had another child, and is now active in prison reform.

In my PowerPoint presentation about Panna's case (to generate support for her clemency), one slide had a spreadsheet-like summary of each Connecticut case and the resulting sentence. People in the audience have asked about the socioeconomic distinctions or a possible racial bias. Even though the sample size was small, disparities were hard to miss. Only I knew the race of each woman. The darker-skinned women had the longest sentences.

———

After three-plus years of researching cases, I called it quits. Including Panna's, I had eleven cases. Seven could be compared to Panna's. The psychiatrist and neonaticide expert Philip Resnick had drawn two distinct profiles of these mothers. In a 1990 article in the *British Journal of Psychiatry*, he split them into premeditated versus non-premeditated. Those in the latter category were emotionally and sexually immature, and faced intense societal pressure. The categories strikingly correlated with age. This was a demarcation I would use. I drew a simple straight line separating my cases: teens, like Panna, versus non-teens, who were demonstrably premeditated.

Two of the teen cases were unresolved and not charged, with no available files—the high schooler from Stamford and the fourteen-year-old student at Miss Porters. I set those two aside, though the evidence was convincing that they should be in Panna's subset, and would weigh in favorably for her. Boiling it all down, I was left with a single legitimately qualifying teen: Julia Gee, the seventeen-year-old from Cheshire. After all that work, I had only one; I needed more.

I'd get two more soon after. They were both teens, nineteen-year-olds. One was an older case from North Haven that had continued to elude me. The other, from East Hartford, would happen in 2014, during our final stages of preparing Panna's brief.

Their sentences would tip the balance on Panna's fate.

CHAPTER THIRTY
TIMBER LANE

For a couple of years, one report sat quietly in my to-do file. From time to time, I went back to it, frustrated that it continued to be a non-starter. I don't remember how I stumbled on it. It was simply a two-inch photocopied article from the *North Haven Citizen*, a weekly community newspaper:

Newborn Found Dead

Autopsy failed to reveal what killed the infant. He was swaddled in towels in the woods near a North Haven home. No obvious lethal injuries were present. The police were contacted by a 19-year-old woman. Sgt. Merrithew declined to identify the woman, although she lived near where the baby was found. The police refer to her as the witness in the case and haven't said whether she is the mother. No charges were filed in the death.

It was similar to many leads I got, with a missing name or date or age of the baby. If not for the word "newborn" in this report, I would have tossed it.

In 2013 and again in 2014, I took what little I had to the North Haven Police Department. No one remembered the case. One told me, "It's gotta be old," because Sergeant Merrithew was now a captain. Merrithew himself had no recall for it. The sergeant behind the glass gave me names and numbers of a couple of officers who might help. One was an old investigator, and the other, a guy upstairs in the file room. I called both, but no luck.

On June 13, 2015, after my first talk on neonaticide before a handful of people at *Books & Co.*, a Hamden independent bookstore, a real estate agent named Eileen Smith came forward to tell me, "There was another dead newborn found in the woods in North Haven." I told her I knew as much and no more. Eileen said, "But I have the name and address of a neighbor who might help. It was in her backyard where they found the baby."

"But that was a good twenty years ago," I pointed out.

She replied, "Oh, but Margaret's still there."

The next day my wife and I went to the address she gave us, on Dent Drive in North Haven. We knocked on Margaret's door. An elderly woman answered. She was immediately wary, staying behind the closed glass door as we explained who we were. Did she remember the crime? Yes. And the year? She gave us that too—1988. And finally, rather reluctantly, the name of the mother: Dana Waite.

I went back to the North Haven police, who knew me by now and were polite and helpful. They assured me that they would find the file and give me a call. Four days later they did; the report was ready to be picked up. While I was at work, Connie drove to the police station, went upstairs to the file room, got the report (some fifty pages in all), and handed over a check for $35. Sitting on the headquarters' entrance steps, she texted me: *At NHPD. Looking at files.*

After several minutes another text popped up: *OMG!*

On October 26, 1988, Elaine Hunter, a social worker at the junior high school, called the North Haven police. She said that she had a student in her office claiming to have seen a dead infant in her sister's dresser drawer.

"What's her home address?" asked Captain Onofrio, who took the call.

"She says Three Timber Lane."

"What's her name?"

"Noreen Waite."

"How old is she?"

"Twelve."

"Twelve? C'mon."

"Officer, she's credible."

"Okay, keep her there. Get her mother there. You got that? How do I find you?"

"The junior high school. We'll have someone waiting out front. The mom's here."

"Just sit tight and don't ask her anything, nothing."

The captain informed Detective Murphy of what little he had and asked him to go check out the Timber Lane address while he headed to the junior high.

Eighth-grader Noreen, her mother, Hannah, and another student, Pamela, waited for the police in Mrs. Hunter's office. Captain Onofrio arrived and questioned Noreen about what she saw.

The previous evening, as Noreen told it, she went into her sister's bedroom to borrow some clothes. She pulled the top drawer out from the dresser, saw a green duffle bag, and zipped it open. Inside was a black bandana. When she pulled on it, a baby's head appeared. It had a plastic bag over it. "It was dead."

The captain asked her, "Was it a white baby?"

"Yeah."

"Did it look full-sized?" He held his arms apart.

"Yeah, I think so."

"And did you see if it was a boy or girl?"

"It was a boy." She added, "The room really kind of smelled."

Noreen said she ran to her 20-year-old brother Michael's room and told him. She stood by while Michael looked into the drawer and called out, "What the hell is that?" He stared at it, poked it, and backed away. He told her not to tell anyone, then called a friend.

Around 10:00 p.m., Noreen's older sister Dana came home, went straight to her room, and turned off the light like she was going to bed. The smell was spreading through the house. Michael knocked on Dana's door, she came out, and they both went into Michael's room. From the kitchen, Noreen could hear parts, but not all, of the conversation. Dana came into the kitchen, looked directly at Noreen and said, "Don't you tell anyone about this."

Noreen asked her, "Whose baby is it?"

"I can't tell you that. But don't worry about it and don't tell anyone."

The next morning, Noreen saw Michael and asked him, "Where's the baby?"

He told her, "Don't worry about it."

Dana followed, pointed at Noreen and said, "You're not going to tell anyone about this, right?"

But Noreen said, "I might. Whose baby is it?"

Dana said, "I can't tell you that. But the mother is a lot younger than you. Now shut up."

The previous night Noreen had called her friend, Pamela (the one now present in the office). At school, Noreen and Pamela decided to tell Mrs. Hunter, the social worker.

Because Noreen was only twelve, before contacting the police, Mrs. Hunter called Hannah Waite, Noreen's mother. Hannah was in the room, sitting quietly. The Connecticut State Police Crime Squad obtained a search warrant for the home, signed by the judge, and headed to the 3 Timber Lane address.

Earlier in the day, after being told of the possibility of a dead infant at that address, Detective Murphy responded. The street was one of the tonier addresses in North Haven, with colonials and farm-style homes set back in well-shaded yards. The North Haven police knew the Waite address. They had had a number of complaints from neighbors, disturbed by the loud music and cars parked on the lawn. Murphy also knew the owner, Eamon Waite, who was in the front yard with a leaf-blower when the detective arrived. He said, "Mr. Waite, we had a report of a little suspicious activity. Mind if I look around?"

"Anything I need to worry about?"

"Probably nothing. I may need to talk to Dana Waite. She here?"

"Yeah, she's around. You're free to go inside." Mr. Waite opened the door for the detective.

In the backyard was a young woman in sweats, hanging laundry. She appeared to be about nineteen or twenty, athletic-looking, with dark shoulder-length hair. "Are you Dana?" he asked.

"Yes." She stopped what she was doing.

"I'm here because of a problem. Seems a baby was found. You know anything about a baby?"

She looked up at him and said, "A baby? No sir. I don't know anything about a baby. I don't even know of any problem."

"I think it was your sister who called." He paused and said, "Noreen?"

"Noreen, yeah, that sounds like her."

"She said she found a baby in a chest of drawers."

"I have no idea. I never believe half of what she says."

"Mind if we go inside, you and me?"

She said, "No." They went part-way into her bedroom. The door was open and Dana's father was in partial view. Detective Murphy said he had a few more questions.

"Go ahead," she said. Another officer, Captain Ori, arrived. They read the Miranda warnings to Dana.

When he instructed Dana that they could stop anytime, she said, "I'm okay." At one point, she got up to get a cigarette, lit up, and smoked while in the house.

"A duffle bag, do you know anything about it?"

"I know I have a green one if that's what you mean."

"Where is it?" She pointed to a drawer on the left side of the dresser.

By that time two C. S. P. Forensic officers had arrived with the search warrant. Murphy directed them to the drawer. The techs, slipping on gloves, didn't see the duffle bag, but did see a shoe box stuffed with bloody clothes. Rancid fluid had leaked to the drawer below.

The detective got up to look at it closely and said to Dana, "What's all this?"

Dana said, "That? Okay, maybe there was a baby."

"Oh. Maybe? Where is it?"

She pointed out the window to a wooded area across the street not far from another house. Minutes later one of the techs walked across the road and, following where she pointed, and found the green duffle bag. He held it up calling out, "Something inside, sergeant."

Murphy said, "Dana, this doesn't look good."

"It's a long story, sir."

The duffle bag, with the bottom wet and stained, was placed on a plastic sheet in the backyard and the area was secured with yellow crime tape. A tech carefully unzipped the bag. A partially decomposed infant was inside. A plastic sandwich bag was pulled over the face. The body stuck to the bag and couldn't be turned over. He told the other tech, "Forget it. Let's get it up to Farmington. Call the ME." Dana's mother arrived and, seeing the scene called, "Dana?"

Detective Murphy explained to Dana and her mother, "I think we need to go to the station. You both will ride with me. Don't say a thing. We'll talk there."

———

In the interview room, Detective Murphy said, "Dana, we've got a little situation here. How about you tell me about this baby?"

Dana said, "The baby. Well. I met this girl, Sarah."

"Sarah? How old is Sarah?"

Sarah was sixteen, she said. Dana said she had met her about two months earlier, on the seawall in the Cove section of New Haven. They met there a couple more times and Sarah called Dana a few times. During September, Dana and her mother were in Ireland. When she got back, Sarah called again. Their conversations were general—girl stuff, nothing important.

Several nights earlier, just before midnight on a Sunday, Sarah called.

She was two blocks away, at the Exxon gas station at the corner of Skiff and Whitney. She needed Dana to come and bring some sort of carry bag. Dana brought her green duffle bag, the one she had used in Ireland. From the gas station, the two girls crossed the street, slipping behind Ted's Cleaners. Sarah had been clumsily holding onto a brown paper bag wrapped with tape. She said something to the effect of, "The baby is in the bag."

Dana became scared, confused, and upset. She left her carry bag, telling Sarah she needed to go for a walk. When she came back, she took the duffle back, feeling something creepy inside. She brought it home, put it in her dresser. A few nights later, her brother, Michael, found it and confronted her. In her letter, she claimed that she took it out to the woods and threw leaves on it.

The cops didn't believe the story and told her, "Look, I need you to submit to an exam by a doctor? A female exam. Okay?"

"If I need to. I'll prove to you what I say."

Detective Murphy told her he would return the next day with a warrant for a complete gynecological exam.

Late the next morning on October 27, Murphy drove Dana and her mother, Hannah, in a squad car to Yale New Haven Hospital. An anxious hour passed while they sat in the emergency room waiting area. Dana was nervous, dying for a cigarette. Several times Hannah tried to comfort her, also telling her smoking wasn't allowed.

Finally, Hannah went to Detective Murphy, telling him, "Dana is ready to talk." The detective got up and asked Dana to follow him. They went outside to the parking lot. It was cool and cloudy. He let her light up and finish the cigarette. Minutes later, Dana's mother located them and said the desk had called her name. Dana, with her face in her hands and weeping, said, "Mom, I told Detective Murphy I'm the mother."

Detective Murphy, feeling a sense of urgency, said, "Sorry ma'am, I need to take her to my car for a statement." Her mother gave her a quick hug and went inside.

In the squad car with heat going and all the lights on, Detective Murphy made a recording as Dana gave her statement.

Sunday evening, October 16, the baby was born. Dana's boyfriend, Vincent Vollano, who was the father, never knew she was pregnant, nor did her family. Cramps started at eleven that night, followed immediately by her water breaking. Taking only a towel, she headed across the road into the woods. After the baby was delivered, it cried. She pulled the umbilical cord with the attached placenta. Leaving the baby and the afterbirth on the towel, she went back home to change and deal with her bleeding. She returned around 2:00 a.m., bringing her duffle bag.

Wrapping the crying baby in the towel, she placed it in the bag. She remained there, shivering, rocking, until 6:00 a.m., whispering, "Shhh. Quiet."

Dana told the detective that after returning to her room, she was unable to sleep. At 8:30 a.m. she went back to check on the baby, taking a black bandana with her. The baby had stopped crying. She thought it was dead. She tied the bandana on the baby's head, telling the detective, "I really don't know why I did that." She left the baby there in the bag and didn't come back until two nights later, Wednesday, close to midnight. Then Friday, she returned to see if it was still there, and again the following Monday, just before daybreak. She carried the bag to her room and put it in the dresser drawer. That's where her sister, Noreen, found it the next evening.

The detective said, "The baby was nine days old."

Dana said, "Yeah, I guess. And I never even knew if it was a boy or girl."

She stayed up, took it outside, this time to a neighbor's backyard.

"That's where you guys found it," Dana said to the police.

After she finished her statement in the squad car, Dana was led inside to the emergency room. An ob-gyn resident examined her, finding a discharge from her uterus and breasts. Both were consistent with a recent delivery and Dana's timeline in her statement. The doctor gave her a prescription for iron pills and filled out the police affidavit for Detective Murphy.

Dana had to wait another two hours for a psychiatry consultation. A resident found her to be coherent, able to judge right from wrong, and not a suicidal risk. The hospital discharged her to her home.

———

Hannah Waite confessed to Detective Murphy that she had seen the weight gain and some swelling in Dana, but it never occurred to her that she might be pregnant. "I don't know how I missed it." She asked, "What's going to happen to her?"

Detective Murphy told her, "We wait for the autopsy. Take it from there. I'm not going to lie to you. It's pretty serious. But let's see what the ME says."

Local reporters knew about the dead newborn in the woods and knew that it was at the medical examiner's office. But the police released no names, claiming they were following "standard procedure." They maintained a "no comment" posture for any questions.

In Farmington on October 27, a medical examiner performed the post-mortem exam in the presence of a North Haven detective. Opening the bag, the doctor saw leaves caked onto the infant, an acorn adhered to the placenta. Upon completion of the exam, for Manner of Death the doctor entered Undetermined.

Then on November 15, after reviewing the police reports, the medical examiner's office stated, "With no outward signs of injury, the Cause of Death was Exposure. Due to the surrounding circumstances, the Manner of Death is consistent with Homicide."

Questioned by reporters about any charges, the North Haven police said nothing—only that it was in the hands of the prosecutor. The police never released Dana's name to the media—a radical departure from what the Danbury police did with Panna.

———

Two weeks later, Dana Waite was advised of an outstanding arrest warrant. With her attorney by her side, she showed up at the police headquarters for a charge of Manslaughter First Degree. The police processed a puffy-eyed Dana—fingerprints and a mug shot—and gave her a court date in Meriden. Released with no bond, she provided a written promise to appear. Furthermore, because of its "sensitive nature," the Superior Court judge sealed the arrest warrant affidavit, making it unavailable to the press or public. The local paper still had no news to report on the suspicious homicide in their town. They printed what little they had.

Dana was looking at a possible twenty years and $10,000 fine. Her attorney, Richard Altschuler, an imperturbable, impeccably dressed man, had her plead "not guilty." He informed the court that in this case, Dana Waite was as much a victim as the infant.

A West Haven psychiatrist later found her to be in a state of shock and depressed at the time of the delivery. He concluded that her actions were not rational.

———

In June 1989, standing before Judge Ronan, Dana Waite entered a plea of second-degree manslaughter, under the Alford doctrine. Attorney Altschuler said a trial would be too much for her. He argued because Dana Waite (eventually) brought the baby indoors, that meant she had intended no harm. He further claimed she tried to keep him alive in the woods, adding, "She's already punished herself."

At Dana's sentencing, some months later, the Assistant State's Attorney insisted she receive a maximum ten years in prison for second-degree manslaughter, describing her actions as recklessly causing the death of a defenseless baby.

Judge Ronan silently listened. He called for the defendant, Dana Waite.

Dana stood before him, flanked by her parents on one side and her attorney on the other. The judge told her, "This is one of those rare occasions when someone didn't have control of their faculties. You were not thinking rationally. Based on your young age, you were over your head, and did not know what to do."

He sorted through some papers, paused, then, leaning into his microphone, slowly pronounced, "Miss Waite, you are to serve a five-year suspended sentence with three years' probation."

Hearing "five years," Dana turned quickly to her lawyer; he leaned her way and whispered, "No jail." The judge continued, saying that Dana Waite did not intend to harm the baby, adding, "The most severe thing that happens to you will be the memory of this incident. I see no point in incarcerating you."

After the proceeding, the Assistant State's Attorney was quoted as saying, "I still feel she should be incarcerated." He cleared his throat and added, "But I'm not going to second-guess Judge Ronan."

Dana, emerging from the courthouse, stood still at the top of the steps. She wore a grey business suit and had a tidy reddish ribbon in her flowing dark hair. She held onto her dad's arm with both of hers, as they remained there—the same girl who in her senior yearbook quoted Robert Plant: "If you die by the roadside, so be it; at least you tried."

As she took a few steps, forcing a smile, Dana couldn't hide her shaking. A few gathered friends and family stood before her. She stopped, trying to think of something to tell them, shrugged, and said, "You know what? I feel okay."

———

I kept Panna and her family abreast as I did my searches with all my findings, including this case. In the late summer of 2015, when Chan visited Panna, she said, "Doug want me to tell you, he find out about that other case. The one in North Haven."

"Mom, before you say anything. I was seventeen when I got here and I'm twenty-six now. Nothing you say can hurt me. Okay? Go ahead. What did he find?"

Chan said, "The girl never went to prison."

"Really? That's good news. Is that what he said?"

Chan smiled and said, "Yes, that's what he said."

PART EIGHT
CLEMENCY

CHAPTER THIRTY-ONE
COMMUTATION

The news out of North Haven was big.

The pieces for a clemency petition were fitting together nicely.

But Attorney Hutchinson and I were navigating without a roadmap. I made inquiries with a handful of defense attorneys and law professors; not one was able to offer any practical insight into clemency. I even ran into Superior Court Judge Jon Blue, arguably the preeminent legal mind in Connecticut, and asked about clemency hearings. He looked pensive and said, "I don't believe we have had one in a long time." By the accounts I had, he appeared to be right: clemencies weren't being done. Hearings by the Board of Pardons and Paroles (BOPP) are held at the Rowland Government Center in downtown Waterbury, so I showed up. But security stopped me; I needed an appointment to get in, they said. I told them that I couldn't get one—a catch 22. I called the office for information, but they were not forthcoming, repeatedly referring me to their website, which had me going in circles. As of this writing, the office has been closed for two years, redesigning their application process and converting to all-electronic.

I began my own research.

———

First, the basics. Clemency power—meaning offering leniency for punishment—dates back to Ancient Rome (Clementia was the goddess of forgiveness), when Julius Caesar used it to spare fallen comrades or enemies on the battlefield. In the United States, there are federal clemencies, which are granted by the president, and state clemencies, which are granted through each governor and/or an appointed board. In a 2015 essay in *University of Chicago Law Review*, Professors Rachel Barkow and Mark Osler, our national experts on clemency, described it as a tool that skirts the adversarial judicial process, offering relief for overly harsh sentences. Another expert, law professor Cara Drinan characterized it as "a way of correcting the problem of our addiction to incarceration." In a 2013 *Georgia State University Law Review* paper, she described how clemencies may be granted for diverse reasons: disproportionate sentence, unfair trial, mental or physical problems, racial discrimination, abuse, advanced age, or even the extent to which an incarcerated person had been a resource for others within the prison system. Despite this broad mandate, Drinan noted that state clemency grants are a rare occurrence.

The numbers show that the clemency process has been failing to do its job, perhaps in part because it has been shrouded in near secrecy. On the federal level, clemencies have dropped off. Franklin Roosevelt granted over 300 sentence reductions in his first term—Obama granted one. Presidents Reagan and Kennedy granted clemencies for more than 21 percent of the federal petitions during their terms. The second President Bush handed out only 11 out of 8,576 (0.1 percent), while Obama, over his two terms, did marginally better, approving 1,715 out of 33,149 (5.1%) petitions, even though he solicited applications and touted the clemency process. President Trump saw it as a tool for cronyism and payback for his political allies, beginning with the man who called himself "America's Toughest Sheriff," Joe Arpaio. By the end of the Trump administration, the number of grants were 237 (2 percent), the lowest total of any president since the start of the twentieth century.

On the state level, the tally of successful clemencies is probably lower. A quick look around the nation reveals a record that is spotty and at times puzzling. For example, Colorado has no record of its clemencies, only "a mess," as the *Denver Post* put it when their reporters investigated. In 2003, Illinois granted 167 commutations in one stroke when the state reduced the death penalty to life in prison. By contrast, Massachusetts had granted only one in the previous twenty-three years, due to the Willie Horton fallout (convicted felon who committed robbery and rape while out on a weekend furlough) and an overly complicated process. Nevada issued one because the person was "retarded." And in Missouri one person serving time was released because Pope John Paul II recommended it. As for Connecticut, records for clemency have lacked clarity, making it a challenge to tabulate them. (Note: Clemency is a broad term, which includes pardon or commutation. Commutation is simply the reduction of a prison sentence. The terms clemency and commutation tend to be used interchangeably.)

In most states, the governor, either alone or with the recommendation of a board, is authorized to commute sentences. In Connecticut that power rests with the BOPP, a panel of men and women appointed by the governor, made up mostly of those, like probation officers, who worked their way up through the corrections system, along with retired detectives or the occasional lawyer, all without clear political affiliation. It is one of only five states (the others are Georgia, Nebraska, Nevada, and Utah) that does not require a governor's sign-off. This can be seen as an advantage, allowing the governor to avoid the spotlight of unfavorable press or jeopardize re-election if the grantee commits another crime. Governors and pardon boards have become notoriously risk-averse.

In Connecticut, two high-profile events might indicate why the BOPP has become gun-shy. One was, as one law professor phrased it, "the Cheshire problem." In 2007, two men with over forty-eight arrests between them, Joshua Komisarjevsky and Steven Hayes, committed what many consider Connecticut's most horrific crime: a rape/arson/triple murder on Dr. William Petit's two daughters and wife at their home in Cheshire. Both of the convicted murderers had been on parole.

In the other case, Henry Price was back on the street after a clemency decision in 1994. Price has been convicted in a drug-related killing to go along with his fifteen other felonies. During his incarceration, he had gotten off drugs, earned his GED and college degree, and had become a minister and a drug counselor—a model incarcerated person. That earned him his early release. He became a preacher-activist and ran for city council. So far so good. But soon he was back to his old ways, becoming a pimp for six sex workers and in 2002 was sent back to prison. Released in 2020, he is in Norwich on parole until 2029.

In the nineteen years following Price's re-arrest, none of the more than six hundred clemency petitions in Connecticut were granted. Was that a coincidence? Or did those crimes by the early-released formerly incarcerated men leave an Arctic chill on the BOPP?

Emerging out of that two-decade drought was Bonnie Foreshaw.

————

Around 2012, when Panna's case first drew my interest, a clemency petition had been in the works for Bonnie Foreshaw. In fact, when I informed my friend Wally Lamb, whose prison writing program brought me to York, that I was doing behind-the-scenes work for Panna, he cautioned me to wait; he didn't want any interference in Bonnie's proceedings. So I did, and used that rare opportunity to study her hearing, hoping it would be a dress rehearsal of sorts for Panna's.

I knew Bonnie from Wally's writing class and was able to talk to her about her past; Panna knew and respected her.

Bonnie was a legend, the elder stateswoman of York, having resided there longer than anyone else. She was revered for her gentle grace, her uncut dreads, standing her ground, and her slow deliberate speech, which added to her perceived wisdom. Over her twenty-seven years at York, she had completed nearly every program and took on many voluntary positions, including hospice care. She was the subject of countless news stories and op-ed columns, had a famous novelist in her camp, was featured in a documentary by an award-winning filmmaker, and had published her own stories. Bonnie had been dragged through the courts, had filed charges which earned her time in seg (solitary confinement), stirred protestors, run through some twenty-five lawyers, and even had a superior-court judge go to bat for her. She fought the DOC and the DOC won. All this without mention of her great-grandchildren on the outside waiting for her to come home.

Pretty amazing for someone who had spent three decades in an eight-by-ten cell.

Sleeping on bare concrete had left her a physical cripple and aged her far beyond her sixty-six years. Hobbled by an arthritic back and moving at the speed of the pope, she rarely left her cell, not for food nor to shower. Women took shifts bringing her meals. The COs and even the DOC maintained a hands-off posture; she was the only one permitted to wear a skirt (a Rastafarian influence). She was also the only one allowed to go by her first name, a carryover from the polite old days. "Miss Bonnie" became a symbol for endurance, even defiance, a sign for the other York women that the system will never break you. The incarcerated women, who were probably closer to the truth than the courts, knew that there were real questions about her crime.

———

By only age twelve, Bonnie's life had begun its downward spiral—she was molested by her stepfather, then delivered their baby. By fourteen, she was on her own, roaming the streets of Miami with daughter Sylvia. Two years later, she was strapped with two more kids by different fathers, one of whom allegedly beat her with a baseball bat. Out of that muck she constructed a life. By her mid-thirties, after surviving three ruinous marriages, she owned a house in Bloomfield, Connecticut, and was a providing mother with a steady job.

For ten years, Bonnie had been a machinist for Wiremold Company in West Hartford. At one point, she had been stalked and punched by her estranged husband. Fearful and in need of protection, she bought a gun on the street for $30. The guy selling it loaded bullets into the chambers and did a pretend shoot for her.

On March 27, 1986, after putting in an extra late shift, thirty-eight-year-old Bonnie was heading home. On the way, she stopped at the Progressive League, a social club for Jamaicans that promoted cultural awareness and island patriotism. The club's reggae music and a cold Guinness seemed like the perfect thing to unwind. Since she did this maybe five times a year, she didn't expect to see anyone she knew.

Hector Freeman, a local with pending charges for assaulting a policeman, spotted Bonnie with her drink, sidled over, and offered to buy. Not interested, she left without finishing her beer. Hector followed her. Outside the club he angrily yelled, "What, you're too good to drink with me?" When Bonnie tried to get into her car, he came at her. Another woman, Joyce Amos, six months pregnant, pulled on Hector to stop him. This is where the story gets murky. Bonnie said Hector was threatening, lunged, and reached into his pockets for what she feared was a gun. She grabbed hers from the glove compartment, raised it, and pulled the trigger—a shot rang out. Overcome with fear, she got in her car and drove off. At her trial, Hector testified that he pulled Joyce Amos in front of him as a shield. Joyce, the only person showing heroism that night, took the bullet and died. Her baby could not be saved.

Bonnie was offered a plea deal in a tidy package: manslaughter and drug crimes, for twenty-five to thirty years. Bonnie rejected it, adamantly stating, "I had never done drugs in my life." The trial attracted huge media attention with a public outcry from placard-carrying right-to-lifers over the death of the unborn baby. Bonnie later told her clemency panel, "I was convicted in the press way before there was even a trial."

The judge at her trial, Paul Vasington, said, "In my experience, this was a deliberate and cold-blooded murder." He handed Bonnie Foreshaw the longest sentence ever for any woman in Connecticut at that time: forty-five years.

However, Jon Blue, who at that time was a public defender, but later became an esteemed superior-court judge, had written a memo to the head of the public defenders declaring that "Miss Foreshaw did not get a fair trial,"—a memo that resurfaced twenty-four years later through the work of an investigative journalist, Andy Thibault. Largely due to that memo and the groundswell of attention, Bonnie got her clemency hearing in 2013.

———

In that packed auditorium, even though clemency hearings are not intended to be retrials, she faced one final assault by the system: a minute dissection by the panel about her homicidal actions. In her slow-paced speech, Bonnie, in describing her counsel for the trial, a public defender named O'Toole told the panel, "When he walked over to the prosecutor's table, why, they looked like they were bosom buddies. It was like I didn't even exist." As for the gun, Bonnie had thrown it from the car across a street, and it was never found. Yet, in the courtroom, as Bonnie told it, "They pulled one out of some envelope to show the jury. Like it was my gun."

Bonnie was questioned over and over about her intention with the gun: whether she was firing a warning shot or taking direct aim at Hector. Joyce Amos's family, all wearing badges with her portrait, stood before the panel and delivered powerful testimonies asking that Bonnie complete her sentence (which meant a release in her mid-eighties). The panel had dug up a DUI and a drug possession from her monstrous files, which Bonnie claimed were false reports. At that point, I leaned over to Wally and said it didn't look good.

The panel had heard enough. It was getting messy. They recessed for forty-five minutes and returned.

All agreed that Bonnie had served her time and was rehabbed. She was granted her clemency and released in November 2013.

———

In the summer of 2014, I contacted Bonnie's lead attorney, Rich Emanuel, asking if Attorney Hutchinson and I might be able to sit down with him and go over his clemency preparatory work. He was gracious and invited us to his office in Guilford, Connecticut. As Hutchinson and I made our way up to his suite in a modern office building, she mentioned to me, "This guy is big time." Emanuel, looking dignified in a tailored suit and trim-bearded, was maybe Connecticut's top appellate lawyer, not a clemency expert by training or experience. Known around Connecticut for his diligent work, he had started his career working in a storefront neighborhood legal service office in the rough section of Bridgeport. He explained to me how, for each new case, he set aside six undisturbed months. "It's not cheap," he admitted. For Bonnie, he was pro bono.

Attorney Emanuel told me a story about a client he had from Danbury, Lawrence Miller, who spent twelve years in prison for an assault he claimed he didn't do. Emanuel believed him and refused to let go. Eventually, an incarcerated man in another prison confessed to the crime. Emanuel described that day: his drive from one prison, where he took the confession, then to the other prison, to deliver the news to Mr. Miller—that he was a free man. A great story.

Surrounded by shelves lined with leather-bound law books and photos of legal luminaries, the three of us arranged ourselves around a large table in his conference room. He opened Bonnie's six-inch clemency file and allowed us to page through it, welcoming us to use it as a template for Panna's. Because he didn't want it photocopied, I committed to memory as much as I could manage. The table of contents on the first page listed some sixty items, mostly letters and her course certificates, a number I was certain Panna's file would surpass. At one point, Emanuel patted it like a child and admitted the obvious: "I did a lot of work on this." He also told Hutchinson, with a tone of warning, that they would first ask if we did a sentence modification, a term that was new to me. By the end of the day, we had a pro bono offer from Emanuel to join us on Panna's case.

Over the ensuing months, Attorney Hutchinson and I inched along in the process, as she was in and out of trial court. As for the sentence modification, I learned that an incarcerated person files a one-page plea, with the argument for a sentence reduction written in the space provided. Connecticut is unique in that the plea must go to the prosecutor (or if the original prosecutor is no longer there, then the same office). The prosecutor alone decides if it warrants proceeding to a hearing before the same judge who did the sentencing. Some tell you not to waste your time—a modification, much like a *habeas corpus* petition, is often attempted, because it's easy to submit, but rarely succeeds. Prosecutors don't like to admit they got the sentence wrong. Also, few lawyers get involved with either a modification or a clemency on big cases. It can be a lot of work and their client is likely without resources or has a violent conviction with strong victim impact statements.

Once the appeals are exhausted and the prosecutor has denied a modification, the only option left is a clemency hearing. To earn that opportunity, one must pass the screening.

———

Clemency screenings are simple affairs, scheduled with a BOPP panel of three who go through a stack of petitions, typically consisting of a one-page application along with a skimpy file of supporting documents, several letters, and numerous prison certificates. They quickly rule on each file, whether to grant or deny a hearing. Very often, the nature of the crime (read: violent) gets it denied. Numerous disciplinary tickets can be a problem. Or if there will be strong victim impact statements. In a typical year in Connecticut, only a couple make it to a hearing, though as of this writing that number is increasing, perhaps due to the influence of Governor Lamont.

In preparation for Panna's hearing, I was able to attend two in addition to Bonnie's. Rather low-key, they are held in the Rowland State Government Center in Waterbury, with the panel behind a table in a small room. Family members gather in an adjoining room, with both rooms able to view the incarcerated man or woman, seated at their prison, via a one-way TV monitor. They might have a lawyer present, sitting quietly at the Rowland Center.

Panna and I were focused on one thing: getting to the clemency hearing, where she and her work would be on display.

First, we needed the screening. But there would be two bumps in the road.

One was a sticky item that I had noticed in Bonnie's hearing: the psychiatrist's statement. He was very much to-the-point, clearing her of any psychological concerns. He added that he would see her in his office at no charge. The witnesses in the auditorium clapped.

I then decided we needed a psych evaluation for Panna. Though it would not be easy.

The other bump would be a surprise in the summer 2014.

CHAPTER THIRTY-TWO

K.H.A

Working in neurology for decades, I got to know the psychiatry service at our medical center—we often saw the same patients and made referrals back and forth. Playing the same game as when we needed a lawyer, in my search for a psychiatrist for Panna's case, I made inquiries with about eight clinicians I knew, in some cases dropping off her file. I made a point that members of the pardon board are not trained in psychology and need an answer to a simple question: is she safe? Some of the psychiatrists were reluctant because they had not done a fellowship in forensics, and a couple had high fees; one estimate was $15,000. But in the end, they all rebuffed me. While making those rounds, I kept circling back to a certain name that popped up on my radar: the Khmer Health Advocates (KHA). I looked at the website. It was a clinic for Southeast Asian refugees—an odd thing for Connecticut, I thought.

A concern about Panna was her home environment, specifically her father, Song. Descriptions of his bouts of rage, though buried deep in the text of one private investigator's report, nevertheless, were there. In the report done shortly after Panna's arrest, the detective was told that if Song had discovered Panna's pregnancy, they feared that he might kick her out of the house—"or even kill her." This fear was based not on

Song personally, but on the previously documented behavior of Cambodian fathers. Those few words, wielded in the hands of this prosecutor, could stop us. Song had to be cleared. Never mind that for the last nine years he had shouldered immense guilt, had had no incidents, no scrapes with the law, was ridiculously pious, and had devoted every fiber of his existence to Panna.

In our discussions, Song had described his behavior or his many symptoms on the PTSD checklist. Those included him banging his head on the wall in the middle of the night. Khmer Rouge survivors had been reported to have an exceptionally high incidence of PTSD, with fifty percent incidence in their American-born offspring as well. Worried about Song, I made him an appointment with the KHA.

On the appointment day, Song arrived with two sealed letters in his pocket addressed to the clinician, both of which I had carefully prepared. The first laid out his traumatic life history, something he would be hesitant to describe. The second letter, two full pages, presented Panna's current situation.

I called Chan that evening, curious about their visit. It went well, she said. They were seen, she thought, by a doctor named Miller. By her account, he took hours with the two of them and kept going back to the letters.

On a follow-up appointment two weeks later, Dr. Miller examined Chan as well, spending more hours with the two of them. Chan told me that he again referred to my letters.

I had reached a state of desperation. The prosecution could cite the risk of Panna repeating the crime of neonaticide, even though, as noted by Michelle Oberman in her letter of support, it's virtually unheard of. Or the board might conclude that Panna being in the home with Song was unsafe. Khmer Health Advocates appeared to be my last chance.

———

KHA was established in the 1980s by three clinical veterans, better yet, willing to stake their careers and forgo any stable income on a high-minded venture in healthcare.

After her last visit, Chan told me the words I longed to hear:

"Doug, the doctor want to talk to you." I made an appointment and located the clinic. The offices were in an unlikely place, a rather tony suburban village, West Hartford. At the far end of a small row of stores and boutiques, I found a glass door marked—or better, unmarked—with only the number 1125. The stairs were steep and just wide enough for one, like those heading up to an attic. The top door opened into a dimly lit hall where I came upon three more doors, each filled with Cambodian script. Just as I was about to pick one, I was greeted by the unmistakable Theavny Kuoch, a saintly Cambodian woman whom I had read up on. She had escaped the Khmer Rouge, losing nineteen members of her family, arriving in the US as a battered eighty-pound skeleton. Part of her remarkable recovery, as she battled through bouts of depression and PTSD, was to establish this clinic, now recognized by the United Nations. She led me into one room and introduced me to the nurse practitioner, Mary Scully, a matronly all-business woman who sported a stethoscope and wore old sandals despite it being November. I had read about her too; for a decade she had lived and worked in the refugee tents on the Thai border.

Four of us sat in a circle around a coffee table with a couple of pizzas, a stack of paper plates, and a two-liter bottle of Coke. Dr. Richard Miller, the clinic's director, and the staff had set up this noon-time conference.

Theavny was short, radiant, and with her heavy accent, tricky to follow. Dr. Miller, very soft-spoken, wasn't much better. When he did talk, it was all Yankee, sparse on words. He was bearded and looked like a Vermont doctor who still did house calls in his 1980s Volvo. On the wall were his plaques, all bona fide: degrees from Harvard and Case Western, and psych training at the Institute of Living. Mary was the go-to person, always on point. Together, Dr. Miller and Mary had over a century of experience doing this stuff.

"Concerning Panna," said Dr. Miller as he lifted the cover on one of the boxes, "this case got by us. I don't know how. We *do* know the Cambodian community. We..."

"A big miss for us." Mary jumped in.

As I took stock of the three of them, the psychiatrist Dr. Miller, clinician Mary Scully, and specialist in refugee health Theavny Kuoch—I said, "I'm going to be blunt. I need help."

"Okay," said Dr. Miller.

"Will you do the psych eval on Panna? Sorry, I'm tired. I don't want to waste time—mine or yours."

With no change in tone and never looking up, Dr. Miller calmly responded, "Yes, we'll do it."

"What about your fee?"

Mary turned to Dr. Miller and shrugged. "We do a lot of things for no fee," she said. "I mean any donation is appreciated." Mary leaned in, narrowed her eyes, then said, "You do realize, we may find something damaging against Miss Krom."

"Fine. It's a chance we take," I said.

"Doug, why the eighteen years for this girl?" asked Dr. Miller. "Seems harsh."

I told him, "The press, the police interview, the prosecutor, the murder charge, like an assault, all wrapped up in, what? Four days?"

Mary said, "She go to trial?"

"No, she took a plea."

"For eighteen. Really?" she asked.

"Everybody pleas. DA knocked off a couple years. It's prosecutor overreach."

"Any other cases like it?" said Dr. Miller.

"A few. She got the longest sentence. We're putting together a clemency packet, myself and a couple lawyers. Her psychological eval will be a big part. Essential really."

Mary, who I believed called the shots, said, "We don't want to know any more. Get us a release. We'll go see her." She got up. "Excuse me, I have a patient."

Theavny took me around. It was a dingy place, somewhat in disarray, with garage-sale furnishings. Waste cans were overflowing and it cried out for a good vacuuming. Perched on nearly every desk were teetering piles of papers and antiquated 100-pound computers. Faded pictures of Cambodia from the 1950s lined the walls, showing temples and jeweled elephants. I poked my head into one room, home base for Lou, the tech guy. Old desktop computers on the floor blocked the way and wires were strung across the room like tenement clotheslines, some tied into giant figure-eight bundles.

This was their labor of love—that was clear. They trained social work students from UConn, published papers, and took care of communities of once-tortured Cambodians, or in fact anyone who walked in the door. It was all managed on a shoestring budget sustained by donations and grants—and those were drying up. Mary had lifted one application off her desk to show me. It ran to a hundred pages.

———

Months later, at a Buddhist New Year celebration at the Bristol temple, Song introduced me to Chithserey, another Cambodian survivor, one of the Khmer Health Advocates administrators. She told me that things at the clinic were dire and sometimes paychecks weren't going out. But no one was leaving. Even with this news, the KHA never wavered in their commitment to Panna.

CHAPTER THIRTY-THREE
MAGICAL THINKER

By the fall of 2014, after spending a few years on the roads in Connecticut, I was running out of new leads. I had a total of nine neonaticide cases. Four of them fell into our target category; teens like Panna. However, for two of those teens the only accounts I could come up with were one-column newspaper clips, in *The New York Times* and a Farmington town gazette. Both girls had attended upscale schools—Stamford High and Miss Porter's prep school—and perhaps because of the demographics normally associated with that (the one at Stamford High had a Park Avenue lawyer), they apparently never faced charges. In fact, I saw nothing in terms of their investigation, nor were their names released to the press. Instead of providing powerful counterbalances to Panna's lengthy sentence, each case was kind of a black box. All suspicions aside, by the letter of the law, I could not use them for comparisons—they weren't crimes.

In time, I did get more information on those two. We made contact with the celebrity lawyer, Mickey Sherman, for the girl who attended Stamford High School. He informed us that since the baby had been buried, the autopsy was inconclusive as to whether it had been alive at birth. No charge could be made in terms of neonaticide (she and her boyfriend may have been charged for improper disposal of a body).

And during one of my talks, at UConn Law School, a woman in the audience told me she had been the lawyer for Miss Porter's School during the time when that freshman student delivered and disposed of the baby in the dorm. One would surmise that within the tranquil well-to-do township, the elite private school and the local prosecutor had no desire to create a spectacle. (It had already been the subject of a national column by conservative columnist George F. Will.) She affirmed that the case was not investigated, not ruled on, and the young girl never faced a court.

It was a different story for the other two teens, the one from Cheshire and the one from North Haven. Both were prosecuted, both took Alford pleas, and were sentenced. Those sentences, each a fraction of Panna's, would become two crucial pieces in our file to demonstrate how her sentence was comparably excessive. Their names were never released to the public, sparing them the added persecution, and prejudice, by the press—something that Panna and her family had to endure.

Although the final listing of teens we compiled was short, adding to it would require more work than the prosecutor, State's Attorney Stephen Sedensky, was likely to expend. Adding to the difficulty, there were no statutes for neonaticide (under twenty-four hours) or infanticide (under one year); prosecutors love statutes. Nevertheless, if his office came up with one case with a long sentence, it would kill our data and our argument.

While Connie created the tabulations and graphics, I kept in constant communication with the psychology people at KHA and other interested parties about our as-yet scheduled hearing date. I continued giving PowerPoint presentations about Panna's case, including background about her family's past and the other neonaticide cases, in a mix of public and academic settings—partly to test the waters on public reaction to her crime story. I received no pushback—no outrage, no protests. Well, just one. A pediatric nurse, who attended my medical school bioethics lecture, boldly declared, "This was murder." It caught me like a left hook. I should have been ready with a reply—"Actually, Panna was charged with murder"—but I wasn't. Otherwise, everyone displayed sympathy for the Kroms (Song and Chan attended a few talks), even standing up and applauding for them at the end.

I was putting final touches on the petition binder, which was neatly divided into twenty sections. Vicki Hutchinson, away in Russia, regularly checked in by email. Panna, fully on board, was gathering her certificates and perusing the file, which had been delivered to her. Connie was added to her visitor's list and was going with the Kroms on Saturdays to see her. An insistent Song, in his charming way of being part of the team and expressing thanks, was up on a ladder refinishing my portico or mixing cement to even out my sidewalk. On all fronts, we were in good shape.

———

One August evening in 2014, I was in the kitchen when Connie called me into the living room. "Doug, come here! You're not going to believe this." I dashed in. "Look," she said, pointing at the TV.

The scroll read: "Breaking News: Newborn Baby Found Dead in Trash Can." A reporter in rain gear stood before the camera. Behind him was someone's front yard, floodlit and strung with yellow crime tape.

"Oh my god," I whispered. We both stared, motionless. "This is not good."

The Channel 3 Eyewitness News lead story was about a new neonaticide, although they didn't use that word. There was a certain grave perspective to this news that only I was focused on—this was the first one in Connecticut since Panna's in 2006. Eight years.

Sadly, it was an all-too-familiar tale, with the starting point an attention-grabbing headline, but short on important details. A teenager checked into the University of Connecticut Children's Medical Center Emergency Room and her exam showed signs of a recent delivery. The girl admitted to very little and denied a birth, so the hospital staff notified the East Hartford Police. At the girl's residence—where the Channel 3 reporter stood—the cops had discovered a dead newborn.

Two days later, the same evening news opened with a press conference. Pam Sawyer, a long-serving Republican State Representative from Connecticut's 55th district, backed by a phalanx of well-suited supporters, stood in the Legislative Office Building, making a pronouncement.

In response to the recent newborn tragedy, she was calling for a task force to find innovative ways to get the word out about the little-known Safe Haven Law. She reminded the viewers that Safe Haven allows a woman to drop off a newborn, up to thirty days, at any ER in Connecticut with no questions asked. The baby would be turned over to the Department of Children and Families (DCF), then to a waiting adoptive family. In 2000, one year after the first such law was enacted in Texas, Pam Sawyer was the lead in drafting the bill in Connecticut. Over the ensuing fourteen-year period a total of twenty-seven babies had been saved. As she pointed out, this still-nameless and unfortunate accused girl, said to be nineteen, with her tragically dead newborn, should have never slipped through the safety net. Representative Sawyer, with the posture and countenance of a field general, spoke into the row of mics, pleading for "creative people from all walks to work together" in order to generate more publicity for the law, so that this incident "will be our last." Connie looked at me.

I wanted to be on that task force. I zipped off an email to Representative Sawyer, including a one-paragraph snapshot of the nine Connecticut neonaticide cases I had identified. I was afraid of my somber image: homicides, adolescent girls carted off to prison, their sentences measured by decades. They are the dark side of the larger picture that includes her otherwise sunny Safe Haven Law with a young couple holding their new baby.

I got an emailed template response. No mention of the crimes, but she did invite me into the group.

My goal was to get the backing of this powerful state legislator for Panna, no matter how many Tuesdays I had to take the day off to trek up to Hartford (the task force met once a month) or how many times I had to ignore the obvious discomfiture when I pushed Panna Krom, this faceless "felon" and her plight onto Representative Sawyer's austere committee. The DCF was always present, as were different department heads, school principals, state legislators, police chiefs, and even a judge. After about a year of this, Pam Sawyer, with her immense political clout, was totally on board. She would pull other passing state senators and representatives into our meetings and introduce me and the young girl at York "who desperately needs our help."

In time, while the committee was regularly checking for any updates on the status of the unfortunate East Hartford girl, Panna's name slowly percolated through the list of agenda items to become its top priority. The groundswell of support and recognition was comforting for Panna.

I kept Vicki Hutchinson abreast of anything new on the East Hartford case. In one early email, I stated the obvious: "Vicki, if this poor East Hartford girl gets a long sentence, even ten years, we're done." Not working in our favor, much less the girl's, were some of her particulars: she was Puerto Rican (though she was light-skinned); as the police chief confided to me, her personal life appeared "pretty messed up;" and she had a stodgy public defender who rebuffed my offer of background data on neonaticide. We could only track it from afar, wait, and hope.

Exactly one year after her arrest, the case was adjudicated. The girl, now named, pleaded guilty to a reduced second-degree manslaughter, which would give her one to ten years. I gained access to more details about her crime.

———

On August 12, 2014, Officer Ian Allison of the East Hartford Police Department responded to a call from an ER physician at the Connecticut Children's Medical Center. The doctor was seeing Ana Castillo-Pichardo, a nineteen-year-old female with a bleeding complaint. She was found to have vaginal hemorrhaging and lacerations, an enlarged uterus, and a positive hCG blood test—all evidence that she was postpartum. He suspected that the delivery had occurred within the last two days. The patient denied that there was any baby. The doctor had no idea where it might be. According to medical records, she had been seen in the clinic in March for the pregnancy, confirmed by ultrasound, but was lost to follow-up. At that time, multiple efforts to reach her were unsuccessful.

The police officer requested that the physician hold the patient in the ER. When he interviewed her, Castillo-Pichardo changed her story. She told of something that came out of her, "a ball," as she described it. Using a plunger she nudged it, but it didn't move.

"What'd you do with that, that ball?" the officer asked.

"Put it in the bathroom trash."

"Is that where it is now?"

"I carried it outside."

"Where outside?"

"The garbage," she said, then hesitated. "I got scared."

"Of what?"

"My mom."

"So, it's in the trash now?"

"Yeah."

The doctor, standing in the back of the room, asked her, "Why didn't you say all this before?"

"Because, you'd tell my mom."

Ana Castillo-Pichardo gave the police the name of the father, Denis Fernandez. She said he knew about the abdominal pain that morning, but might not have been fully aware of, as she put it, "the details of the pregnancy." Fernandez had urged her to go to the hospital. Soon after that, she texted him a selfie of herself, in a hospital bed, smiling and holding up her arm with an IV.

Based on that testimony in the ER, a search warrant for the Castillo-Pichardo home on Andrews Street in East Hartford was prepared by detectives and signed by a judge.

However, a few hours prior to that warrant, two detectives showed up at the Castillo-Pichardo house, a fairly new suburban colonial on a treeless lot. Concerned about the vague tip of a missing newborn, one possibly in distress, they were carrying out a check welfare complaint. The uncle of Ana Castillo-Pichardo answered the door and invited the detectives in. He told them that two families with nine kids lived in the house. He directed them to Ana's bathroom on the lower level, where the detectives found several baby wipes on the floor and blood in several places: on a towel, in the wastebasket, and in swirls on the floor. A red-stained mop was leaning in the corner.

On one side of the house, by the garage, was a blue plastic garbage can. From within it, they pulled up a dark plastic bag that was near empty. Beneath that bag was another, a white one. Opening it, they discovered a baby. It was male, full-term, pale-skinned, with dark hair; the body was rigid. After a STAT call to the East Hartford Fire Department, the paramedics arrived and pronounced the baby dead. The area around the house was secured with yellow tape by the Criminal Investigations Bureau team. Within twenty minutes, a team from the medical examiner's office arrived and transported the body to their office in Farmington.

The autopsy was performed the following day, with the medical examiner paying particular attention to the lungs for any water, which she did not find. On Thursday, October 16, Detective Allison was informed about the findings: the Castillo-Pichardo newborn had been alive at birth. The cause of death was asphyxia and the mode of death was listed as homicide.

The East Hartford police issued an arrest warrant for Ana Castillo-Pichardo.

The next day in Hartford Superior Court, Ana Castillo-Pichardo was arraigned on second-degree manslaughter with another three charges—the four charges together carried a sentence of up to ten years. Her public defender, Paula Waite, sketched out a wholesome picture of her client—a full-time college student, from a good family, no priors— and asked the court that she be released on a promise to appear. The judge denied the request and set the bond at $500,000. With that, the nineteen-year-old was taken by van to the York Correctional Institute in Niantic.

The *Hartford Courant* ran a front-page blown-up mugshot of Ana Castillo-Pichardo. Underneath the grimace she looked to be attractive, her hair tightly pulled back, but now with a taken-hostage stare, eyes puffy and nose reddened. As reported by the *Courant*, she and her boyfriend knew months ago that she was pregnant but never told anyone. The article went on to say that medical records had refuted the story she gave, claiming she had lied to the police when she told them she had lost the baby months before, in March. On Facebook, she had posted recent photos of her pregnant belly.

———

The women at York told me that she would have been assigned to either Two North or PC, where she would have better protection.

Ana's sentencing date was November 13, 2015. The court had considerable latitude in her sentencing, anything from zero to ten years. Being about thirtieth on the day's docket, her case came late in the afternoon. Minutes before she entered, a TV camera crew quickly set up. She was led in by two marshals from a side door, with cuffs and leg shackles, in a gray sweatshirt and clean tight jeans. Her hair was brunette with blond ends, hanging straight past her shoulders, and her head was held down like she was watching her feet. The entire time, those in the gallery could see only a trace of her cheek and she uttered no sounds.

Judge Joan Alexander, when handed the pre-sentence investigation, gave it a passing glance and asked each side if they had any changes to make. Both indicated they had none. The judge thumbed through the psychological evaluation. She noted that the grandmother and father of the baby had submitted letters to the court but both declined to speak. The prosecutor informed the bench that the father would have raised the child and held no animosity, adding, "Ana suffered from some sort of 'magical thinking,' was fearful of her parents, clearly not able to take care of the baby."

Judge Alexander asked the defendant if she wanted to speak. She shook her head. The judge said, "The court will record that as no." I was shocked that her public defender did not help her prepare a statement expressing remorse.

The judge continued, "A step you need to take, on behalf of the child, is to get the message out to other women who may be similarly situated, that there is a different option other than like what you did, ignoring the child and letting it die." Ms. Castillo-Pichardo gave a barely perceptible nod.

Judge Alexander issued the agreed-upon sentence, ten years, suspended except for eighteen months, with five years' probation. With time served, Ms. Castillo-Pichardo would be released on March 24, 2016. She had four months remaining.

As I sat in the back of the courtroom and listened to Judge Alexander hand down the sentence—eighteen months, the low end of the recommended guidelines—I was curious: Why? I thought of how one could be easily repulsed by Ana's crime, only worsened by the unsavory aspects of her behavior: the months of deception, refusing medical advice or any prenatal care, the bold web of lies to authorities, the premeditated procedure for a final disposal, and the reported mirth that she shared with her boyfriend post-delivery. This type of conduct is not atypical. It is seen over and over in youthful neonaticide cases—a disconnect with the tragedy. In his brief to the Supreme Court concerning teenage crimes, Psychology Professor Laurence Steinberg characterized the teen mindset as being "like a car with a good accelerator but a weak brake."

As law professor and neonaticide expert Michelle Oberman wrote in her support letter for Panna: "Neonaticide is a disturbing crime. The death of a newborn seems to cry out for harsh response. Yet, throughout history, those called upon to judge these cases find that they are different from ordinary cases of manslaughter. The girls and young women who commit this crime do so out of confusion, isolation and desperation. They should be punished for their terrible mistakes, but that punishment should be tempered by our recognition that they are fully amenable to rehabilitation." She added, "Justice has long since been served in the case of Panna Krom." At the time of her letter Panna had done eight years.

A certain segment of people in our society are unwavering in their beliefs, many tied to their faith. They can be vociferous and self-righteous, not swayed by any mitigating factors—they want the harshest penalties. They don't ascribe to the idea of "second chances" unless of course, it involves themselves or their loved ones. Judge Alexander took a noble stand in not giving in to that faction. She seemed to be acting according to the intention of Professor Oberman's well-chosen words, without ever having read them.

———

One Saturday evening in early 2016, Panna was in the visitors area with her parents when from farther down her table, she heard the name Ana and turned to look. There she was, Ana Castillo-Pichardo, sitting across from her parents and her brother, all neatly dressed. Panna had noticed her with her family at every Saturday visit. She was cheery, laughing with them—a scene somewhat out of place in the stifling, somber atmosphere of York. Panna also recalled having seen her several times around York and locking eyes with her, but because they lived on different tiers, she was never able to talk to her. "For a long time, we said hi to each other, smiled. She seemed so scared. We had no idea we were in for the same thing," she said. Once Panna learned about Ana and her crime, she knew that if she had tried to talk to her that would make her suspicious and Ana probably would not talk. "That's totally understandable," said Panna.

One Saturday, Ana was not there. She had finished her eighteen months at York. Her release made no news. For Panna, after working through the inner pain of seeing Ana come and go in such a short time, this was good news. In fact, it was a huge relief and a celebratory event. Panna said, "I should write a letter to Judge Alexander and thank her."

CHAPTER THIRTY-FOUR

SCREEN

In 2015, the Second Look Bill, for teen offenders with long sentences, made it through both the Connecticut House and Senate. This new law secured a parole date for Robin Ledbetter, the woman I met on my first trip to York, who had been charged in a felony murder at age fourteen and was serving a fifty-year sentence. Panna's eligibility date would come up in January 2019, twelve years into her sentence, far from a guarantee she would be released. Although good news, it did nothing to slow our efforts for her clemency petition.

In the fall of that year, I took my documents to Attorney Hutchinson's home, a country-style house on the outskirts of Danbury. Seated at her kitchen table, we spread out our documents, compared and combined what we had. It included the court filings, police reports, the presentence investigation, plea agreement and sentencing, certificates of prison courses, and Panna's diploma and transcripts from Wesleyan and Quinnipiac Universities. I had included her bio and summarized her medical and the three voluminous psychiatric evaluations onto two easy-to-read pages; the memo mentioned President Obama's and Connecticut Governor Malloy's efforts at prison reform. A printout from York showed her prison record with no disciplinary reports. We had her artwork and recommendation letters from counselors at York. In addition, there were twenty-one support letters, from a star-studded mix: faculty at Wesleyan, the University of Texas, including Michelle Oberman at University of Santa Clara Law School; Pam Sawyer, the Connecticut state representative; author Wally Lamb; and even Professor Edward Zigler (now deceased), founder of Head Start and head of the Edward Zigler Child Study Center.

It was a heady lineup, but no letter writer captured the moment quite like that of Philip Resnick. He was the Case Western University psychiatry professor who did the seminal research on neonaticide. Any bibliography on that subject starts with references to his work. He'd been the expert witness for national-headline cases, like Andrea Yates and Susan Smith (both murdered their children). Since his work dated back to the 1960s, I had assumed he was long retired. But in 2015, the Yale Forensic Psychiatry Department invited me, along with a cadre of British psychiatrists, to present and discuss Panna's case. The keynote speaker was Dr. Resnick. He and I actually shared the stage. In discussing her case, he brought attention to the mitigating factors. Before he left, I pulled out a support letter for Panna, pre-typed and ready for his signature, leaving space for his comments. Rather stone-faced, he gave no hint of his intention and let it slip from his fingers into his briefcase. Two months later, I received it in the mail, signed (with no comments).

In the stack of documents one matted page was artfully-designed to catch one's eyes. It was filled with haphazard signatures of some sixty members of Panna's family. At the top was a statement, a pledge of support, and below, everyone signed their names or left marks or scrawls, from a three year old all the way up to Chem, Panna's exalted grandmother, who at the time was suffering mid-stage dementia.

With the neat three-inch binder adorning her kitchen table, the normally stoic Vicki Hutchinson shook her head and admitted, "It's impressive. I think we're set for the sentence modification."

Hutchinson was going on vacation but decided to let the state's attorneys know she was planning to drop off the file. She opted not to target Stephen Sedensky, but instead selected his Assistant State Prosecutor, Colleen Zingaro. Her sense was that Attorney Zingaro, on her way to another county in Connecticut, would be less resistant to a hearing.

Days later, Hutchinson forwarded an email to me. Attorney Zingaro responded: "I don't care what's in that file, I'm not reducing the sentence." We had yet to send it.

At first blush, it was a blow. Final word from the prosecutor was to follow, but we anticipated that it would be the same—or worse, if that's possible.

On December 15, 2015, Hutchinson forwarded another email and told me: "It's official. The state attorney's office rejected the sentence modification request."

We were down to our final card, our petition for the clemency hearing.

Secretly, both Panna and I wanted that hearing, an open forum for showcasing and debate, not a quiet backroom deal as is typically done for modifications.

———

During this phase, the *Phnom Penh Post*, an English-language paper in Cambodia, ran a front-page splash on Panna, written by Brent Crane, an ambitious American reporter. Weeks prior, via Skype, he interviewed me. The article was sympathetic, if a little flawed, but my real concern was his reporting of my role orchestrating the clemency petition. I had worked with utter vigilance to ensure I was not traceable to Panna. Throughout our binder, my name had been meticulously deleted. Since Crane had interviewed Sedensky and the *Post* was accessible online, I worried that the state's attorney would spot my name and wonder, who is this guy? Could he accuse Panna of soliciting the aid of a "staff member" (what they would likely call a volunteer)? I supposed he could, if he bothered to make those connections.

Sedensky's interview with the *Post*—his first I was aware of in the last ten years—did give us a peek into his mind. Had he softened? The answer was no. As if wearing blinders for the twenty-odd sections of her petition, he told Mr. Crane, "She intentionally killed a child, so do we believe that people need to be held accountable for that? One of the interesting things that I find in the clemency application is the avoidance of what the behavior was: drowning her baby girl in the toilet."

Panna's petition for a pre-screen hearing was basically the same file as for the modification, only going deeper with the memorandum, the argument. Late into the evening before filing, Hutchinson and I exchanged a flurry of emails, as I composed paragraphs that she pasted in, then added the proper legal language. With limited programs and courses offered to all women in the prison, it was hard for any one woman to look "exceptional," which is the word the paroles and pardons board often said they wanted to see. What we had instead was the sentence comparisons to other teens, showing hers to be twelve times longer than the most severe, that of Ana Castillo-Pichardo. That, hopefully, was our knockout punch.

On March 9, 2016 Hutchison was ready. Early the next morning, she dropped the file off at the prosecutor's office.

By nine the following morning, some twenty internet news sites, including all the Connecticut newspapers and some radio stations, had picked up the story.

On her next visit to York, Hutchinson gave a copy of the file to Panna, which she was able to keep in a locked drawer in her cell. Only her roomie, Shannon, knew about it. Panna said, "Every time I came back to the cell, the first thing I did was check to make sure it wasn't gone." The letters impressed her—Sawyer, Zigler, Lamb, Lawrence, and, of course, Resnick. Every night she re-read them.

She got her first look at the police reports. She couldn't believe what she had "confessed" to. Through her parents, she told me that she wished she could do it over, realizing that she had unknowingly signed her life away. She now gets it, and the mantra repeated by the other women—refuse to talk!

Dr. Zonana, the Chief of Forensic Psychiatry at Yale, told me that in Panna's traumatic state and subject to the common persuasive interviewing techniques of the police, including implicit permission to lie to subjects, Panna's memory of the crime event, both then and now, may be one of misjudgment. Panna did recall the police constantly assuring her: "We are not going to hurt you. We are here to help you."

I asked Dr. Zonana, "So, with no tape of the interview, and now you tell us we can't rely on what Panna remembers, what you're saying is that the so-called facts from the scene of the incident, basically what's in the police report—is suspect?"

"Right. We'll never know what really happened. That's why since 2014 it's a state law to have recordings for all statements in Class A and B felonies. According to that statute: 'Failure to record results in a presumption that the statements are inadmissible.'"

The essence of Panna's case.

———

As soon as news of the petition hit the wires, the York prison rumor mill was in high gear. When other women asked Panna about what they had heard, she ignored them. A couple of them asked her for her attorney's phone number. She scribbled Hutchinson's actual number and said, "Here. Good luck." In a staff meeting, all the COs were briefed on her petition. Panna was surprised by how many wished her luck. One particularly religious CO came into her cell, placed his hand on the file and blessed it. The majority of the women were also supportive. The same one or two still hurled negative slurs, something she had grown immune to. Chan explained, "We don't care anymore what they say. We focus on us."

On March 12, 2016, the *News-Times* front page ran a headline, "Danbury Woman Who Drowned Her Baby Pleads for Clemency." However, a week later, the editor Jacqueline Smith took a brave stand and wrote an op-ed recommending her release. Still, when the *News-Times* called us about interviewing Panna at York, we told them no. Panna later described them as being "like TMZ." I was particularly bothered by their unmonitored and anonymous comment threads, some of them vicious—to me, no more civil or accountable than graffiti on a bathroom wall. I assured Panna, no one reads that trash. Still, for the first time, Panna had a favorable piece in the news.

During this period, State's Attorney Sedensky seemed to be basking in the new spotlight. He fed more quotes to the reporters, though he offered no new insight. Because Panna's original charge was murder, he opposed reducing her sentence, explaining, "Many of these things were addressed at the time of disposition." He added, "She was already given tremendous consideration. You have to remember that she drowned a newborn baby girl."

———

The board gave us a date for the screening, June 14, 2016. At the Rowland State Government Center on Main Street in Waterbury that day, the docket had eleven names. David Owens, the crime reporter for the *Hartford Courant,* sat next to me and was the only other witness. Mr. Owens had been following her story, but curiously never asked me who I was or what I knew—in fact, I interviewed him. Three panel members were at the table. Pulling the file off the top, one of them said, "Who's this?" Another said, "Krom." My heart jumped. I sensed that they had already reviewed it. The lead, Jennifer Zaccagnini, said, "Let's have an executive session." With that, Mr. Owens and I were ushered out of the room. While we sat in the only two chairs in the hallway, he muttered, "That's always a bad sign."

Assuming he was a veteran and knew the ropes at these hearings, I asked, "Why?"

He shrugged, as if it was some sort of ethics breach to divulge the reason.

Minutes later, we were called back in.

In quick succession, they announced the name of each applicant, slid the file over, opened it for a quick peek and said, "Denied." One by one, they did this: ten names, ten denials. One remained—the thick one. "Panna Krom," said Zaccagnini. She looked at the other two women and said, "All agree to grant a hearing." I heard two barely audible yeses. The room we were in was a government room, small, unadorned, hush like a library. I was afraid to move a muscle. In fact, what I wanted to do was leap up and down on their table.

Over the last decade, the Krom family had prepped themselves for a few big days—this was one. The night before, Chan talked to Panna, both weeping, and told her, "Just expect the worst, baby." She and Song did their routine, stayed up late into the night praying to Buddha, then were up at 4 keeping the flame going.

I left the hearing room, sat alone in the hall, in a trance. The people were exiting the room. I tried to absorb this moment. I knew Chan had gotten special permission at her workstation to have her cellphone propped up in front of her. I also knew she was on a knife's edge, probably trembling, making a mess of her assemblies. I had informed her that by 11 I should know. It was 10:50. I sat out the ten minutes, then typed: *Panna got the hearing!* waited another several seconds, and pressed SEND. Then I texted Connie: *We did it!*

Connie was my foot soldier, my rock, and had talked me down from the precipice more than once.

When my text popped up on Chan's phone, she crumpled to the floor and uncontrollably sobbed. Operations at the Danbury campus of Hologic, the football-field sized mammogram machine factory, whirred to a hum. Everyone gathered around Chan hugging her, crying with her. She reached for her phone, gathering herself enough to press Song's number.

At Imperial, the same thing.

Panna knew that by 11 a.m., we would have our answer. Her plan was to call Chan. But she didn't. Not then, nor for the rest of the day. York was on an unscheduled lockdown.

At ten the next morning, her cell door snapped open and she and several others sprinted down the hall to the phone. She rapidly punched in the numbers for her mom and waited impatiently to get through the DOC recordings. Shannon, Chasity and others were grouped around her with their ears inches from the receiver. Suddenly Panna collapsed to the floor convulsing with joy and, like schoolgirls, they all jumped up and down. Panna later told me, "We had to make sure we didn't hug, that's a big ole no-no." She laughed and said, "But we did anyway."

CHAPTER THIRTY-FIVE
BITE OF THE APPLE

In the Fall of 2015, about ten York women, half of them already released, received a nice surprise: an invitation to display their artwork in the Brooklyn Museum. In their own creative way, they had replicated the Judy Chicago Dinner Piece display, which sits in the Brooklyn Museum. Theirs would sit in an adjoining room.

The museum invited two political outliers in the prison reform movement: Connecticut Governor Dannel Malloy—a former district attorney—and his wife Cathy to be keynote speakers. Both were known for their unabashed stands against mass incarceration, well ahead of a more reluctant public. Cathy used her VIP status to make frequent visits to York. The governor, along with the DOC Commissioner Scott Semple, visited an area north of Berlin, to study the Neustrelitz Prison to see why modern German prisons work so well. What he discovered was a key ingredient that was being dismissed in the American penitentiary system—the human connection. Upon his return, at some political risk, he and the commissioner introduced that concept, involving open cell doors, communal healing and mentoring, in two prisons in Connecticut, one of them being York (a program called W.O.R.T.H.).

Aware of Cathy Malloy's sentiment toward the York women, I

planned to seize the moment in the Brooklyn Museum. I crafted a letter which laid out the particulars of Panna's situation; my singular purpose was to get Panna's name into Cathy Malloy's hands. Following her speech, as she was coming down the stairs, I stationed myself at the bottom, where I could get her attention. As soon as I uttered "this woman at York," she cut me off. "What's her name?"

"Panna Krom."

"I know Panna." She smiled and, to my delight, slid the envelope into her purse. "What are we looking for?"

I said, "She shouldn't be there."

She looked at me and said, "I will definitely read this. I know some people." What I wasn't aware of was that some months before, Cathy Malloy was on one of the tiers at York where she led a let's-let-our-hair-down chat with the women, making a mental note of each name. Panna, in particular, impressed her.

A few weeks after that quick exchange, I attended an open forum on re-entry challenges at the Hartford Public Library, featuring a panel of four formerly incarcerated. As it was winding down, I spotted Cathy Malloy across the auditorium. She was leaning against the wall, by herself, without an entourage or her usual state trooper bodyguard. After I made my way over to her, she gave me a warm embrace and asked, "Where are we with Panna's hearing?"

"Still waiting for a date," I said. "Few weeks, I figure."

"This should be a slam-dunk," she said.

I wondered if she knew something I didn't. I told her, "Numbers aren't exactly on our side."

"What do you mean?"

"They've only granted three."

"Three?"

"Out of the last 189 applications."

———

The *Connecticut Law Tribune* (where I found those numbers) ran a lead article on Panna's clemency petition, with a cover shot of a windblown-haired Vicki Hutchinson gazing into the horizon. That piece brought her renown within the criminal defense community, well-deserved, even more so, since she was pro bono. The reporter, Megan Spicer, did a careful job of weighing the data on sentence disparities. Plus, she interviewed the DA, Sedensky. His position, going back to 2007, when he originally charged her, had not changed, regardless of Panna's exceptional record. In fact, he used her achievements against her. "Too much was focused on Panna and her accomplishments," he told Ms. Spicer. In his eyes, the suffering of the baby was ignored. "The facts in the case are pretty horrendous," he said. "She's looking to say, 'Well, I don't like that plea agreement, and I want another bite of the apple.'"

Panna's upcoming hearing continued to generate interest from journalists. The next to contact me was Maura Casey, who had been an editorial writer for the *The New York Times* and had won numerous awards. She was intrigued by the story and thinking about an op-ed for the *Hartford Courant*. She needed details, so she drove to my house in North Haven. In the den, I showed her two desks with stacks of binders, and on my Ipad we scrolled through the PowerPoint that Connie had created. It began with the crime scene, touched on the psychological factors and life in Cambodia, described the other cases, and brought us to where we then stood. I could see she was moved.

During the late summer, as we waited for a hearing date from the board, it seemed every week we were thrown another curveball. Hutchinson heard that Sedensky had canvassed judges and prosecutors throughout the state for other neonaticide cases. I knew that in one click of the mouse he could get the kind of access I had dreamed of. He needed only one case to invalidate our data.

Interestingly, the only case he notified us about concerned a college girl who received a life sentence for neonaticide, probably adjudicated so harshly because after the crime she texted her boyfriend, *It's done.* However, the case was not relevant to our data—it occurred in the Midwest.

He brought up some other points, like when Chan was notified of Panna's pregnancy during the motor vehicle accident. And he questioned whether the DNA testing established the identity of the father (not done). In addition, he now had a different guardian ad litem (for the baby). None of these points were of any consequence. All in all it was a mix: some craftsmanship, a lot of noise, rumor, and more than likely, desperation, maybe even confusion.

———

The BOPP gave us a date for the clemency hearing: September 7, 2016.

For a locale, they settled on the hall at Gates, the decommissioned men's prison—the same spot used for Bonnie Foreshaw's hearing three years earlier. The facility, a quarter mile behind York, now sat abandoned, overgrown with weeds and saplings.

So we had a date and a place. Around the "yard" at York, the word got out that this was a parole hearing, something fairly routine. Panna's tight circle knew the truth, but they did nothing to quell the rumor. Two York women were assigned to do cleanup in the Gates building. They came back and described to Panna exactly what it looked like and joked with her about the "terrific news," that it now had a fresh coat of beige paint.

I sent out a flurry of informative emails: to the psych group, to Hutchinson, to the family for any late add-on names, and for any last-minute support letters. I did get two from Panna's fellow incarcerated women. There's a certain us-against-the-DOC sisterhood among the incarcerated: they readily write the best support letters.

Attorney Hutchinson sent me the BOPP-issued rules for the hearing. Only one reporter and cameraman would be allowed inside, likely a response to Forshaw's media crush. Doors would open at 7:30 a.m. Each name had to be approved, with IDs required. I had a total of sixty names, including thirty-seven from Panna's family. The only items allowed in the room were car keys: no cellphones, no purses. No one was to have contact with Panna. Prosecutors would sit on one side, Panna and her lawyers on the other, with the psych team seated behind them. Panna was to be led in by a CO; they hadn't revealed which one. She would be in her prison uniform, the t-shirt and jeans, but uncuffed. I conveyed to Song that family members were to dress up, shave, cover tattoos, and not say one peep to Panna. There would be no cries of "We love you, Panna!" from the back of the room.

For Panna, the tension was mounting. Once a day, she called Chan, scared and crying. By the end of the fifteen minutes, she gathered herself enough to proclaim that she was ready. "I just want it over," she told her mom. Every few days, I tweaked her prepared statement and texted those changes, if any, to Chan, who then read them over the phone to Panna. I followed it with an urging to "put it in your own words," which she did. For two months, with Shannon as her voice coach, she practiced the five-minute statement. Shannon was attentive to her delivery, guiding her when to pause and take a breath, when to look at the panel, and when to turn to the prosecutor. Speak up so they can hear you in the back, she said, and try not to look at your notes. Never peek at your family, and don't cry—although getting a little teary-eyed and dabbing is a plus. Using nail clippers, Shannon did a layered cut on Panna's hair.

Late in the game, Hutchinson sent me an email asking if I wanted my name mentioned in her introduction. As much as it hurt—since the file, the data, even the memo, represented years of my work—I said no. I feared my name might raise a flag, since I had been officially banned at York (more on that later).

Days before the hearing, Attorney Emanuel visited Panna to walk her through the process and allay her fears. Just as Attorney Tunnard had done for her pre-sentencing hearings, he felt compelled to show her a photo of the dead baby he had obtained from the prosecutor's file, to desensitize her. Afterward, he remarked to me, "This young woman was smart but tough, did her homework, said 'Yes sir' to everything. She's a star. I'm not used to that."

The first of September, I got a rushed call from the *Hartford Courant*'s opinion-page editor, Carolyn Lumsden. They were going with Maura Casey's article and needed a recent picture of Panna. I called Chan and Connie, to see what we had. Over the past decade there were only three or four photos of Panna, all with her mom and dad, taken by the prison staff. We sent one of them. The op-ed ran the day before the hearing.

The *Courant* titled it "Mercy for Panna Krom." It pleaded for

Panna's release, asking that she be granted five years parole. That last part was taken directly from Vicki Hutchinson's request in the petition —a meaningless slip, as commutations attach no parole. Would the prosecution pick up on this and use it as a bargaining chip for more prison time?

I reminded myself, we weren't going up against Clarence Darrow.

CHAPTER THIRTY-SIX
SEVEN MINUTES

The morning of the hearing, September 7, 2016, was crisp, bright and breezy, in the low sixties. In the parking lot at the Gates prison facility, Connie and I spotted Song and Chan. Chan, in a fine dress and jewelry, beamed with optimism; Song, in white pants and black jacket, looked like Charles Bronson. I was wired, jumpy. Connie used her steady hand to calm me. We all hugged and watched as the cars rolled into the lot, plenty of dark SUVs with tinted windows, and more than a few out-of-state plates. To them, this was formal; everyone came in suits and dresses. As they got out, Connie and I guessed at their names or how they were related. We knew about half. Song helped us with the rest and took me around to shake hands and greet each one—thirty-seven Kroms in all. Panna's grandmother, Chem, the grande dame, was in a wheelchair, escorted by two grandsons.

Of course, Pam Sawyer and Wally were there, as were neurologist Lori Cretella, second-year law student Carolyn Lipp, State Representative Gayle Mulligan, Tiffany Quinn from Safe Haven and her dancer daughter Lindsay, Hutchinson's husband, a couple of neighbors, and others who had picked up on the story. A truck pulled up to the entrance and workers in CT-N shirts, the state's political television network, unloaded their video equipment.

I finally was able to lay eyes on the prosecutor, Attorney Sedensky. He was actually a decent-looking guy, square-jawed, solid in the shoulders with a self-assured swagger, short-haired and wearing a light-gray suit. He was paired with Attorney Sharon Wicks Dornfeld, his guardian ad litem. She wore retro-frame round glasses and had a pixie hairdo. Both of them armed with bulging leather satchels. She matched him athletically, as they were stride for stride, fully engaged and strategizing. They looked emboldened, like odds-on favorites to win and ruin the day for everyone else.

When we queued up for check-in, Sedensky stood inches behind me. Little did he know that the nondescript guy in front of him was the architect for this production. Since my first day in Song's living room, I had imagined a target on this fair-faced district attorney. I recall going into the Danbury courthouse and locating his office at the far end of the hall. I just wanted to know: who were we dealing with and where did he work? I found out he was in a family line of Danbury prosecutors—his dad was one, as was his sister. This case seemed like a nuisance to him. Even if he was misusing his power, Connecticut state's attorneys have no real accountability. They are not elected—Connecticut was one of only three states (New Jersey and District of Columbia the others) that don't elect district attorneys—but fall loosely under the governor, being appointed by the governor's Criminal Justice Commission. The gubernatorial office has no oversight should there be any misdeeds. In fact, across the nation it's unheard of for a district attorney to be prosecuted. The clemency power stroke was our only remaining means of redress.

Moving past the entrance, I stood before a small check-in table where a CO ran his finger down the alphabetical list of names, searching for the H's. I was in utter fear my name would have a big red stamp: "Entry Denied"—I would be blocked while Sedensky waltzed around me.

I had good reason to worry.

About a year earlier, a group of volunteers and incarcerated women were talking in a hallway at York, when someone mentioned something about my "helping Panna." Neither Panna nor I was there. The one CO who was most protective of Panna was. He sternly rebuked her: "If something's going on, shut it down." The next morning, I got an urgent call at work from Chan, who was on the verge of a breakdown. I felt a chill. My number-one rule was: do no harm to Panna. According to the DOC, as a volunteer, I was considered staff, and staff were not "advocates." We did "shut it down" for a couple of weeks. I stopped my visits to Bethel and skipped a month of writing classes. After the noise quieted down, we slowly eased back into our routine. At York, gossip and rumors disappear as fast as they appear.

My real troubles came a few months before the hearing.

The DOC sent me a letter dismissing me from York, even banning me from visits. I forwarded the letter to the others in my writing group. "It's pretty pathetic when you're a volunteer and you're fired," I mused, in an attempt to find humor. I loved that writing class and the trust I had gained with the women. Having a front-row seat watching Wally was priceless. He was the equivalent of Jack Black in *School of Rock*, making music out of chaos.

Wally read the DOC letter to the women. Chasity, the de facto leader, demanded: Why?

I called the guy who signed it, DOC's Chief of Volunteers. He was a master of double-talk. Initially, he claimed that it was because of a letter of support I wrote for one of the women in our class. That letter was written three years before. There may be times when a volunteer gets a small taste of the same treatment as the incarcerated: subject to an autocratic police state system of nebulous, ever-changing rules with no court, no appeals board, just an unseen judge who delivers the ruling, and it's final. I decided to drop it and not make an issue.

But the DOC memory has a short half-life and within months I was back, doing visits.

———

Standing nervously at the check-in table, I swelled with relief when the CO's finger stopped at my name and calmly put a line through it. I was never so happy to see a metal detector.

Our row of chairs included Pam Sawyer, Wally, Connie and in front of us were Song and Chan. Further up, the opposing legal teams settled into their traditional sides, prosecutor to the left, defense on the right.

The Khmer Health Advocates psych team sat immediately behind the defense.

The BOPP panel of three women—Jennifer Zaccagnini, Rufaro Berry, and Joy Chance—entered, set down thick binders of documents, took their seats, made small talk, then called for order and established the standard rules. Two of them were Black and all three were casually dressed and looked relaxed. Each had a degree from a local college and had moved up the ranks presumably after showing a certain star power. One had been a legal assistant, one a social worker, and the other a probation supervisor. They were veterans, well-versed in the prison and judicial system, and as panel members, wielded considerable power over individuals' lives.

A CO led Panna in. She wore her prison-issue jeans and t-shirt. He uncuffed her and they swore her in. She looked to her left—it had been ten years since she last faced Sedensky. Over that time, her memories of him had induced many nightmares. The chairwoman of the panel, Ms. Chance, invited Panna to give her statement.

Panna rose and spoke. While her eyes stayed fixed on the panel, three pages of notes were lying on the table below her. From the back, we couldn't see her face and had to listen carefully to her soft voice.

First, she thanked her team and family.

"When I arrived at York in 2007, I was just a kid, naïve, frightened, in utter shock. I spent almost two years in Protective Custody, depressed and hating myself. I exhausted the maximum amount of daily phone calls, on each one spending the whole fifteen minutes crying with my parents on the other end. I realized I couldn't go on like that. I had to decide—do I continue, give in and become institutionalized, artificially disabled and part of the prison culture? Or do I find strength and use my years to be a good person and open the opportunity for a second chance? From that moment, I did everything I could to make myself better and become someone my parents would be proud of. Fortunately, York provided those opportunities, the courses, the education, the work ethic, the many ways to volunteer, to do art and put on shows, and be a mentor for others. I tried to do them all.

"York has been a harsh blessing. I am not sure who I would be if not for York. Prior to my incarceration, I lived a nice life, which, with the pregnancy, became a reckless one, entangled in a web of lies. I was not honest to my parents, friends, or even to myself. Prison experience has instilled vital lessons that I practice daily. Irresponsible actions can result in dire consequences, a notion that my seventeen-year-old mentality could not accept."

Here she paused. I feared she forgot where she was. Her head was down. We couldn't see. Was Attorney Emanuel going to bail her out? She started again. "I've learned to be honest with myself and my loved ones. We have grown very close. My family deserves immense credit for helping me meet these challenges."

She talked about her sentencing and the promise she made to Judge Ianotti, to help other young pregnant girls, letting them know there is a safety net.

"At hearings such as these, there should be a victim or the family of a victim sitting over there [she pointed at the prosecutor's table]. That is not lost on me. My family grieves over their granddaughter, or niece, or cousin. Angel, I took your precious life away. Today, you would be nine-and-a-half, going into fourth grade, attending birthday parties and dance classes."

Again, she paused, gathering herself. "I always hold the pain inside me and deep remorse for you. A day doesn't pass without thoughts about you. I am so sorry for being a selfish and irresponsible mother. I own and carry what I did. Please understand my sorrow and accept my pledge to work in your memory.

"My family is Thai-Cambodian, proud survivors of the war. Life for us was never easy—especially the generation of my parents. They were child rice farmers with no education. We are quiet, simple people. We take care of ourselves. Every Saturday evening my parents drive here from Danbury and have done so for the past ten years. They sacrifice simple daily basics—using the saved money to pay for my phone calls home and my commissary. They are faithful, believe in karma, and lead a pure life to bring fortune for their children. I did not make their lives any easier. But they are honorable people. They never questioned me. I am a blessed woman at York."

Panna talked about her work at York and her plans for when she's released, starting with paying back her parents.

"Mom, Dad, I look for the day when I can finally tell you: your grief and suffering over me—it's over. Members of the panel: I thought this day would never happen. Make no mistake, this has not been an easy ten years. I have done the best I can. I have no regrets about my time at York, but I am ready to go on. No matter what your decision is, I am a very content and proud young woman. I thank you for hearing me."

———

Ms. Chance said, "Thank you Miss Krom. I can see you put a lot of time and thought into that. And I see you have a lot of family here to support you."

Attorney Hutchinson stood. She was dressed in a tidy powder-blue suit, with a modest gold necklace, her hair in a swept-back shag.

"I need to correct an error, when we asked for parole in our petition," she said. "The board does not do that. They only grant a shortening of the sentence, a commutation."

She continued, "Panna committed the act under the stress of extreme emotional disturbance, or EED. EED is where an individual is exposed to an overwhelming state, a loss of self-control. Reasoning is overwhelmed by intense feelings of passion, anger, distress, grief and excessive agitation, panic or similar emotions. So there was a reasonable explanation.

"The maximum for that statute on her crime was twenty years-to-serve with a minimum of one year. After admitting guilt and taking a plea bargain, she got eighteen years, not after a trial or with any denial. Panna, at the time of her sentencing, promised Judge Ianotti, the state's attorney, and the courtroom that she would become a better person, that she would take advantage of every opportunity, of every program in prison. At that time, mid-2008, nobody knew what kind of person Panna would turn into. Would she be amenable to rehabilitation?

"Children often lack the experience, perspective and judgment to recognize and avoid choices that could be detrimental to them and others. Look at the institutional records of Miss Krom, her record of rehabilitation. I submit that it is amazing. She did not have a single disciplinary report. Although she spent her first two years crying and depressed, she did not do a single thing wrong. After she cleared her head at about nineteen, she did all that the DOC asked her to do. In fact, she did everything she could possibly do.

"We are asking the board to look at what she has done and the person she's become, to consider the risk she might pose, if any, to anybody on the outside, and what she can contribute to society if released. After reviewing all that, we ask the panel to commute her sentence. Thank you."

———

State's Attorney Stephen Sedensky stood. He pushed his sleeves up and adjusted his glasses with both hands, dropped his notes and leaned heavily over them, fists resting on the table. In a whisper, he began, "School started last week in Ellsworth Elementary School." He paused and straightened up. "Miss Malterellos, a fifth-grade teacher, looking at her class list, probably did not realize she was missing one girl, a girl that would never be in that class, this year, next year, or ever." Gesturing with a pen in one hand and at times removing his glasses with his choirboy face muscled and his neck veins bulging, he continued. "She will not be in that class because on December 28, 2006, the defendant—"

He stopped and pointed at Panna and began, "She intentionally and repeatedly flushed the toilet to drown the baby girl, a purposeful killing of a totally innocent baby. That's why we are here today. The defendant was arrested and charged with murder. Make no mistake, she was charged with murder because she intentionally killed a baby girl. I provided the board with a photograph of the baby girl. I disagree that the person who killed the child can name the child. I wish I had a photograph of the baby girl, had she lived. But I only have a photograph as she was in that closet. I provided the board with a photograph of the toilet that she was drowned in. The defendant was appropriately charged with murder, a sentence which carries a mandatory minimum of twenty-five and a maximum of sixty-five years. That's where we started in this case: *murder*. There was no dispute.

"With the board's standards for clemency, the legislature's mandate, and the defendant's agreement, what stands out is the state's consideration when the defendant entered her guilty plea to that intentional killing under a far-reduced charge. So, that suggested to the board that discretion has *already* been taken.

"The defendant in her material submitted to you cites different cases, and yet when you look at the cases where the defendant was charged with murder, the sentences are very similar. There is a fifteen-year sentence. There's a seventeen-year sentence, cases where the defendant was charged with murder. I suggest that apples and apples should be compared. This was a murder case. And in those cases, there was a very similar sentence."

He continued. "At the sentencing, Judge Ianotti said the defendant avoided a murder and he took a huge step in exercising the discretion. Certainly, the defendant's positive conduct while in prison should be considered. But consider it when she'll be eligible for parole in January 2019.

"The board is not an alternative avenue to complain about the quality of legal representation, the legality of the conviction, or the length of the sentence. You are being asked to act like a sentence review panel. Only most compelling circumstances of miscarriage of justice should be entertained, and only after exhaustion of all judicial remedies. There's the judicial remedy of writ of *habeas corpus*. If it's indeed a wanton and freakish sentence, as has been put in the materials submitted to the board, there should have been a *habeas corpus* petition filed. And there was not. Why? Because it was *not* a miscarriage of justice. Okay? It was an appropriate sentence worked on by the state, the court, the defendant and her attorney.

"I looked at the letters submitted on behalf of the defendant," he continued. "No one addresses the toilet flushes that the defendant took to kill the little girl. It's always about the defendant. They don't know the baby girl and the life she didn't have. They don't know the circumstances and the horrendous nature of the crime.

"The board is being asked to make this a compelling situation, but what is really compelling is the death of a baby girl. Please respect our legislature, our court for the job they have done, and deny the application. Thank you."

———

What Sedensky chose to ignore were the comparative graphs of all the neonaticide cases. He cherry-picked the worst cases, older women with children who were premeditated and calculated in their homicides. He chose to ignore the teenage cases, the whole point of the study. I suspect the board saw through that.

And when I heard his description of the board's narrow mandate, I wondered if it offended them. The prosecutor was wrong. The board actually is an alternative avenue for justice, as he stated, in the executive branch, and they are given broad latitude and can entertain sentence reduction for any reason whatsoever. He was also incorrect about *habeas corpus*. It was not appropriate in her case—she was not contending that her imprisonment was unlawful.

———

The guardian ad litem, Sharon Wicks Dornfeld, seated next to Sedensky, stood. She described to the panel the odd nature of her position. "Since 1988, I have limited my practice to representing children in Connecticut's probate, juvenile, family and criminal court. So I find myself here today in a rather unusual position for several reasons. First, in almost thirty years of representing children, I've never before had a client who was a mere abstraction. It is possible to gain a sense even of preverbal infants, but in this case, there was no one to visit, no one to observe, no one who could tell me anecdotes about the child. I struggle whether there was a foundation on which I base my comments today. But because the victim's family has at best conflicting loyalties, I agreed to speak for the child who is not here.

"Second, in reading the materials submitted by both the state and Miss Krom, it is clear to me we are mostly focusing on Miss Krom as a seventeen-year-old. I would ordinarily be representing the interest of a seventeen-year-old. In that role, I spend a lot of time talking about frontal lobe development and adolescent magical thinking. So, the material Miss Krom submitted resonates with me and evokes mixed feelings.

"Third, as a lawyer, I'm accustomed to relying upon specific legal standards and definitions when assessing a situation. In this case, I am unable to find any Connecticut law which specifies the circumstances meriting clemency or sentence commutation.

"So it seems the question boils down to whether there is a subjective feeling that Miss Krom has served enough of her sentence for the crime of causing the death of her newborn daughter. I've carefully read Miss Krom's own statements both at the time that she gave birth and more recently. I also read the police reports and the school personnel and friends who spoke with Miss Krom about her pregnancy. And I read the reports of the psychiatrists, psychologist, and social worker who have evaluated her. I was struck by the glowing reports of Miss Krom's behavior in prison and her efforts to take full advantage of every possible opportunity. She is to be commended. I am persuaded she poses no risk to the public in the future, and her desire to help other young women who find themselves with problem pregnancies, as genuine.

"But at the same time, I am also struck by the statement of Miss Krom directly and by her evaluators, that no one reached out to help her. By implication she deflects some blame of her own actions. Aside from being simply inaccurate, it reflects minimizing her own responsibility for her crime. The fact is that a teacher, guidance counselor, and the assistant principal all raised the topic of her pregnancy, and she lied to each of them about her parents being aware and helping her with adoption plans. The mother of a friend of hers also reached out and offered guidance and Miss Krom refused to accept it. I am further struck by the absence of certain details of her crime when she related her story to her two evaluators in 2015. In both of those cases, it appears she failed to state she observed the baby to move her arms and legs, that she flushed the toilet more than once to drown the baby, and left her in the toilet while she showered to ensure the baby was in fact dead. Failure to include those details again seems to me to minimize her responsibility.

"So despite Miss Krom's sterling record as an inmate, I am left with the fact that the nine-year-old who should be here simply isn't. While the objectives of rehabilitation have certainly been satisfied, retribution or punishment is also a legitimate goal. But it just doesn't feel to me that she has served enough. On behalf of the nine-year-old who is not here and won't ever have a life, I respectfully and regretfully object to the petition. Thank you."

Pam Sawyer leaned and whispered, "Both of them elected to disregard the psychological dilemmas of these young mothers."

———

Ms. Chance, the chair, asked. "Ms. Hutchinson, do you have a rebuttal?"

"Yes," she replied and stood up. "What you have to look at is Panna's mental state at the time she gave birth. Not only was she seventeen years old, her mental state being less than ideal. She was a seventeen-year-old who was in labor. She was a first-generation American. A very strict family. Her parents did not know she was pregnant. She had raging hormones, horrendous pain, and gave birth by herself in the bathroom as quietly as she possibly could. She had no prenatal care and was bleeding. And didn't know what to do. She made terrible decisions.

"At the time Miss Krom was sentenced, it was anticipated she would be asking for a modification. Our judicial system contemplates almost any term of prison, other than mandatory, might be subject to future reduction, revision, modification, or termination. At the time of the sentencing, Attorney Tunnard said, 'I will be continuing to fight for Miss Krom because in my heart I know that eighteen years is not appropriate for this young girl.' And Judge Ianotti responded, 'I have no doubt Attorney Tunnard will continue to work on your behalf, and I encourage her to do so.'

"Attorney Tunnard was not able to follow through with it, but Attorney Emanuel and I are doing that. So this was something anticipated at the time. Clemency is not overwriting the statutes. There's a long history of clemency. Clemency is deeply rooted in our traditions of law. It is the failsafe in our judicial system. It's not overwriting any legislative intent. It is looking at a particular case, a particular set of facts, a particular individual, and making a determination as to whether the needs for justice or the purpose of sentencing have been fulfilled. And the facts of this case warrant an early reduction of the sentence. In January 2019, she may be eligible for parole, depending on how long it takes. It could be January 2020 before she has that hearing. I'm not sure what purpose, other than punishment, would be served by further lengthy period of incarceration for this individual. Thank you."

The panel recessed and all stood. Everyone was afraid to comment—we had no idea about the decision. I saw Rich Emanuel and asked him, "Well?"

"Will the panel overturn a prosecutor? I don't know the answer to that."

Seven minutes into the break, the side door quietly opened—the room immediately hushed—and the three women entered. The only sound was them sliding their chairs. They took their positions at the small table while everyone found their seats. Connie grabbed my hand and squeezed tightly.

What we couldn't see was Rich Emanuel nudging Panna, signaling for her to look down. On a scrap of paper, he had printed in block letters, "STAY CALM." The CT-N camera zoomed in for a closeup of Panna's face. She remained stony as the panel delivered their decision.

In a calm voice, Chairwoman Joy Chance said, "In the case of inmate Panna Krom, number 347106, I make a motion to grant you commutation effective September 30, 2016. Is there a second?"

One panel member said, "Second."

"All in favor."

Both other members said, "Aye."

I closed my eyes and let my breath out.

As the panel got up to leave, Panna was led out. She never turned to look. Witnesses in the audience hugged and cried. A TV camera and roving reporter cut through the crowd to find Chan, who was twisting back and forth hugging family members. Tremendous tears ran down her cheeks.

CHAPTER THIRTY-SEVEN
WINDBLOWN

Minutes after the panel's decision, and in the midst of the commotion in the auditorium, Panna was cuffed and unceremoniously led out a side door. They placed her in a lockup, a portable three-by-five steel cage, which sat by the door. She waited there for the COs to escort her back to York. A trickle of officers went by, a couple of them giving her a thumbs up. Minutes later, it was the three women from the panel. She thanked them and they returned reassuring smiles. In the auditorium, Attorneys Sedensky and Dornfeld were standing over their table sheepishly packing documents into their briefcases. With a wary eye for the newly-arrived Channel 3 reporter and ducking down as if there was gunfire, they circled around to the far side of the room, never speaking to anyone, then slipping out that same side door. Immediately to their left, only feet away, was Panna. Sedensky told her, "Good luck to you in your life."

Panna said, "Thanks."

"No, I mean it."

Attorney Dornfeld added, "Yes, Panna, good luck."

Panna told them, "Thank you."

That exchange, the first Panna had ever had with him, a warm one, made me think—if only Sedensky had known her—maybe he would have been sympathetic. This is no accident—it's intentional, a reason that district attorneys rarely meet the person(s) they are prosecuting.

———

Inside the York prison, the women were aware of the 10:00 a.m. hearing but lacked any means to get a live feed. Many kept their TVs on Channel 3, anticipating that the daytime programming would be interrupted. At about 11:30, it was—a "Breaking News" flash came on and reported on Panna's commutation. While the announcement was made, the camera zoomed in on Panna's face, catching a few people behind her. To the regular TV viewer, the clip, only seconds long, must have looked eerie. The message I had Song relay to the extended family was to show no emotion no matter what, and Panna had her message from Attorney Emanuel, instructing her to stay calm. So at the precise moment the panel gave the release date, instead of an eruption, there was a funereal silence and cut.

Then off camera, the eruption.

Elbowing her way through the chaos, roving reporter Susan Raff interviewed Vicki Hutchinson, Chan, Song, then me, labelled as a "family advocate." With her cameraman over her shoulder and a microphone planted in front of me, she asked, "How did this come about?" I had about ten seconds to organize my thoughts and come up with a cheery sound bite about Panna's three-year battle for fairness.

At York, where the news had moved fast, there were shouts of joy, and even a few cheers from the COs. When Panna was led through the facility, it was "like Shawshank," said one. Women stopped work, lined the hallways, pressed against the plexiglass and bars, cheering, raising defiant arms and pumping their fists. Panna, a bit confused, asked herself, "How did they know? It was literally minutes ago." The York women saw Panna's commutation was a jab at the DOC, something for which all current and formerly incarcerated women lock arms.

During the time leading up to her release on September 30, the two roomies on Zero South counted down the days. Shannon saw her role as bodyguard for Panna. Her fear was that other women would mess with her just to see her go to seg. Shannon, a street-smart woman with a biker build, made no secret about her assignment: "If there's a fight it'll be with me, or someone going down, it'll be me." Panna quit her programs and jobs, pretty much to lie low in her cell for the three weeks. She waited until the last night to sort through her stuff. She didn't want to bum out Shannon—who had eight more years—seeing her area look as if it was never lived in.

———

On that long-awaited morning in late September, Pam Sawyer, Rich Emanuel, Connie and I met in the parking lot at York. The weather, a brilliant New England autumn day, matched our mood. Connie went inside to be our on-scene reporter. Vicki Hutchinson parked nearby and we briefly exchanged a few pleasantries before she proceeded into the front entrance. Then six of the Kroms, including Song and Chan, hurried over to us, sporting big smiles. Squared-jawed Song had on his shades, dark shirt and dark jacket, hair gelled, looking cut and classy, like some kind of Cambodian secret service. He and I seemed to find a comfort zone being side by side. Panna was expected to be released at 10:00, in only a few minutes, so after some light talk and our man-hug, Connie and the Kroms all rushed inside. A Department of Corrections pickup pulled up and the driver informed me and Emanuel, "We can't let you congregate in the parking lot. For security reasons." We apologized, got in our cars, and headed to the parking lot next door at the Samuel M. Peretz Park, where the Channel 3 crew was setting up a TV camera.

A stream of text messages from Connie appeared on my phone, informing us of what was happening inside the York visiting area.

Panna had been led by a CO from her cell. As was the custom, she left her things behind for others—TV, books, toiletries, hot plate, hair dryer—everything but some papers, which she carried in a see-through plastic bag. Since she had more than $50 in her account, she received no "gate money." She and Shannon had been up the previous night laughing and crying. With a wink of the eye from the COs, Shannon was allowed to walk with Panna to the last gate. The two gave a final hug, something the COs let slide.

Panna entered into the glassed-in CO office in the visitors waiting room, wearing her cousin's black suit, which they allowed her to send to A & D. The cousin had asked her, "What size?" and Panna laughed, "Size? I have no clue." It was a tight squeeze.

The last door snapped open. Song, Chan, and other family members all smothered her with a group hug. One at a time, they tied bracelets made of sacred *Sai Sin* white thread onto her left wrist, each having been blessed by a monk specifically for her purity and good fortune—similar to the bracelets cut off on the day she entered York. After hugging Connie and Vicki, Panna stepped outside, did a Mary Tyler Moore spin and exclaimed, "Where do I go?" She gazed up at the facade portico and remarked, "Wow! I've never seen the front of this place."

While waiting in Peretz Park, I had time to chat with the two crime reporters from the *Hartford Courant.* I already knew David Owens from her screening in June. I fed them particular details about her case, trusting that they would get the story right. When I asked if it might be on the front page, they shrugged and said yeah, depending on any other news. "Above the fold?" I asked with raised eyebrows.

After receiving word from Connie that Panna was on the way, I informed everyone, and the Channel 3 crew began filming. From our parking lot a few hundred yards away, we could follow the black, official-looking SUV with its small motorcade circling around the York visitor parking lot and headed our way, much like a celebrity live shot on CNN.

Within minutes the black Tahoe pulled in beside us, but before it rolled to a stop, Panna jumped out, dashed over, and gave me a hug. As we stood together, all eyes were locked on her, expecting her to talk. She was at a loss for what to say. The wind whipped her hair across her face, which she pulled out of her mouth and eyes. The Channel 3 reporter, Susan Raff, stepped forward with a microphone and asked her, "Well, how do you feel?" Panna displayed a puzzled face and quipped, "Great!" The next question was, "When people say this was a terrible crime, what do you say?"

Panna strained to smile and shrugged, a little dumbfounded. She said, "I understand. I need to readjust to being free right now. It's a question I know I'll get asked." She paused and said, "You know what? The wind blowing my hair in my face feels so liberating." Then as she pulled a folded sheet of yellow paper out of her pocket and flattened it out, she explained, "If it's okay, I need to thank some people."

She began reading.

What a wonderful day!

First, I want to say I would not have survived without the love and absolute dedication of my parents, Song and Chan. Exactly what I mean by survive I am not sure, too scary to think about.

As I walk out of York, I owe a debt to many.

Let me be clear about this. There would be no clemency were it not for one person: Doug Hood. Doug stumbled on my case and started working on it three years ago. I never asked him to. In fact, I've never really talked to him. He did the research, found the lawyers and psychiatrists, got support letters, and came up with the strategy for clemency. There were many obstacles and frustrations. And he did it all, until this moment, anonymously.

Doug, what can I do to thank you?

And of course, my lawyers, Vicki and Rich. You guys are amazing. True heroes against injustice. Wally Lamb, Pam Sawyer, Chasity West, thanks for backing me. And Connie Xu and Tiffany Quinn who visited me, keeping my spirits up.

You learn some odd lessons in prison. One is that some women with horrific crimes can be very generous people. So good, you wonder if it balances out. That's a bigger question for those smarter than me. But no denying many at York helped me with my clemency. One was my cellmate. Shannon selflessly protected me, knowing she was losing her best friend. Shannon, I hope I can help you. I will be right here the day you get out.

Now I need to spend quiet time with my parents in our new apartment, see my cousins, aunts and uncles. I'm looking for work—if you know any—and I need to get a driver's license.

Very soon I'll get started on the work I promised—to help pregnant teens in distress.

It's a joyous day for my family and myself.
Thank you for coming.

———

The next morning, Connecticut's flagship newspaper would get it right —all in a single image. The front page of the *Hartford Courant* had a blown-up shot of a tearful Chan hugging Panna. It encapsulated a certain noble end for the Kroms.

On a wintry evening in 2012, I made a pledge to the Kroms. We were in their Bethel apartment; it was our first meeting. They had just spilled out disturbing details about what sounded like police and prosecutorial misconduct and I had no reason to not believe them.

At the end of that first evening, I was stirred, enough so that there was little chance that I would walk away from their story—not just their story, but them. I was sufficiently moved and overcome with the same awareness, I suspect, that had led James Foley, the journalist quoted in this book's epigraph, to choose to immerse himself in war-torn villages in face of the peril. He paid a price—he was brutally murdered, caught on film and distributed by ISIS. But he left a statement and I quote it here, because it works for me: *The plight of the little people who are walked upon like grass.*

I was surprised how they held back nothing in their personal lives, trusting me. I was offering a sympathetic ear and was constantly fearful that I might be fueling false hope. I tried to lower their expectations, but the objective was freeing Panna. They were brave and full of determination. They were not *little people*—Foley knew that.

As I was learning about the clemency process and compiling the necessary documents, Panna became a steady resource, someone like myself who attracted little attention. Over the ensuing months and years, she and I, though worlds apart in every way, had kept our ties, which were through Chan, and we stayed on target, even while sharing many fitful nights of sleep and fighting back waves of pessimism.

As I thought back on that period, it occurred to me that beyond our brief encounter in that prison hallway, Panna and I never had a private conversation nor did we correspond. Our only hug came the day of her release, and within minutes of that embrace we were parting ways, returning to our lives—our worlds—as we once knew them. Both of us were profoundly changed. Over time, she had convinced me of her one desire: to return to the embrace of her extended family and resume her life in Bethel.

While I felt rewarded on that breezy day, seeing the radiance around Panna flanked by her parents, in a selfish twist an unexpected something weighed on me. There would be no more Saturday lunches with Song and Chan, no more Khmer festivals and funerals and no more fishing lines bobbing in the still water of the reservoir— events all steeped with unintended teachings about love, endurance, and a call-to-arms about fairness.

Panna got into her cousin's car, looked down and exclaimed in humored puzzlement at a FaceTime video handed to her, then waved to everyone as the window was rolling up, and they drove off.

EPILOGUE

"The one thing I was really dying to see was the stars," Panna told me only days after gaining her freedom, which came with considerable notice.

Her mother's embrace on the front page of the *Hartford Courant* included an article by veteran crime reporter David Owens. Given access to her petition, he wrote an even-handed piece. Panna's sudden attention was something I believe she enjoyed, certainly initially, as well as what came with it: the letters, calls, gifts, and requests for appearances.

One of the letters to Panna, came from the BOPP by way of Attorney Hutchinson, stating that her sentence, compared to similar crimes in Connecticut, was lengthy. By design, the board is freestanding, practically faceless, and not accountable to anyone, not even the governor—but particularly not to the incarcerated. Attorney Rich Emanuel pointed out that no one directed them to provide that explanation to Panna and called it unprecedented.

Acting on a tip from Wally, a producer for the *Colin McEnroe Show* on Connecticut National Public Radio had booked Panna for a live interview. In early October, Panna sat across from Colin in his soundproof booth at WNPR. As usual, Colin had done his homework and after taking measure of his uncertain guest, decided to dial back his usual style of rapid-fire interjections. Given this time for thought, what listeners got to hear was an imperturbable young woman, possibly dispelling their notions that a calm voice of reason could not emerge out of the state's prison apparatus. The episode, "Neonaticide is an Act of Desperation," won the 2017 PRNDI, a national award.

More articles followed. John Curtis, the retiring editor of *Yale Medicine* and Randall Beach, a seasoned features reporter for the *New Haven Register,* chose to do fall foliage shots of me and Panna to match their refreshing takes on our odd collaboration.

Next in line was OWN, the Oprah Winfrey Network. A resourceful production agent wanted to fly Panna and her mom to LA for a live TV interview. As he pressed and sweetened the deal, she retreated. I had watched her slowly inching away from the buzz. This instance marked a clear departure. When Panna ended the call, she turned to me, smiled, and said, "No more interviews."

———

A few weeks after that, I drove to Oak Woods Estates in Bethel. The Kroms lived in the same tidy complex where I first met them. Now they were on the ground floor, in a corner apartment with two bedrooms. For the first time in her life, Panna had her own room. And a mini-deck. It doubled the rent; for that Song and Chan were dipping into their 401K.

Panna and I cut through the woods behind her apartment, then onto the grounds of Bethel High School where we were the only two on the track. Warmed by the October sun, we did laps, old 440s as I knew them in my racing days, completely immersed and lost in conversation. I could see that she was torn. On one hand, there was an utter desperation to repay her mom and dad, meaning to chip in her share. But any work would steer her away from Song's dream for her: going off to college. She also told me, "Doug, I'll never get over Angel. It's my private anguish. Makes me question myself to be a mother again."

She missed the girls at York. She felt lucky. Others had been there longer for less, she said. I told her that I got a letter from her old roomie. Shannon must have spent an entire page on her "deepened love" for

Panna. She claimed that we two sent shock waves through York. "Now everybody wants clemency," she said in the letter.

"Did you actually hear from others?" said Panna.

"About a dozen."

"What did you do?"

"Took on half. You know one thing I found? Every case is messy—sloppy investigation, ineffective counsel. You know."

"Yeah, I know." Panna and Shannon talk regularly. Shannon's had a rough go. "Obviously, if I'm there, that's not happening," Panna said. "We were grounded."

Panna hadn't started thinking about her life plans: nothing concrete about college, no brilliant ideas about a career. "You dream up all these big plans, but the day you walk out, they evaporate," she told me. Mutual friends had confided to me: all Panna wants is a hubby and a few kids. I didn't bring it up, but she did. "I think about it a lot," she said. After a few seconds, she shrugged and with a look of resignation, added, "I have to deal with it."

———

During Panna's incarceration, to gain support for her, Connie and I updated the ninety-slide PowerPoint presentation, which we took to many universities. We depicted her crime and prosecution, her family's wartime escape, the eleven other neonaticide cases, and her path to the clemency hearing. Song and Chan had been coming. Now Panna would be there and prove to be the principal draw. Women in the audience were especially quick to spot the judicial pitfalls and to decry the impulse to vilify a minority female. They identified with her plight and wanted to hear what she had to say.

Panna's cool handling of the post-talk Q&As earned her a scholarship offer from the president of Post University. At Yale, a professor of Southeast Asia studies, Eric Harms, invited her to his seminar and for a lunch conversation with his students at Mory's, a Yale-only private club. Amy Smoyer, a professor of social work at Southern Connecticut State University, had her as a special guest at her all-day program about forgiveness. Impressed, Smoyer tried to interest her in their social justice curriculum. I had championed these overtures and was at the time disappointed that Panna was not stirred. She demurred, and for each, politely let them know that she would give consideration.

———

Song's mother, Chem, the family matriarch and the only survivor from her embattled generation, had been living with out-of-state relatives. In her mid-eighties, she was deep into her decline, in need of sponge baths, spoon feedings, and being lifted everywhere—but she still had what I regarded as an inextinguishable regal air. Because everyone in their household worked, Panna wanted them to bring Grandmother to Bethel. For the first few months, the full-time duties of her care helped Panna erase York memories and recalibrate her life. But soon the decompressing no longer worked. Isolation was eating away at her.

"It didn't help that I was cooped up in one room all day, even with Grandmother," said Panna. "I had to force the idea that I'm out, I'm free. It got to be February and March, so we couldn't go anywhere. The clock constantly reminded me where I should be at York."

Panna was waking in the middle of the night fumbling for her bearings. She flipped on the light and, like a CO, checked on her parents. Approaching a closed door, she balked, assuming it was locked. On the streets in tiny Bethel, she got impossibly spun around. For a decade her universe had been a mini-world of several hallways and tiers—the same faces, the same shrill noise and dull gray color, the steel bars and snapping doors. Nearly robotic, at York at most she made two or three decisions a day. Now, being on the outside, she felt angst from the need to handle a flow of micro decisions. One time in a deli, when the butcher asked, "What kind of cheese?" she froze.

Stressors mounted. Failed job searches. No insurance. Everywhere she went, she wondered, do they know me? She needed a root canal, new contact lenses, a gynecologist. She had a letter from the IRS, hit a cone in her driving test and tanked the SATs. It was similar to what I heard from other newly released women. One guest who had spoken at York, Jennifer Gonnerman from *The New Yorker,* came to that conclusion in her book, *Life on The Outside*—that it can be tougher than on the inside. Panna said, "At York my job was pretty basic, go to class and get an A. The rest was making it to the next day."

In June, Grandmother was returned to family and she and her untold story slipped away. Panna felt the time she spent taking care of her over her last few months never made up for her missed decade. While reading a eulogy at the funeral, she sensed something palpable beside her. It caused her to draw on the teaching of Buddha concerning the dead: They have four spirits. One will always be with you.

———

That spring, Panna went back to filling out work applications. She said, "Once they asked about my most recent job, then as subtle as a tire around my neck, there was that ten-year gap. I was totally up front. Lotta good it did. I got no calls." Finally, a physical therapy office wanted to hire her after her first interview. They loved her, a perfect fit for a supervisor job. They said they needed a background check. Panna called me, "What should I do?" I said, "Call them right now and tell them your story. They are in the healing business. They'll understand. Or maybe they'll say they already knew." A few hours later, Panna texted me: *they withdrew the offer.*

Eventually, Dick's Sporting Goods hired her, as a Retail Sales Associate, working a checkout register. She quit when an opportunity popped up at Radial Bearing. The manager promoted her to the front office, where she learned billing, ordering, and, payroll.

———

In May, 2017, Panna and I met in her onetime defense attorney's office for a sort of a celebratory get-together. I took delight in seeing Jennifer Tunnard and Panna hugging. Sitting in the book-lined conference room, the three of us replayed the 2007 plea negotiations. Twenty years had been sitting on the table. Jennifer said that State's Attorney Sedensky's tirades killed any dialogue. She couldn't go to trial and he knew it. She fought to knock off two.

I said, "You know I've read a lot of reports and listened to a lot of experts and have had time to think about this. The story we have of what happened that night is Sedensky's narrative, all according to his detectives. The truth is we don't know." I looked at Panna. "It's not even fair for us to say what we think. But we don't know. It's taken me a long time to come to that conclusion."

Panna said, "I don't know what to say."

I asked Jennifer Tunnard, "You couldn't challenge her confession?"

She replied, "Going by the rules of evidence at that time, there was no misconduct. Besides, the risk was high. It's still a confession. Still a jury."

"It keeps coming back to the interview, doesn't it? We don't know how much of it was coaxed out of her. Sorry guys. Just can't let it go. You know, I spoke with a retired detective and told him about their interviewing a 17 year old. He told me, 'Seventeen, no one there? No, they'd throw that out.'"

Changing the subject, I reminded Tunnard of her testimony in the LOB that winter of 2011-12, explaining, "That's when I first heard the Panna Krom name, from your lips that day, and got involved." I asked her, "Why did you take the day off, drive to Hartford, wait the whole day and testify?"

"I can't remember," she said, giving it little effort.

"The case was closed," I added.

"I know. I know. I just did. I barely recall being there."

"So, is that it?" I said with a laugh. "For four years, I've been dying to ask you."

———

In May of that year 2017, a newborn was discovered in Danbury, crying and half-hidden in the bushes behind a grocery store. Panna told me that it was the talk of the town and that she was fearful the press was going to drag her name into it. Sure enough, a *News-Times* reporter named Dirk Perreforte, seeking her comments, tracked me down. I let him know, "Your paper has never been kind to her." Within seconds he pulled up past articles about her, reading the last one to me: "Clemency Granted to Danbury Woman Who Drowned Baby."

"See," I said. "And that was the happy story." He did agree but informed me that that particular reporter who wrote those stories left years ago. Still, Panna had no interest in talking to them.

According to reports, the baby was admitted to Danbury Hospital and did fine. The Department of Children and Families (DCF), which oversees Safe Haven, took custody. The court arraigned the mother, later identified as a twenty-two-year-old Hispanic, on charges which included abandonment of a child, and released her on a $1,500 bond. She admitted that she had hidden the pregnancy, delivered the baby alone in her apartment, and left her behind the store hoping someone would find her. She was unaware of the Safe Haven law. While she was pregnant, she informed the father on Facebook. He blocked her.

She is now serving a three-year sentence at York.

In the legislature, there had been a new bill pending, requiring all high schools in Connecticut to include the Safe Haven law in their health-education curriculum. Some legislators saw the news on this crime as an opportunity to push the bill through.

According to the *News-Times*, some years before, Danbury High School had introduced Safe Haven into their health classes and implemented ways to ensure pregnant students were connected with the community services. Clearly, this was the legacy of Panna Krom.

———

Months went by and I heard little from Panna. I figured things were settling down, getting back to some level of normalcy for the Kroms, meaning things are good. Chan did tell me that they bumped into Stephen Sedensky in Stop & Shop. He was cordial and asked how Panna was doing.

Then in September 2018, Panna shot me a text, *you changed my life forever... you are my hero*. She insisted that we all get together. It was the two-year anniversary of her release.

That Saturday, Connie and I met the Kroms at Pad Thai restaurant in New Haven, just like old times. Chan was beaming and spirited, and Song looked his usual youthful self. With both of his hands clasping mine, he repeated, "How *are* you, Doug?" Panna was accompanied by a young man—they had gone to a Giants game together. She was now matriculated at Post University, taking online courses, studying business management.

They all looked content and unbothered. Theirs was a tight family, loving and supporting, one that has, and will endure, I thought.

I said to Song, placing my arm on his shoulder, "Tell me, is everything paid off?"

Song laughed and said, "Yeah. We're good."

"You're squared away?"

"Yeah, yeah, we square."

I eyed Panna and her partner, laughing and lost in private conversation, and realized that she was in the exact spot where she had longed to be.

Halfway through dinner, Panna announced, "Hey everybody! Good news!" With a big smile, she leaned across the table grabbing her friend's hand and said, "We're expecting."

That marked the end of the Krom saga. At least my part; my idea of a good place to stop.

But there was another message.

Considered Removal

On January 22, Panna sent me a text: *Hi Doug, I really need your advice on a very serious matter.*

She was at Danbury Hospital. She had been admitted the night before, at thirty-seven weeks with preeclampsia, a condition which threatened her and the baby, and they induced her with Pitocin. After an all-night labor, she delivered a beautiful healthy baby.

Early that afternoon, two doctors she had never met before entered her room. They told her they were taking her to a conference room to talk, alone. This did not look good. She knew she had been sitting on a time bomb.

The two MDs, both hospitalists, closed the conference room door and without bothering to sit, one opened by telling her they knew about her history. The other cut in, "We called the DCF." A trembling Panna scrambled to explain. The crime was twelve years ago and she had paid her debt. When her obstetrician had asked about previous pregnancies, she was up front and volunteered the details. Panna told them, "It should all be in my medical record."

Minutes later, a social worker from the DCF entered. His name was Kevin and he upped the tension. "Are you different now than twelve years ago?" was one question.

Panna sensed a trap. She said, "Different? Where do I begin? I went through the criminal system, was sentenced, did ten years in prison, all the rehab, convinced the pardon board I had exceptional behavior and was granted a commutation. They took eight years off my sentence. Am I the naïve lost girl I was in high school? No, not at all. I am back with my family, have been working, and now my boyfriend lives with us. I have a lovely baby." She paused. "Did I answer your question?"

He seemed dismissive.

She thought, Did I say too much?

"Tomorrow, we have a meeting," he said. "Here. 10:30."

"What kind of meeting?"

"It's called a Considered Removal Meeting. You can invite your family."

"Removal of what?"

"The baby."

That's when she texted me.

The following morning, alone in her room, Panna and I spoke at length. She assured me that she had made all her appointments, did her ultrasounds, took her vitamins, and she had done the birthing classes. A gynecologist who knew her full story followed her and was supportive, as was Danbury Hospital's chief of obstetrics, who had stopped by earlier. He had voiced his opposition to this meeting but had no official say in it. As we talked, family members were arriving. We headed into the conference room.

Seated together were four DCF staff. Close to twenty members of Panna's family—ten cousins, three aunts, Song and Chan—plus her partner's family filled the room and lined the back wall. The panel, turning to each other and synchronizing their nods, said that they had never seen a showing like this. Beyond that, the tone was adversarial.

Panna outlined her plans. She had quit her job, while her partner had eight weeks of paternity leave. After that, Chan planned to take two weeks off. Following her leave, Song would pick up with two more weeks. They had applied to a nearby daycare facility. Cousins and others said they could help. One spoke up and explained, "We all live within a block of each other. We are a village. We take care of each other. We don't depend on anyone else. We never ask for anything."

I told the staffers that Panna had had three full psychiatric evaluations, all clearing her of any psychopathology and stating that she presented no danger to herself or anyone else—including babies. I informed them that repeat offenders for this type of crime, known as neonaticide, are unheard of.

At one point, one of the DCF members proclaimed, "I've read the police report on this crime. It's very ugly. We can't forget that." That comment was a tell. First, they were poorly informed on Panna's case. And second, their decision was made—nothing in this meeting would change that. They expressed no reaction to Panna's outpouring of family support nor to her stellar rehabilitative record. Instead, they asked for copies of her psychological reports, which amounted to over a hundred pages of highly privileged material. They got up to go and Kevin closed the meeting with, "We will get back to you."

In the cafeteria, I ran into a cousin. We sat together and had a bite. She told me, "Doug, if we were from Westport, this is not happening."

"I thought of that."

"It's eighteen years all over again." She paused. "But we'll get through it."

"You *will*."

Later that evening, Panna called me, sobbing. "They're coming up with more rules!"

A DCF social worker had informed her that she was considered an "unfit parent." They had a convoluted plan for the baby with a visitation schedule. Panna had no answers to my questions about their imposed plan, the length, the requirements, or possible outcomes. She did know, however, that she could no longer nurse.

The next day the DCF obtained a court order signed by a judge. More court hearings followed and Panna was advised to get a lawyer.

The Public Defender office told me that with no crime or arrest, they could not provide counsel. I reached Jennifer Tunnard in her car, who was appalled. She said she had had legal disputes with the DCF before. She needed some documents: a diary of Panna's daily life, an ob-gyn physician's note about her compliance, and copies of the psychiatry reports handed over to DCF.

Later that day, the obstetrics service discharged Panna and she followed their plan to the letter.

Panna, while going through security at the Danbury Superior Courthouse for her first hearing, said, "I can't believe it. I'm back at this place." During the next few months of unproductive hearings, the DCF provided little clarity. She and her family were complying—the supervised visits, the parenting classes, drug counseling, and additional psych evaluations—all at their own expense. Despite that, a DCF social worker Panna had never met before told her that there were other more severe plans in the works. That sent Panna into a frenzy of crying.

Tunnard infused some calm; she told me, "Once we step into the courtroom, they will quickly realize they don't have a leg to stand on."

The DCF counted on them tripping up. But they didn't.

The arrangements were working.

In June of that year, I got a text: *We are all home.*

The DCF had left a voicemail at Attorney Tunnard's office: "We're terminating the Krom case." They sent no letter, no explanation, no apology, no advice, nor did they offer compliments or a closing salutation with encouraging words.

––––––

Lately and happily, Panna has never strayed far. She and I text every few days. Usually, it's something playful with Song or myself as the fall guy.

Panna posted a video. Shot through a dream-like filter, she was in a field with sunflower stalks, behind her glints of sunshine. Panna wrote: "I am stronger because I had to be, I'm smarter because of my mistakes, and I'm happier because of the sadness I've known—and now wiser, at 31, because I've learned."

ACKNOWLEDGMENTS

I owe my greatest debt to Panna and her parents, Song and Chan, who spent hundreds of hours with me, opened their lives and trusted me to get their story right. We have become close friends. Getting to know her entire extended family has been enlightening. I have been fortunate in this regard.

Wally Lamb is known by those of us close to him for opening doors. He allowed me to get access and begin work on this story, sometimes at his own peril and personal cost. This is what Wally does, often parlaying his literary fame to help those like myself who are lost and struggle to get a start.

My two closest old friends were there for me. Mark Lawrence in Austin, a superb craftsman of nonfiction, gave me a hand when I was hopelessly stuck, nudging me back on course. Leslie Farqharson, a master of literature in Ontario, did a final thorough read, and offered sage advice and encouragement.

The amazing staff at the Khmer Health Advocates in West Hartford Connecticut who devoted many free hours to helping us get Panna released: Theanvy Kuoch, Mary Scully, and Richard Miller, with Megan Berthold of the University of Connecticut.

Thank you to my first agent, Donald Gastwirth, who sadly passed away in the beginning of our work, and the second, Gina Pannettieri, who, from the first day we met, championed the story.

I am grateful for many others who read the manuscript and provided advice. Included are those in my writing group, all accomplished writers: Wally Lamb, Sari Rosenblatt, Jon Anderson, Denise Abercrombie, Pam Lewis, Leslie Johnson and Bruce Cohen. A special thanks to Thomas Duffy, Yale Medical School's endurable and eloquent voice of humanism. He pushed to get the manuscript into the hands of other influential readers. Michelle Oberman, the noted author on neonaticide, was a constant mentor. Rachel Barkow, world expert on clemency also encouraged me. Ben Kiernan, John Merriman, Mark Mercurio, Randi Epstein, Kathleen Zeidner, Rachel Broderick, Karina Xie, Pam Sawyer, Suzanne Gold, Howard Zonana and Edward Zigler were generous and provided ideas. Early on, Ann Froelich cheered me on. Recognition goes to those of our York writing group: fellow writer, Careen Jennings, and our students: Mary Ames, Liz. P., Kelly Donnelly, Susan Braig, Angelina Jamelle, Ms. O., Shannon Simperi, Chasity West, Chandra Bozelko, Tracie Bernardi—women who taught us a lot about life.

And thanks to Vicki Hutchinson (lead attorney), Jennifer Tunnard, Richard Emanuel and Clinton Roberts who graciously donated many hours of their time to make this whole thing a success.

When you do a project this long and involved, inevitably there are times you feel alone or abandoned. But no matter how bleak it got, I always had my family—my smart, dogged and adorable wife, Connie, and our charming kids, Suki and Lee Clyde.

For several years, whenever I talked to Maxine, the first words out of her mouth were, "How's the book?" I wish I could finally let her know, "Mom, it's good."

BIBLIOGRAPHY

1. Affonco, D., *To the End of Hell: One Woman's Struggle to Survive Cambodia's Khmer Rouge*. 2007: Reportage Press.

2. Becker, E., *When the War Was Over: The Voices of Cambodia's Revolution and Its People*. 1986: Simon and Schuster.

3. Criddle, J.D. and T.B. Mam, *To Destroy You Is No Loss: The Odyssey of A Cambodian Family*. 1987: The Atlantic Monthly Press.

4. Fadiman, A., *The Spirit Catches You and You Fall Down: A Hmong child, Her American Doctors and the Collision of Two Cultures*. 2012: Farrar, Strauss and Giroux.

5. Him, C., *When Broken Glass Floats: Growing Up Under the Khmer Rouge*. 2000: W. W. Norton & Company.

6. Lawrence, M.A., *The Vietnam War: A Concise International History*. 2008: Oxford University Press.

7. Rierden, A., *The Farm: Life Inside A Women's Prison*. 1997: University of Massachusetts Press.

8. Short, P., *Pol Pot: Anatomy of A Nightmare*. 2005: Henry Holt and Company, LLC.

9. Ung, L., *First They Killed My Father: A Daughter of Cambodia Remembers*. 2006: HarperCollins Publishers.

10. Meyer, C.L., Oberman, M., *Mothers Who Kill Their Children*. 2001: New York University Press.

11. Raab, Selwyn, "Ruben (Hurricane) Carter, Boxer Whose Murder Convictions Were Overturned, Dies at 76," April 20, 2014, *New York Times*.

12. Herszenhorn, David, "Police Await Autopsy Results in Stamford Newborn's Death," December 20, 2002 *New York Times*.

13. "Miss Porter's School For Young Ladies Faces Shock of Death in Dormitory," December 12, 1976 *Herald-Journal*

14. Graham, Victoria, "Questions Unanswered in Baby's Death, Decorum and Death at Miss Porter's School," December 19, 1976 *Prescott Courier*.

ABOUT THE AUTHOR

Doug Hood was born in Detroit and growing up in a military family went to schools overseas. He attended the Univerisity of Florida and Yale University. He was a Lecturer in Neurology at Yale.

He has published short stories and essays. This is his first book.

Doug lives with his wife, Connie, and two children, Suki and Lee Clyde, in North Haven, Connecticut.

Printed in Great Britain
by Amazon

40512378R10187